—•⟫ ⟪•—

About the South

An Aging Southerner Recalls Life
Tragic and Triumphant in a
1900s-Era Rural Farm Family

By R. Olin Jackson III

Published by Whippoorwill Publications, LLC
Woodstock, GA 30189

ISBNs: 979-8-9900211-8-1 (jacket); 979-8-218-70053-9 (hardcover);
979-8-9900211-9-8 (softback)
Library of Congress Control Number: 2025906420

Publisher's Cataloging-in-Publication Data
provided by Five Rainbows Cataloging Services
Names: Jackson III, R. Olin, 1951- author.
Title: About the South : an aging Southerner recalls life tragic and triumphant in a 1900s-era rural farm family / R. Olin Jackson III.
Description: Woodstock, GA : Whippoorwill Publications, 2025.
Identifiers: LCCN 2025906420 (print) | ISBN 979-8-9900211-8-1 (jacketed hardcover) | ISBN 979-8-2187005-3-9 (hardcover) | ISBN 979-8-9900211-9-8 (paperback)
Subjects: LCSH: Country life—Georgia. | Farm life—Georgia. | Family life—Georgia. | Polk County (Ga.)—Biography. | Autobiography. | BISAC: BIOGRAPHY & AUTOBIOGRAPHY / General. | FAMILY & RELATIONSHIPS / General.
Classification: LCC PS3608.A7 A36 2025 (print) | LCC PS3608.A7 (ebook) | DDC 814/.6—dc23.

Author of:
A North Georgia Journal of History, Volumes I – IV
Georgia Backroads Traveler
Tales of the Rails in Georgia
Moonshine, Murder, & Mayhem in Georgia
Mystery & History in Georgia, Volumes I & II
Some Genealogy Keys to Some Georgia Family Trees
Memories of Army Life and MPs of the 529th
After All That We've Been Through
Gunmen, Lawmen and Wild Men of Early Georgia
Historic Rails and Forgotten Trails of Early Georgia

Copies of Whippoorwill Publications, LLC books are available online at Amazon.com; BarnesandNoble.com; IngramSpark.com; and other fine booksellers. For more detailed information, please visit www.georgiahistorytraveler.com

The road to a career in journalism is paved with crushed matrimony.
—Anonymous

This book is lovingly dedicated to my brother Guy,
whose flame of life flickered far too briefly.

Table of Contents

—•≻≻ ≺≺•—

Foreword

Travel with the author back through time in the 19th and 20th centuries as he retraces the humorous, poignant, tragic and sometimes triumphant life of his family - the Jacksons - who have resided in northwest Georgia now for generations.

Zimri W. Jackson (1824 -1894), was born in North Carolina, and migrated southward circa 1835-1840 to Pickens County, Georgia, with his father, Thomas Frederick Jackson (1782-1850) and the rest of their family to seek a better life. Both Thomas Frederick and his wife, Elizabeth Ann Patterson, are buried in old Hinton Cemetery in Pickens.

Accompanied by his brothers, Zimri later migrated from Hinton to Cassville, Cass County (later renamed Bartow County), GA, in the early 1850s, no doubt shortly after the death of their father in Hinton. By 1849, Cassville, the seat of that county's government had grown into the largest town in northwest Georgia, with four hotels, two colleges, four churches, a two-story brick courthouse, and many commercial and private endeavors. Business was booming there and it was a powerful magnet for young men searching for their destinies. Cassville was a place in particular which offered many new construction opportunities for builders such as the Jacksons.

Zimri would have been 26 years of age at that time, and already skilled in the building profession, no doubt having learned his craft at his father's knee, judging from the impressive Hinton home which still survives today in photographs. In all early censuses in which Zimri appears, his profession is listed as either "master carpenter," or "builder," or "master builder."

On page 21 of the ***Bartow County Heritage Book, Volume I,*** Zimri W. Jackson is listed as *"among the important persons entering the Civil War from Bartow County."* He had enlisted circa 1862 in Company I, 40th Regiment, Georgia Volunteer Infantry, but when his prowess as a builder was discovered, he, according to tradition, was sent instead to Savannah, Georgia, where he reportedly built ships for the Confederate Navy.

Back in Cassville, on separate occasions between May 19 and November 5 of 1864, the entire town – including most of the residences – was ultimately erased forever, after being torched by federal troops. Only the churches and a smattering of homes used for hospitals and the quartering of troops survived. Following this utter devastation, the town was never re-built, the charred chimneys standing in mute testimony to the unconscionable destruction wreaked during Union Gen. William T. Sherman's infamous *"March to the Sea."*

Just as had his great-grandfather, Ralph Olin Jackson Sr. (1893-1986) also migrated westward, to better land in northwest Georgia's Polk County in 1920. At this time, the South was still recovering from the devastation of the U.S. Civil War, and considerable raw acreage still existed in this area at a very economic price upon which a man could stake his claim to a livelihood for his progeny.

On the pages which follow, the reader has the opportunity to enjoy numerous events and experiences "about the South," as many tragic, heart-rending, adventurous and comedic moments experienced by his family are recalled by the author:

Suffer with them as the author's youngest brother is tragically accidentally poisoned to death; the youngest sister is beaten, robbed – and worse; and alcoholism almost destroys the family. Then savor the comedic and hilarious moments in this family and their triumphs over the forces dragging them toward destruction.

Enjoy a recollection of the author who, as a child of five years in age, exercised a small tyke's vengeance to "imprison" his grandfather in the family's dairy farm milk-house for some five hours where the elder Jackson was forced to "cool his heels" after having chastised the fearful tiny youngster for a perceived innocent activity.

Learn about a devoted elderly Black farm worker who meticulously and lovingly cared for the Jackson youngsters during their formative years, experiencing with them many adventures and subsequently earning their unwavering love and respect.

Read the detailed description of the destruction of a beaver dam on the Jackson farm property with dynamite in the mid-1960s, and how the demolition "expert" almost eliminated more than the dam in the process.

Listen to the respect and admiration the youngsters in the *Boy Scouts of America, Troop #14,* had for their leader, a highly-decorated World War II veteran, who took his young charges on adventures throughout the state of Georgia, the memories of which have remained with them for a lifetime.

Roll in laughter at the descriptions of the Jackson boys, and the comedic games they created with a gasoline-powered "Go-Kart" they "collectively" received one Christmas, and the hijinks they experienced with this device.

Enjoy the abject hilarity of one of the youngsters' friends and his buddies who set out for a "frog-gigging" adventure, only to see the entire episode devolve into utter chaos which created a memory not to be forgotten.

These and some 19 additional episodes of unusual high adventure and heart-rending tragedy await the readers of this semi-autobiographical account of the author's rise to manhood where even then he continued to experience oft-hilarious incidents which defy description.

The author's great-grandfather (William Anthony Jackson) and four of his six siblings pose for the camera. Pictured (L-R) are: Edward L. (1867-1935); Thomas Arthur (1857-1939); George Milton [(1854-1928) (death date also recorded in some records as 1940)]; William Anthony (1852-1936); and Robert Zimri (1864-?). Brother James Walter, born in 1850, relocated to and died in Oklahoma, date unknown. A sister, Fannie, born in 1860, also is not pictured.

─◦}{◦─

"Grandfathered In"

My earliest memories about my life are centered around an old pre-Civil War farmhouse on Hutchings Mountain Road outside what then was the tiny burg of Rockmart, Georgia. Though this aged dwelling undoubtedly was one of the earliest abodes in what today is Polk County, in its day, it was one of the more prominent. It had been constructed by an early family in the area named "Hutchings."

It is one of the very few farmhouses in Georgia (and possibly in the South) with what then was a very fashionable and durable "slate roof," which, even 175 years later, still shields the old home from the elements. Other antebellum and turn-of-the-century homes in nearby historic Vanwert and Rockmart also boasted these roofs, being supplied with slate shingles from the local stone quarries in that area which gave "Rockmart" its name.

In the early days, the drafty Hutchings farmhouse had only two large hearths as sources of heat – one in the main bedroom and one in the "sitting room." A large floor furnace which burned oil was later added in the center of the old home probably in the 1940s, but even when my family owned and lived in the home in the 1950s, my father quite often kept a fire going in one or the other (and sometimes both) of the two hearths to add heat to the un-insulated old home during frigid weather.

Just off the back porch, a cistern provided the home with water in its earliest days, but the inhabitants must eventually have found this to be inadequate, for a well had been hand-dug in the lower pasture in later years sometime around the Civil War for better quality water. It, too, was eventually abandoned for another well in the barnyard, and still later for a more-refined drilled well which we used.

A full unfinished basement had been dug out of the ground beneath the home. During this excavation, the owners – or perhaps a slave – apparently

1

struck a long-buried aboriginal war-axe, breaking the weapon into two roughly equal portions. The worker apparently recognized the smoothly-finished stone as an ancient implement, and tossed it up next to the stone foundation of the old home where it laid for perhaps 100 years before I rediscovered it and added it to a growing collection of flint arrow- and spear-points, stone fire-starters, atlatls, and other ancient remnants of the forebears of that area who no doubt had once called the little knoll "home."

The pre-Civil War farm on this site was literally a "land of milk and honey." Across the pasture from the front of the old house and down to the left, a pecan orchard of some six or eight trees - all huge and towering by the time we occupied the property - produced an abundance of pecans each season. The nuts on these trees were so numerous that my brother and sister and I would fill large bags with these delicious nuts and then my father would take us to town - loading our little red wagon into the rear of our station wagon - and we'd sell the pecans door-to-door.

Beneath the pecan trees, blueberry bushes had been planted which towered some eight or ten feet, and they also produced so many berries that we never came close to exhausting them. My grandmother occasionally made delicious pies from them.

Out in the pasture to the north of the house, an apple orchard had been planted in the vicinity of one of the first freshwater wells for the home. There were five or six of these trees, and they also produced abundant fruit each year on which we thrived.

In the rear yard of our farmhouse, three varieties of grapes were so voluminous that the ground beneath them was often damp from the dropped berries. This delicious treat came in the form of red and white grapes and a thick-skinned scuppernong - a Southern delicacy - all growing up into the trees edging the yard and onto an arbor built by my father.

Near these grapes, the original farm owner had planted a small orchard of five or six peach trees, all of which produced extremely-large, but very hard fruit each season. Though we never enjoyed these peaches (due to the inedibility of the hard fruit), had we known that these only required proper pruning and/or treatment for peach mites, we would have had yet another mouth-watering summer delight.

A hundred feet or so from the peach trees, a large patch of fig bushes existed which - almost daily - also produced far more sweet figs than one could possibly eat.

And a few hundred feet from the fig bushes stood a large black walnut tree and a large persimmon tree, both of which also produced abundant food.

Altogether, these multiple fruits, berries, and nuts provided all the summer treats my brothers and I needed in our youth.

I cannot recall whether it was my father, or my grandfather, who had actually purchased the old Hutchings farm, but in all likelihood, it was my grandfather. In 1950, being freshly-married during his pursuit of a law degree at the University of Georgia, my father simply did not have the funds.

My grandfather had also recently purchased another farm of sizeable acreage nearby which had been originally owned (the aboriginals notwithstanding) by the Simpson family, who were prominent in Van Wert, Georgia history. "Grandpa" must have often perused the monthly "tax sales" on the Polk County Courthouse steps, because I know for a fact that he purchased the Simpson farm under these auspices, and he possibly purchased the old Hutchings farm in that manner as well.

I have no doubts about the fact that my grandfather was a very honorable man. He lived a Christian life and had a substantially positive impact upon our family and community in northwest Georgia's Polk County. Grandpa and I, however, invariably seemed to be at odds with each other during my childhood. Perhaps my siblings and cousins experienced this uneasiness around him as well.

I'm certain the fault – if any – for my lack of a loving relationship with my grandfather lay completely with me. Like I said, he was a pillar of the community and highly respected throughout his life.

Though he never advanced any further than the 10th grade (in an 11-grade school system) in Bartow County, Georgia, where his family lived for generations, Grandpa was destined to become an active participant in the development of the school system in neighboring Polk County. He was a member of the *Polk Board of Education* for twenty years, serving as chairman for more than a decade. He served on the board which initiated the first county-wide, nine-month school system, and was chairman when the board consolidated the schools countywide, eliminating the tiny sub-standard classrooms which had been used since pioneer days.

Grandpa was also a charter member of both the *Cedar Valley Farmers' Club* and the *Rockmart Rotary Club*, serving as a charter director of the Rockmart Rotarians. He was a deacon and Sunday school superintendent of the *First Baptist Church* in Rockmart for decades, and instrumental in its development from the 1940s thru the 1960s.

Grandpa had been born on October 23, 1893, and moved from his native Bartow County to Polk County in 1920, only 48 years or so after the town of Rockmart had been founded. He was the son of William Anthony Jackson and Cornelia Fricks Jackson, and had already been a successful farmer before moving to Polk County where he sought new opportunity beyond his father's shadow.

Just prior to his move to Rockmart, Grandpa had married Isabelle Neel of the prominent family of Judge James Monroe Neel of Cartersville. Grandpa and his new bride traveled with the couple's possessions via six or seven mule-drawn wagons to a 300-acre farm he had just purchased for cash on the dusty one-lane pig-trail which would one day be enlarged into the Rockmart-Aragon Highway section of modern GA-101.

The farm was located at the site at which a stone quarry was opened (now long abandoned) in later years – destroying the pastoral quality of the property Grandpa had purchased some 60 years earlier. By that time, however, Grandpa was long gone, as were most of his children, so the devastation of his former home by the quarry was immaterial.

In 1920, many folks in rural northwest Georgia still traveled by a mule or horse-drawn conveyance, and nearly all of the streets (except Main/Marble Street) were dusty trails in dry weather and muddy quagmires in rainy weather. There also weren't any bridges across the Euharlee Creek in Rockmart for any forms of conveyance. Most people in northwest Georgia, however, didn't own automobiles, and they just crossed the creek in their wagons and buggies at the shallow ford near mid-town during fair weather.

Grandpa had what was known as a "three-team farm" in the 1920s and '30s, keeping up to three teams of mules busy plowing, sowing, and harvesting the crops he grew. His laborious, but perceptive farming practices in Polk proved successful once again – at least temporarily.

Aside from being reasonably-productive land, Grandpa's farm was also – probably to the surprise of modern residents in that vicinity – a historic site as well. A number of artifacts from the U.S. Civil War were uncovered by Grandpa's plowshares over the years, including a Civil War-era bullet-mold, the conical and devastatingly-destructive .58-caliber musket bullets, and even a musket bayonet, all of which are still in the possession of this author.

The right branch (*Army of the Tennessee*) of Gen. William Sherman's troops marching upon Atlanta, was commanded by Gen. James B. "Bird's Eye" McPherson. In early 1864, prior to burning Cedartown and destroying Van Wert in Polk County, McPherson and his men had camped on the land which later became Grandpa's farm, leaving the relics that were later discovered by Jackson family members.

Grandpa initially raised cotton – with which he had been very successful in Bartow – in the rolling pastureland opposite his substantial Polk County home. However, following the onslaught of the boll weevil plague of the late 1920s and early 1930s, Grandpa – who was anything if not an exceptionally-savvy businessman – converted his cotton farm into a dairy farm.

When *Goodyear Mills* opened a large facility in Rockmart in the 1930s, Grandpa was able to obtain an exclusive contract for the sale of milk to the residents in the new factory's associated mill village. He also sold his products to the residents of Rockmart and nearby Aragon.

By 1943, assisted by a number of successful real estate investments and a limited but shrewd acumen for stock investments (He purchased shares of a product called *Coca Cola* a few years before it found markets worldwide), Grandpa was able to retire at the moderately-young age of 50 and live for the remainder of his life on the income from his investments. In 1951, he sold the Aragon Highway farm property to *Southern States Portland Cement Company*, then purchased a residence on Elm Street adjacent to the *First Baptist Church* in Rockmart where he was a member.

As explained above, it was at about this same time that Grandpa also purchased - for taxes - a 700-acre farm south of Rockmart known as "the old Simpson place" at the foot of Vinson Mountain. This property – which also included the now-historic Simpson Falls, the old Simpson farm residence, barns and out-buildings and a substantial orchard of peach and apple trees – was used by Grandpa to raise beef cattle.

Throughout our youthful and adolescent lives, my brothers and I hunted and camped upon, and regularly explored Grandpa's farm. This included the remains of a pioneer-era water mill (*Simpson Falls Gristmill*) where corn and other grains had once been ground into flour and meal.

It has been documented through folklore that in addition to the mill, a pre-Civil War government-licensed distillery as well as a tannery and a cobbler's shop, also once existed in this Simpson Falls vicinity, all of which, according to an 1884 Columbus, Georgia newspaper report were destroyed by an immense flood. It, too, is quite possible that the mill had also been burned prior to the flood, since charred timbers from the structure could still be seen as recently as the 1960s – vestiges, perhaps, of McPherson's destruction 100 years earlier.

In 1947, Grandpa built Jackson Lake and a lakeside cabin (now long gone) on this property. He and Grandma used this residence during the summer months. In later years, my brothers and I spent countless days fishing, frog-gigging, camping and swimming in and around this lake as well.

Grandma and Grandpa ultimately produced two females and one male – Mary Ann (1922), Julia (1925), and my father, Ralph, Jr. (1923). Grandma passed away in 1982, and Grandpa in 1986, and their children have all long since passed away as well. At this writing in 2025, many of the grandchildren have passed too.

In his earlier years, Grandpa just naturally became the object of much general family "ribbing," particularly at holiday gatherings. Though he took this teasing reasonably well, Grandpa nevertheless brooked no nonsense from his grandchildren in earlier years who he felt basically should be "seen" but not "heard." As a result, my brothers and I, in general, tended to avoid him.

Though he wasn't playful, and would quickly snap at us if we seemed – in his judgment – to be "out of line," he always carried an extra pack of *Wrigley's Beechnut* chewing gum – which he loved – in his pocket specifically for us, since he knew we loved chewing gum as well. As a result, though we avoided him, we'd initially mob him for a stick of gum and were very appreciative of that little treat.

Over the years, there were numerous incidents which undoubtedly gave rise to Grandpa's aloofness from his grandchildren, particularly his male grandchildren. One such memorable occasion has been recalled in family lore as *"the time Grandpa got locked in the milk-house."*

On this particular day – which, even in my 70s now I can still partially recall – I was hanging around in the cooling-house where all the cows' milk was stored in large shiny stainless-steel holding tanks. A large condenser/compressor cooled the milk in the tanks and maintained the ambient room temperature somewhere around 60 or 70 degrees. It was always a really refreshing spot on a hot summer afternoon – and a favored rest-stop in which a sweaty youngster could cool off.

On this day, Grandpa happened to be making his periodic inspections of my father's little enterprise which no doubt had been initially constructed with funds provided by the elder Jackson. He would just stop by unannounced and begin "making the rounds," which even we children could see that Daddy didn't really appreciate.

When Grandpa entered the milk-house and discovered me cooling down on the damp concrete floor, he immediately took umbrage, and commanded me to "skedaddle." As far as he was concerned, the milk-house was solely a place of "enterprise," not "leisure." Looking back, that is a completely understandable assessment. Grandpa, however, could have been just a tad more tactful in his approach when dealing with a painfully-shy little boy.

At this time, I was approximately five years of age – still just a little tyke easily frightened. For this reason, I quite often was actually afraid of my grandfather, particularly since he wasn't what one could describe as "kindly."

The author's grandfather was photographed here at a Christmas dinner in 1955 at the elder Jackson's home in downtown Rockmart. This was approximately 6 months prior to the elder Jackson's "unexpected detention" in the Jackson dairy milk cooling room in 1956.

I'm sure he meant nothing by it. It just wasn't in his personality to be a warm and loving individual.

As a result, in a little five-year-old's eyes, "scary Grandpa" was to be avoided. And in this instance, it was also judged by "frightened little five-year-old" that "scary Grandpa" needed to be "contained" where he couldn't engage in "scaring" anymore.

So what did "frightened little five-year-old" do? Why he did exactly as his grandfather had abruptly commanded, but as he was leaving, he paused just long enough to lock "scary Grandpa" in the milk-house.

Now at the time that I flipped the latch over the hasp to lock Grandpa in the milk-house, it was approximately eleven o'clock in the morning. Dad was away doing something else, and my brother (the youngest not having yet been born) and sisters were inside our home attending to life there. No one knew that Grandpa had been locked in the milk-house, nor would they become aware of it until the passage of a good five hours when Dad came to milk the cows at 4:00 pm that afternoon.

Grandpa, of course, having owned and operated a dairy himself for many years, was abundantly cognizant of all of the above. There was nowhere to sit in the milk-house except upon the cold wet floor. He certainly couldn't break out through the heavy wooden door now securely locked. The only other openings in this sturdy concrete-block milk-house were three small slit-windows located high up on the wall to allow natural light into the room and there certainly was no hope of escaping through them. No... Grandpa knew full well that he was going to be "cooling his heels" in the milk-house for several hours until milking time arrived that afternoon at 4:00 pm, and he was definitely an "unhappy camper." If I had not already had a poor relationship with my grandfather prior to that day, I didn't have to worry about that circumstance going forward. I now enjoyed permanent banishment to Grandpa's "crap-list."

My elderly grandfather sitting upon the cold wet cooling-house floor, however, did not give up without a fight. One has never heard such banging and loud admonition as was emanating from that milk-house on that day. One in his position should also have known that he was not helping his case one bit by threatening to whip the crap out of me. That did nothing but convert a frightened youngster into "winged Pegasus" fleeing across the barnyard to the safe confines of our home, leaving "scary Grandpa" to fend for himself.

Interestingly, though they hid it well from Grandpa, Mother and Daddy apparently found more hilarity in his confinement than a need for punishment for me – particularly from Mother's perspective, since she and Grandpa never enjoyed a close relationship either. Mother and Daddy nevertheless explained very carefully to me that I should not have committed such a deed, and that if I ever did it again, I would be punished.

That was all fine by me. "Scary Grandpa" had been dealt with. Needless to say, I avoided Grandpa like the plague for several years thereafter, and he – to my knowledge – never again entered the cooling-house to make an inspection. I was also pretty-much banished from the chewing gum brigade in perpetuity too.

—•⟩⟩⟨⟨•—

The "Reuben James" of My Days

"Reuben James,
you still walk the furrowed fields of my mind;
the faded shirt, the weathered brow;
the calloused hands upon the plow;
I loved you then and I love you now, Reuben James."

Kenny Rogers & The First Edition (1969)

T he truly lucky people in God's wonderful world are the ones who have known an individual who has had a profoundly positive impact upon their lives. It doesn't have to be a wealthy person, or a beautiful woman, or a celebrity. It doesn't have to be a person who makes one rich or powerful or famous. It can merely be a humble layman from the everyday walks of life who understands and shares what is truly important in this life so fleeting.

Photographed a few weeks prior to his death, Hilliard Gibbons squints into the morning sun at his home, the ubiquitous smile ever-present. Hilliard raised some six children to adulthood, one of whom - Murray Crews - became a two-time state wrestling champion at Rockmart (Georgia) High School and a Greco-Roman World Champion, earning a scholarship to Iowa State University where he was a 1983 All-American in wrestling. Murray ultimately transferred these talents to the education forum, becoming an assistant wrestling coach at California Poly-Technic State University in San Luis Obispo, California. His wrestling clinics continue to be sought-after today.

9

In 1901, *Southern States Portland Cement Company* began business operations at a large deposit of limestone located just off what then was a dusty Rockmart-Aragon Road which later became GA Highway 101 in Polk County. Pictured here are some of the first structures and employees from this venture. It was here that Hilliard Gibbons found early employment circa 1933-1940. In 1953, a more expansive operation here was purchased by Marquette Cement Manufacturing Company, and it continued the production of cement products at this site until 1982.

As explained on previous pages, my brothers and sisters and I grew up on a small farm in rural Polk County in the 1950s and '60s. My dad always employed a laborer to help him with the rigors of farming. Over the years, several individuals came and went as they fulfilled that role. Most all of them were good men, but one I will always remember as "a cut well above the others" was a fellow by the name of Hilliard Gibbons.

Hilliard grew up hard. By that I mean that he was raised in the *Jim Crow South* of the 1930s and '40s, and he could have been very bitter about his relegated status in life. To the contrary, however, Hilliard was an honest firm realist who was determined to make the best of any situation – no matter how bad it might be. To him, an honest day's work, devout good deeds and a Christian existence were the building blocks of life, and he focused upon these every day – almost to the very end.

Hilliard also had an iron-clad "John Wayne" attitude about what was "right" and what was "wrong." And there was no such thing as a "gray area" to him either. The thought of dishonesty or the commission of a crime or evil deed was completely alien to him. He attended church – literally "religiously" – every Sunday, and he was one of the most patient, generous, and kindly individuals I have ever known.

Beyond his strength of character, work ethic and honor, there was nothing particularly special about Hilliard. In his younger years, he worked in some of the most arduous and demanding jobs one might imagine. I don't think he ever finished high school. He may not have even attended high school, but he could read and write quite well.

Hilliard often told my brothers and me stories of his early days working hard labor at places like a local cement manufacturing plant. One story which remains with me to this very day involved some of his co-workers who he said died after somehow becoming trapped inside a huge oven in which limestone and clay were cooked at high temperatures to create the ingredients of concrete at the plant.

The ovens apparently occasionally had to be cleaned, and this required physical entry inside the huge cookers by manual laborers. On the day in question, the workers were inside cleaning the ovens when the huge doors were suddenly closed and the heating systems ignited. The workers had no chance whatsoever for survival.

"When we went in to get 'em," Hilliard explained to my wide-eyed brother and me, "we could hardly hold 'em to carry 'em out because they were burnt so bad that the skin slid off they bodies when we tried to get a grip on 'em." The description was horrifying, and Hilliard was very obviously profoundly disturbed in revisiting the incident.

A New Job

By the time he went to work on my dad's farm, Hilliard was already known by everyone in my family. His honesty, intelligence and ever-happy demeanor had won him many friends over the years, as well as a weekend job at a small downtown retail shop in our town, where he was a fixture in the community every Saturday. His quick bright smile and ever-helpful attitude were great sales tools, a fact which had not gone unnoticed by the astute wealthy business owner who I suspect paid him exceedingly modestly to work each weekend.

My brothers and I patronized this shop regularly, usually purchasing odds and ends with which to repair our bicycles, or pellets for our air rifles, and later, ammunition for our shotguns for dove and quail hunting in my father's pastures. Hilliard had thus become ingrained in our lives long before he came to work for my dad, and we were quite happy when he and his sweet wife, Ruby, became members of our "family."

My father and grandparents had known Hilliard – and his reputation for honesty and geniality – for many years prior to that. They employed him and Ruby often as cooks on special occasions, because their culinary skills were widely-known and appreciated.

I can still remember the day my father drove us over to Hilliard's home near the cement manufacturing plant to ask him to come to work at our dairy. I don't know why that day is so ingrained in my memory, but it remains special to me to this very day.

Before he remarried (his first wife, Ruby, died tragically from an illness – probably cancer – and he grieved for her for years thereafter), Hilliard would occasionally offer a modest lunch in his humble home to my brothers and me if we had happened to have missed lunch at our own home. *(Hilliard's house was the old Hutchings farmhouse, which my family previously had occupied from 1951 to 1957. It was located approximately one-half mile from our new home.)*

Hilliard's lunches for us were always very simple fare – perhaps Vienna sausage, applesauce, a slice of bread, maybe some fresh carrots and fresh milk – but we always took him up on his offer. The food was good and Hilliard was just plain fun to be around.

That was the thing about Hilliard Gibbons. He'd give you the shirt off his back and be glad he had done so. He had no possession too valuable to lend or give to my brothers and me, and he was never too tired to help us, no matter the task. And poor as we were in those days, Hilliard was infinitely poorer.

> *"The gossip of Madison County died with child;*
> *And although your skin was black*
> *You were the one that didn't turn your back,*
> *on the hungry white child with no name, Reuben James"*

Deuce-and-a-Half

On one occasion, when my younger brother, David, and I were teenagers, we were riding on some of the country backroads with several friends in an old *U.S. Army* surplus "Deuce-and-a-Half." This large truck – complete with its canvas covering over the rear portion – had originally been designed by the Army to transport troops. Its dependable six-wheel drive could pull immense amounts of weight through the absolute worst terrain.

The engines in those Deuces were extra-special too. They could function on gasoline, diesel, plain oil, cooking oil, and practically anything that had a combustible potential. Those engines were durable too, lasting for well over 150,000 miles, even after brutal treatment.

This particular Deuce had been purchased for *Troop 14* of the local *Boy Scouts of America* of which we were all members. It was the pride of our troop. When we attended jamborees or camps across the state at which other troops participated, everyone took note when we came rolling up in that big old six-wheel-drive Deuce-and-a-Half. No other troop in the state at that time had transportation that special. *(This was obviously also way back prior to the present-day seat-belt restraint safety requirements now mandated by the government.)*

On this day, we were out joy-riding in the Deuce. It was being driven by one of our friends who was just barely old enough to have what was known as a *Learner's Permit*, but not an actual *Driver's License*. He therefore wasn't actually "legal" as a driver, but we were out on backwoods dirt roads where no other traffic existed, essentially trying to see if it was possible to get the Deuce irretrievably mired in mud. *(Kids. Go figure.)*

On this day we happened to be successful. On one particularly treacherous stretch, our teenage driver failed to turn the wheels fast enough on a soft, muddy mountain road, and the big old truck mired up in the gooey red earth on the right lip of the road, hanging over just enough so that the wheels on the left side were lifted off the ground (high-sided) and the wheels on the other side were deeply mired in gooey mud. Despite all our best efforts, that truck wasn't coming out on its own accord. It was finally definitely "stuck."

At that point, a tow-truck should have been summoned to extract the heavy Deuce, but since that was expensive, and since our driver was out in the truck "without permission" and legally "un-licensed," one of our friends volunteered that "old Hilliard might be able to drive the Jacksons' tractor over and pull the truck out," thereby saving the offending driver from the parental punishment he was sure to receive. *(I knew those folks had brought my brother and me along for some reason. . .)*

To make a long story short, one of our crew hitch-hiked back to town where he obtained another vehicle. He then drove back up into the mountains to pick us up and then out to our farm where we indeed asked Hilliard if he would bring the tractor to pull out the truck. This was in the days after my father had pretty much decided his life and career lay beyond our small town, so he was far from Polk County during the week and basically unaware of what was going on "back on the farm," and by that point, I don't think he actually cared anymore anyway. (*More on that later. . .*)

Since it was my brother and me making the request of extraction of the Deuce by our tractor, Hilliard did not turn us down. I'm certain he had reservations, knowing our tractor was far from a tow truck with snatch-block pulleys and special extraction cables, etc. He nevertheless was the same good old Hilliard – always willing to give his best effort to help someone in need – especially my brothers and me.

Several hours later – after he had driven our tractor all the way back into the mountains to the backroad where the Deuce was mired – it had become painfully obvious after an hour or so of mechanical effort that the tractor was woefully inadequate for the extraction of the big Deuce-and-a-Half. Since he didn't wish to disappoint us, Hilliard had used every possible manner to move the truck, but that heavy Army vehicle needed greater leverage than a simple farm tractor for removal.

My brother and I weren't disappointed at all. We didn't really want to involve Hilliard in *"our friends' problem"* in the first place, and only did so to please them. At the conclusion of his efforts, we gladly thanked Hilliard and he responded with his patented wide white-toothed smile. *(He always had that big happy smile.)* He then backed the tractor up and began driving away.

Our compatriots, however, weren't anywhere nearly as satisfied as we were. They now knew they had no choice but to go back to town and "face the music." They would be compelled to reveal to their parents that they had taken the truck without permission and in an obviously-illegal driving status. Even worse, someone was now going to have to pay an expensive tow-truck bill. They were grumpy, disappointed, worried, and even a bit angry, thinking that Hilliard had somehow let them down.

We all piled back into the other vehicle which had been acquired. As they were driving my brother and me back home, we passed Hilliard who was cautiously taking his time with the tractor. The driver of our car drove dangerously close to the tractor, then roared around it, leaving Hilliard in a cloud of dust. They hadn't even thanked him for his effort, and now they were disrespectfully dismissing him without so much as a wave of gratitude. I couldn't help feeling bad.

Hilliard, however, was undeterred, continuing to drive carefully and cautiously up the dusty dirt road. And when I waved to him as we passed, he flashed his trademark bright smile once again.

Hall-Marks of the Man

Another thing I remember indelibly about Hilliard Gibbons was his amazing strength. My brother – 15 or 16 years of age at the time – was trying to hitch a heavy harrow to the tractor one day in order to plow a pasture. "The tongue of that harrow was far too heavy for me to lift up onto the tractor hitch," my brother stated in later explanation. "Hilliard walked up and said 'Heah Davit (He always called him "Davit," not "David"). Don't hurt yo'sef.'" As he said this, Hilliard reached down with one heavily-muscled big arm, picked up the long heavy-gauge iron tongue of the harrow and easily slipped it over the hitch.

I'm sure his immense strength was at least part of the reason Hilliard had considered becoming a professional boxer in his youth. He occasionally mentioned his boxing career desires to us. As with many youthful goals, however, life ultimately led him in a different direction. He met a pretty young lady named "Ruby," and steady work suddenly became more important to him than a boxing career.

Another of Hilliard's trademark features was his pipe and tobacco. We never had any trouble whatsoever in finding him on the acreage at our farm. All we had to do was follow the sweet smell of his pipe tobacco.

Hilliard smoked a very particularly fragrant brand of tobacco. It was what was known as "cherry blend," and was the most aromatic and pleasant-smelling tobacco I have ever encountered. In fact, it was the *only* pleasant-smelling tobacco I have ever known.

Back in the late 1950s and early 1960s, kids were exposed to all types of secondary tobacco smoke by their relatives and others around them. None of it smelled "good." In fact, virtually all cigarette, cigar, and pipe tobaccos of those days – and still today – had an exceedingly unpleasant smell as far as I'm concerned.

Hilliard's tobacco, however, was decidedly different. And there was always a steady stream of exhaled smoke wherever Hilliard was located too, making it quite simple for us to track him down. Unfortunately, Hilliard's love of pipe tobacco would later turn out to be a deadly habit which would come back to haunt this good man.

Boundless Humor

Oftentimes, Hilliard's stock-in-trade was pure humor, and it was one of the numerous things that made him so popular. He could take the simplest of incidents and turn it into a comic event.

Hilliard often talked to himself as he worked, and if he happened to bang one of his fingers with a hammer or mash it in a door, his quick exclamation would be "Look out Hilliard! Can't buy dem at *Sears-Roebuck!*"

As a very young child, my youngest brother Guy had a penchant for biting. It was one of his few defenses against his two older brothers, and had become his stock weapon. If you happened to irritate or anger him, you had to exercise extreme caution for at least an hour or so, because Guy would invariably exact revenge by locking down on your arm or leg like a pit-bull. And I'm here to tell you too, it wasn't a soft lock-down either. He'd leave a purple welt on you in a heartbeat before fleeing to avoid getting swatted.

Now Hilliard and his wife, Ruby (who were childless) doted on Guy. They would occasionally take him in and prepare him a small meal if they saw him wandering around on our farm. On one of his anger binges, Guy once even bit Hilliard, and for years thereafter, Hilliard still chuckled at the memory. "I just bit him back," he said. "Never had no worry bout it after that."

Over time, my brothers and I sometimes looked for ways to innocently tease Hilliard, simply because we loved being around him. We learned that he was deathly afraid of snakes, and as far as he was concerned, no snake – not a King Snake nor Black Racer, nor Rat Snake, nor any non-venomous snake – was a "good" snake. No matter that they kept the rats and mice from overwhelming our farm and some – such as the King Snake – even killed their venomous brethren. To Hilliard, the non-venomous snakes were "the devil" just as surely as were the venomous ones, and became instant hoe and axe targets for immediate execution.

After learning of Hilliard's phobia, the lights came on for my brother and me. We should have known better than to listen to the little mischievous voice speaking to us, but we were just kids.

One day we discovered a particularly large harmless King Snake that had been killed in the road by a passing car. We instantly decided to take it to

Hilliard's back steps where we coiled it up in a particularly-menacing fashion. Now Hilliard always used his back door to exit his house each morning, and we had placed the dead snake on the top step where Hilliard would walk out of his house and actually be stepping down upon the snake before he realized it was there. *(Looking back, I cringe today when I recall some of these things.)*

The next morning, we hid and waited. Sure enough, we soon heard Hilliard whistling a tune as he opened the back screen door to step down upon the top step. He had actually stepped on top of the dead snake before he realized what he had done. At that point, Hilliard literally sprouted wings. I've never seen a human jump as high and as far in one amazing leap in all my life. Michael Jordan had nothing on Hilliard Gibbons, and he (Hilliard) was not a young man at that point either.

Hilliard had also jumped from the top of the stone steps at his back door, which was a height of at least six feet off the ground. Mortals simply aren't supposed to be able to leap like that. It was a true testament to this amazing man's strength and agility at which we couldn't help but marvel.

By the time he hit the ground, Hilliard was anything but a happy man though – uttering strange staccato words and acting oddly. At that point, we knew we had carried this thing way too far. Convinced that we had damaged Hilliard for life, we pleaded for his forgiveness, which he of course immediately gave us, knowing by that point that he had been the object of a child's innocent prank.

Nevertheless, I couldn't help noting on the day of his snake encounter that it did take a number of minutes before the color came back into Hilliard's brown face which had turned the strangest shade of light gray. We never again teased Hilliard with snakes. In fact, we never again teased Hilliard about anything at all, such was our respect for him.

A Devoted Guardian

I will always believe Hilliard truly loved my brothers and sisters, because he demonstrated it time and time again. We were almost like his own children, and he treated us that way.

On Saturday afternoons, Hilliard always took his meager earnings to the local market to buy his week's-worth of groceries. His salary from employment at our farm couldn't have been much. My father wouldn't part with more than $2.50 per day for his own sons who worked at least four hours every Saturday and Sunday helping to milk the 50 or 60 cows in our herd.

Hilliard, nevertheless, was able to "make-do" on whatever it was that my father was paying him. He was a marvelous gardener, and my father allotted him a plot of land where he grew more vegetables each season than two or three families could consume.

I'll never forget Hilliard's delicious yellow-meated watermelons, huge cantaloupes, squash, tomatoes, butterbeans, corn, carrots, okra, and other delights. Even though he eventually had a sizeable family (six or seven children) after his second marriage (following Ruby's sad death), Hilliard nevertheless always shared his bounty with us even though we never requested it. He wouldn't have thought of doing otherwise. It was the Christian thing to do in Hilliard's mind.

> *"With your mind on my soul and a Bible in your right hand;*
> *You said 'Turn the other cheek*
> *There's a better world a-waitin' for the meek.'*
> *In my mind these words remain from Reuben James."*

Passage of Time

Some years later, when times turned bad for our family, my dad lost our farm to bankruptcy. Honestly translated, this means he was a pathetic and even foolish manager of his money. Dad had essentially abandoned us long before then, choosing to live with another female in Atlanta *(though we had no inkling of this at that time in our young lives)*.

Prior to the bankruptcy, Dad had returned sparingly on Fridays to free-up Hilliard on the weekends *(which had been part of their original working agreement)* and keep a bit of money coming in from the sale of milk from our dairy. Even though he was working full-time for the U.S. Department of Agriculture in Atlanta (beginning in 1968) and still drawing modest income from the dairy, he nevertheless was unable to save himself (and our family) from bankruptcy, because he was so far in arrears financially.

Dad, quite frankly, was deeply in the throes of alcoholism by that point, and had simply given up on us. He and my mother had both gone their separate ways years earlier.

Hilliard, meanwhile, was forced to find other employment following Dad's bankruptcy and loss of the farm. Did he turn to crime, or allow his misfortune to bring him to despair? No. Of course not. Hilliard did what Hilliard had always done – survive. No job was too small for him; no task too humiliating if it meant it would put food on his table. Many individuals today – both black and white – would scoff at such behavior, choosing instead to take some easier less-humiliating route to obtain funds, or just refusing to work at all and become a ward of the state. Not Hilliard.

Years later, after I had returned home from a stint in the *Army (to which I and my brother had both resorted – at least in part – to avoid the hunger and limited opportunities with which we were confronted at home)* and re-entered college on the *GI Bill*, I occasionally saw Hilliard when I rejoined my family during holidays.

By that time, Hilliard had obtained a job with the city, driving a street-sweeper down the dusty byways of our town – usually in the evenings, after the traffic had died down. I always stopped my car and flagged him down to chat for a few moments to find out how he was doing. We were all struggling by that point, and Hilliard was family to me. It was always difficult each time for me to say "goodbye" to him yet again, because I knew what a struggle his life had to have become.

Things were doubly-difficult for Hilliard too, because after Ruby's passing, he had married a very nice lady from Rome, Georgia, named "Marilyn." The new marriage included Marilyn's children by her former marriage: Michael, Marshal, Mark and Murray. Hilliard and Marilyn also produced several children themselves. Despite all his hardships, Hilliard always provided a home for all of his children.

The years came and went. I finally finished college; found a job which barely paid for the gasoline required to reach that job each week *(these were the devastating and depressing Jimmy Carter presidency years)*; raised a family and watched as friends, family and acquaintances drifted into the mists of time as old age, disease, and misfortune took their toll.

With strong enduring individuals, it is easy to forget that they eventually grow old and wear out too. Even as strong as old Hilliard had been, *"Father Time"* eventually began catching up with him as well. It had been easy to think that he would just "be there forever," but that, of course, was not to be.

Final Visit

I'll never forget the last time I saw Hilliard. It was Christmas sometime in the early 1990s I think, and I had a small gift for him. I wanted to do something to try to bring a little sunshine into his life. I had heard that he had been stricken with cancer and was gravely ill.

When I arrived at his home, I called out to let him know it was me. To my surprise, he appeared at his doorway immediately and walked briskly out to meet me in his yard, no matter the recent major surgery which had opened up his body to discover the cancer hiding there.

Without hesitation, Hilliard wrapped his once-strong, but now-diminished arms around me to give me a big hug, his trademark wide white smile lighting up his face yet again. That was the first time Hilliard had ever expressed any emotion of that nature in my presence. I later realized it was his simple way of telling me goodbye for the last time.

I gave him his gift, and spoke with him a few moments, asking about the family and other odds and ends, making small-talk as old friends often do when there isn't much to say and things are a bit awkward. I had heard that he was terminally-ill and I wanted desperately to tell him what he had meant to my life. Hilliard, however, was only interested in putting me at ease. In the end, I was able to tell him that I'd never forget him, and that seemed to please him. Again, the bright white smile.

Today, the legacy of Hilliard Gibbons is a meager one. Two of his adopted children still live in Georgia. One, Mark, is deceased. Of his natural children, one son died in his youth from brain cancer, and I do not know the present-day circumstances of the others. I have lost track of them. I do know, however, that he loved and painstakingly cared for them all.

On the day of his funeral – despite all his goodwill during his lifetime – I remember being surprised that there were so few mourners in the little church for this humble, kind and wonderful man who had been so helpful and loving to everyone around him during his lifetime.

My mother, brother, and I took a seat in the little funeral home. Perhaps by that point, there simply weren't many individuals in Polk County who remembered or knew him. I hope that was the reason attendance was so sparse. Hilliard Gibbons deserved much better.

This admirable individual will always walk the furrowed fields of my mind; remembered for the kindly, generous, God-fearing soul that he was, back in the days when his fatherly attentions were present for three young boys with little direction, whose own father had been preoccupied elsewhere.

—•⅋ ⅋•—
Old Scoutmasters Never Die

O ccasionally in the course of a young boy's life, an adult (other than the youngster's father) has a significant impact upon that impressionable mind. . . Sometimes the impact is of considerable proportion, lasting a lifetime. Such was the case with my friends and me when we were members of *Boy Scout Troop #14* in Rockmart, Georgia, in the mid-1960s.

For us, our scoutmaster was just such an individual, and in our eyes, he was almost mythic in stature. Whispered stories about his courage in battle during World War II had already made him a virtual legend in our community, so we knew he was special. But as adolescents, we didn't really care about those things. . . . No, what we cared about were the great adventures to which he introduced us. He literally filled our lives with outdoor fun during those scant years.

His name was James C. Ezzell, but everyone just called him "J.C." or "Jay." He was already in his mid-forties *(middle-aged is what they call it)* when we met him for the first time, and we of course felt that he was ancient. I now am in my early 70s (as of 2025), and I would trade quite a bit to be mid-fortyish again.

When we first were introduced to Jay, it was as an assistant scoutmaster. Jay was a local postal deliveryman who was very well-known around our community. He had already raised one step-son who had become a Georgia State Policeman, so we became his "second" family.

Though he had initially volunteered only to "assist" with our troop, it wasn't long before Jay had taken over totally in the leadership role. And it also wasn't long before he demonstrated to us all that age is merely a state of mind too – at least when one is in his 40s. Jay was a titan of strength and endurance.

Beyond his thinning hair and wrinkled face from a lifetime spent outdoors, nothing else about J.C. bespoke "oldness." His physical strength was unchallenged in our community, but that was never really an issue, because at heart, he proved time and again that he was just an old softie.

Long before any of my friends and I were introduced to Jay, our parents had known him and his family. As an athlete at Rockmart High School, Jay's prowess in sports – particularly on the football field where he had been a fearsome opponent – had been long established. There was no sport in which J.C. Ezzell did not participate in high school from 1938 to 1941, and he was a letterman and a star in them all.

Jay, however, had come up in life the hard way, just as did many individuals in our small northwest Georgia mill-town. As a result, he had learned at an early age that he would have to fight for much of what he achieved in life, and he gained a reputation in his youthful years as a person one simply did not cross.

As an adolescent himself, Jay had sometimes allowed his quick temper to get him into trouble. Though we never knew the exact circumstances of his infraction, Jay had committed a transgression of some type which had caused local judicial authorities to give him the choice of either being disciplined by the legal system or enlisting in the United States Army. Jay – always on the lookout for adventure – of course took the second option.

In short order, the young man from northwest Georgia was serving a tour of duty during the darkest days of World War II. Even as an enlisted man in the U.S. Army, J.C. Ezzell asked no quarter from anyone, and gave none in return if challenged – not even from his superior officers.

Though his resentment of authority apparently soon became clear to his chain-of-command, so also were his abilities at marksmanship and survival. It wasn't long before he was assigned to a special unit of U.S. Army scouts – the Field Artillery Reconnaissance Company (FAR) of the 601st Tank Destroyer Battalion. During World War II, FAR was one of the most dangerous units in all of the armed forces.

The men in Jay's platoon were assigned some of the toughest duty of the war – quite similar to that portrayed by the misfits in the major motion picture *The Dirty Dozen*, starring Lee Marvin (a decorated Marine veteran in real life during the war), Clint Walker, and a number of others. It was only later – much later – that we all learned what Jay had actually endured and the courage he had demonstrated in battle.

J.C. Ezzell and a number of other individuals had been organized into a special unit, working behind enemy lines and living off the land while learning the location of vulnerable German troops, their supply depots, and any other strategic targets. Jay and his men would then either attack the sites themselves, or call in the locations to Allied air support or to his radio contact. As a result of their destructive capabilities, Jay and his fellow scouts were despised by the Nazi troops they constantly harried and stalked.

"I was just an old Georgia country-boy who could spot things and made 'First Scout,'" Jay once was quoted in an article in the *Atlanta Constitution* newspaper. *"It is a terrible thing to take a man's life. I just don't like opening up the doors to those memories."*

According to a lengthy article in the *Constitution*, *"At 11:00 a.m. of August 17, 1944, near Hyres, France, Sgt. J.C. Ezzell's platoon was halted by a furious cross-fire from a German roadblock. Sgt. Ezzell crawled forward 40 yards to assault the nearest machine gun.*

"Just at this crucial moment, his rifle jammed. Undaunted, he dashed 10 yards through a continuous chain of automatic fire and jumped into the enemy emplacement. Using his jammed rifle, he clubbed the gunner to death...

"He then turned his attention to the second machine gun. He killed its rifleman, after which he quickly put the rest of the enemy to flight."

This was hardly the last time a heroic incident was recorded about J.C. Ezzell. On September 8, 1944, another engagement in which he was involved was described in an article in the *Rockmart Journal* weekly newspaper:

"Spying an enemy convoy of more than 30 vehicles approaching on the road, Ezzell manned his .50-caliber machine gun and when the lead vehicle was only 200 yards away, he opened fire and completely destroyed the first three vehicles. About 400 Germans dismounted from the remaining vehicles and deployed on both sides of the road.

"Despite the tremendous odds against him, Ezzell remained at his machine gun in an exposed position and with no regard for enemy small arms fire which bounded off his scout car only a few inches from his head, firing every available

round of his .50-caliber ammunition. His accurate fire killed 35 enemy foot troops and formed a roadblock, enabling a U.S. Army tank destroyer to take out 25 of the remaining 27 enemy vehicles."

J.C. Ezzell served a total of 32 months (2 years, 8 months) in heavy combat, much of it spent behind enemy lines in North Africa, Sicily, Italy, France and Germany, often working completely alone, surviving only by his wits and courage in some of the most dangerous duty of the war. Aside from earning a **Purple Heart** for being wounded in action, and the French **Croix de Guerre** which is the highest award for valor in France, J.C. Ezzell was also awarded the **Silver Star**, the third-highest combat decoration in the U.S. Army. In this veteran's opinion, it wasn't enough. Lesser men exhibiting less courage have been awarded the **Congressional Medal of Honor** – the nation's highest award.

Jay served until the day Germany surrendered in 1945. After returning home, he bounced around in several jobs before settling down as a postal deliveryman, dependably carrying the mail – rain or shine – six days a week to a portion of our community. He did that for many years, and was a fixture in town. On any given day, he could be seen walking briskly down the sidewalks of town and the residential neighborhoods, issuing a friendly greeting to everyone he met, always seemingly eager to somehow bring a ray of sunshine to them whenever possible.

Though somewhat quiet vocally, Jay was actually gregarious by nature, and a sportsman/fisherman by gene-pool. If someone from town wanted to go on a hunting trip that would be discussed in awe for months and years to come, all that individual had to do was enter Jay's "inner circle" of friends.

Jay's toughness, however, kept most people in admiration from a distance. Even when in his 50s, his physical prowess was still the stuff of legend. He was anything but ordinary, but his gruff exterior was all a ruse, belying his kind heart.

His daily foot patrols with the mail kept him in top physical condition. He wasn't a slow walker by any stretch of the imagination, since he intended each day to complete his "rounds" in time to get home for some fishing and hunting in the afternoons, and to spend every Monday with local *Troop 14* of the *Boy Scouts* where he was the leader.

When he volunteered to become our scoutmaster, we understandably were somewhat stand-offish at first, but that didn't last long. Since his family had lived in the community for generations, he knew all of our parents, and none of them had any doubt that their children would be safe with Jay.

He taught those who weren't already aware of it all about the "great out-doors," leading us on adventures that were remembered for the remainder of our lives. He hauled us around in his old U.S. Army-surplus Jeep, exploring areas far back in the Blue Ridge Mountains of our native northwest Georgia.

Jay, in fact, had a good bit of old Army equipment. We often wondered if he didn't have "O-D Green" blood. *(As is the case with many veterans, he had become accustomed to the Army and the tools of its trade, continuing to use them in civilian life.)*

Jay never volunteered any information to us of any of his heroic exploits during the war, but we all eventually overheard whispered descriptions from the adults and parents in our association. He would discuss some of the happier memories he had of his days in the Army, but rarely any of his combat memories.

But just as entertaining as Jay was to us, so also were we to him. He was constantly amused at our antics. I think that was a big reason he took on the responsibility of *Troop #14*. We brought about as much liveliness to his life as did he to ours. And depending upon just how unintendedly comedic we became, Jay's characteristic scratchy laugh would conversely permeate the air in degrees. He'd either be loudly guffawing or else moderately chuckling, and always amused. But regardless, Jay always laughed "with us," not "at us."

One aspect of our adventures in *Troop 14* lay in a big U.S. Army-surplus two and one-half ton *"Deuce-and-a-Half"* truck. Jay helped to find funding to pay for this immense six-wheel-drive behemoth for us. It could easily hold all of the members of our group and all of our camping gear in its cavernous canvas-covered rear section. When we came pulling up to a *Boy Scout Jamboree* or other camping event involving other northwest Georgia Scout troops, all eyes turned in our direction in admiration as that big truck came rumbling into camp.

Everything was an adventure with Jay. We camped in forests primeval near cascading waterfalls. We traveled to remote areas where we searched for ancient Indian pottery, arrow and spear tips and other relics. We even camped at Jay's ancestral family cabin – long abandoned – far back in the mountains, weathering a deep winter snowfall and staring in amazement at honey from a huge beehive in the chimney dripping down into the equally-ancient hearth as the wax comb was melted by the fire we had built. Bees very obviously had been storing their sweet liquid there unimpeded for decades. These were simple pleasures and glorious times to which Jay introduced us.

From his own youthful experiences at home and in the Army, Jay taught us survival skills that could be used to persevere under conditions which could be life-threatening to others. He took us on camping trips far out in the mountains, teaching us how to find food and live off the land, surviving on berries, nuts, fruit and fish. He taught us how to persevere in extremely cold weather; how to build a simple bed-frame out of downed branches from trees in order to keep our sleeping bags off the wet ground.

We were all so impressed with Jay that we'd go to great lengths to avoid letting him down too. One year when *Troop 14* went to a large camping jamboree at *Camp Sydney Dew* – the primary summer camp for *Boy Scout* troops in northwest Georgia at that time – *Troop 14* took home top honors not only in firearms and archery proficiency, but also in pioneering skills, such as the tying and use of specific rope knots for emergencies – and we were competing with some fifteen or twenty other *Scout* troops. To this day, I still recall several of the knots.

At our *Scout* meetings every Monday night, we'd start off with a competitive game of softball. Jay loved baseball/softball, and, when running the bases, he always limped from an old injury. He had been deer hunting on remote Blackbeard Island far down on the Georgia coast one autumn, and while climbing down from high in a tree-stand, he had fallen a considerable distance, snapping the bone in his leg. *(This was back in the early 1960s, when deer, contrary to today, had been extremely rare in most any forest in Georgia, having been hunted almost to extinction by that time. One had to travel to remote corners of the state such as Blackbeard Island to find deer to hunt.)*

Despite the terrible pain from the injury Jay had sustained in his fall, he had refused to mention anything about it to the men who had accompanied him on the trip, preferring to endure the pain in silence. It was only after his swollen leg had begun turning ominous shades of grayish-green and black – signaling much more dangerous circumstances – that he had relented and sought medical attention. After all, it's difficult for a walking postman to deliver the mail with only one leg.

As it turned out, Jay was fortunate with his broken leg *(if that's actually possible)*. His doctor had explained to him that had he waited any longer to seek medical attention, the leg would have required amputation. For the better part of a week, Jay had endured the pain and suffering just to avoid disappointing those hunters in his group who ultimately had to sacrifice their cherished hunting time in order to transport their close friend off the island in one of their boats to the hospital. Though he retained his leg, he, never-theless, walked with a substantial limp for the remainder of his life.

The unspoiled beauty and scenic landscape of Blackbeard must have made an impression upon Jay, because it wasn't long before he was arranging a camping trip there for our *Scout* troop. Blackbeard is one of several islands off the Georgia coast that continue to be a protected environment filled with an abundance of wildlife today. Bobcats, deer, armadillo, alligators, endless waterfowl such as pelicans, osprey, and ducks; skunks, raccoons, eastern dia-mondback rattlesnakes, cottonmouths, and multiple other forms of wildlife proliferate there.

While on our trip, we went on long hikes throughout the island. We skied in the brackish inter-coastal sound between the island and the coast *(dodging floating alligators)*. And just as always, our leader roared with laugh-ter as we lost our balance and bounced off the waves as he towed us with his speed-boat.

Our seasons with Jay seemed to stretch forever, but just as is the case with all young boys, we eventually grew into young men, moving on to things more interesting than the *Boy Scouts*. Females, automobiles, high school sports, summer vacations in Florida, and eventually departure to college unerringly took us – one by one – away from our indomitable leader.

In all honesty, I don't recall the day I ceased attending *Boy Scouts*... As with the rest of our group, I eventually just seemed to drift away. Jay, how-ever, never missed a beat, taking on new charges and teaching them the same things he had taught us, and, no doubt, enjoying their antics just as much.

As my life took me farther and farther from my hometown, I lost track of Jay but I occasionally thought of him and wondered how he was doing. Near the end, I went to visit him one Christmas to take him a gift. He was well into his 70s at that point *(not too much further along than I am now)*, and his family genes had not engendered long life.

Just as with our beloved family friend Hilliard Gibbons who is detailed on previous pages, I had heard that Jay was very ill – suffering also from can-cer – and I wanted to pay him a visit before it was too late. By that time I was all grown up into my 40s, married, and steadily pursuing a career as a writer.

When I knocked upon his front door, Jay suddenly appeared, still em-anating that indomitable presence and quick merry laugh. I couldn't help being shocked, however, by how small and shriveled this once-muscular and indomitable man had become. Cancer does that.

He welcomed my wife, Judy, and me into his small home on Lake Doreen near Rockmart. I couldn't help recalling that as a youngster I had learned to ski in that lake right there behind his home, and I looked wistfully out over the dark water as we chatted, recalling some of those adventures all those years ago.

Despite his illness, Jay's kind nature and warm demeanor still shone brightly. He seemed genuinely glad to see me.

We exchanged pleasantries and I caught him up on what I was doing and where I now lived. Not much had changed, however, with him. He still lived in the same little home in which he and his wife had always lived since the days of my youth. His wife had passed away several years earlier.

We talked and reminisced about old memories, laughing anew. He wanted to know everything that I was doing and had done since last he had seen me. We talked for an hour or more – until the shadows began to gather and I knew it was time to take my leave.

Almost exactly one year later on December 8, 1999, J.C. Ezzell passed away peacefully in his little home at the age of 78. I learned his sisters had sat lovingly around him, caring for him in his last moments.

I later also learned that on the day he was dying, J.C. had been asked if he wished to take Jesus Christ as his Lord and Saviour. He initially had declined.

During the years following the war, Jay consistently disavowed Christianity, stating that he couldn't understand how a loving God could allow the carnage that he had witnessed in World War II. He said he had on one occasion heard a fellow soldier praying to God for protection from a foxhole, and then almost immediately, that soldier's life had been snuffed out by an in-coming round from enemy artillery.

Nevertheless, later on his last day, when the end was clearly near at hand, it is my understanding that Jay ultimately relented, and departed this earth as a Christian. Well done old friend. Well done.

Old scoutmasters never actually die. They just grow ever larger in the minds of the "youngsters" they once led.

At War With Beavers

B ack in the early 1960s, my father – now long deceased – had a problem on our farm which needed attention. As I look back on the various and sundry incidents we experienced during those years, I sometimes just have to shake my head. One of those was Dad's war against a bevy of beavers.

For the uninformed on this form of wildlife, beavers exist throughout the United States except in California, Nevada, and parts of Utah and Arizona. They proliferate in the southeastern United States, particularly in places like Georgia, and though their activities represent many good qualities for nature, they also can be quite problematic.

Part of the routine business of raising dairy cattle and producing cow's milk for sale in public markets involves the production of food for those cows. One method Dad used a great deal was the cultivation of crops such as corn which he would harvest with a large mulching mower. After cutting and pulverizing the cornstalks and ears of corn, the resulting matter would be blown by the mower up a large tube into the rear bed of a large truck which followed behind the tractor and mower. This harvested product would then either be stored in a farm silo where it was pickled into "silage," or else fed immediately to the cows.

Dad spent a great deal of time and money planting and growing one moderately-sized field of corn for this purpose, and when beavers in an adjacent stream began damming up the creek water and flooding Dad's cornfield, he took particular umbrage. Dad's irritation eventually turned into rage against the pesky beavers, and things became somewhat lively.

The beavers had been in the vicinity of our farm for a number of years, but had never previously been much of an irritant. I guess their numbers eventually reached the proportions that their work in the creation of dams just took Dad by surprise. Whatever the circumstances, Dad reached his breaking point when his cornfield was flooded.

We tried initially to "still-hunt" the beavers by sitting up all night with shotguns to await their appearance, but they were just too wily. They always seemed to sense our presence.

We next tried tearing down their dams by hand, but that inevitably proved to be a far more laborious chore than anyone could handle when pitted against what must have been at least as many as six or eight (or more) beavers denned up in this one corner of my father's 500+ acres, adding still more branches and mud to the dam each night.

Dad eventually realized he was going to have to call in more "professional" help. I don't know from whence he enlisted the services of "the dynamite man," but with the announcement of his impending arrival, matters began to get really interesting. There were several rock quarries in our county, and explosives experts therefore were not in short supply at that time. Perhaps that's where Dad found his helper.

When the "explosives expert" appeared on the scene, Dad was unable to hide his pleasure. Not only had the beavers been eating his corn, their dam had flooded at least an acre of his field, making it impossible for him to harvest the feed in that area for his cattle.

We took the explosives guy out to the beaver dam, and he researched the site, noting where the "beaver den" was located and the size and fortitude of the very substantial dam the energetic rodents had by now created to impound the water from the creek. After he had made his projections and decided upon a strategy, the man departed. He returned the next day with his "tools of the trade."

Now back in the early 1960s, there just weren't a whole lot of restrictions on the use of high explosives in Georgia. If you could get your hands on dynamite *(which wasn't easy for obvious reasons)*, there were very few restrictions on its use for reasonably legitimate purposes. I don't know what kind of training this ordnance professional had been given, but he seemed to know what he was doing – at least at first.

Now given the fact that he was dealing with high explosives, as the "expert" began his installation of the dynamite, Dad, my brother and I moved back a good 60 yards or so from the site of the dam. I don't recall if that position was where the explosives expert had told us was a safe zone or what, but that was where we perched as the guy bored holes and mounted the sticks of dynamite beneath the dam all along its length. He also planted the explosives beneath the beaver lodge in order to cut down on the population in that manner.

Just as there were not a whole lot of restrictions on the use of high explosives in rural areas back in the early 1960s, there also were not a lot of restrictions on the elimination of beaver either. In fact, I don't believe there were any restrictions. Today, these oft-irritating rodents are highly protected and the penalties for their "execution" are quite stringent.

Dad took complete advantage of the system as it existed. We watched this guy as he ran detonator cords from the line of explosives, connecting it all together into one single series. He then laid down a single length of wire from the interconnected explosives all the way back to the 50 or 75-yard mark where we were observing his activities. When he re-joined us, he connected the wire to his device which supplied the electric current to detonate the dynamite.

Now we of course had zero experience in a situation of this nature. We had no idea what to expect other than the fact that it was supposed to be a nice little explosion which would remove the obstructing beaver dam and house. I suppose we perhaps thought the resulting destruction was going to be reasonably modest.

Looking back, it seems to me that the "explosives expert" also apparently was not fully appreciative of the import of his actions, nor, even more importantly, of what to expect once the dam had been removed. He just matter-of-factly went about the task of preparing for the detonation of the dynamite.

When the big moment arrived, I recall this guy turned around and asked my dad if we were ready.

"Ready?" we thought. "Ready for what?" As things turned out, we simply weren't "prepared" for anything. As far as we were concerned, we were merely observing this "expert" in the pursuit of his profession.

Anyway, when my dad just smiled and nodded, the guy cranked current to the detonation devices. To say that we were stunned, does no service whatsoever to the word "stunned." There is no word to describe what we experienced at that moment. Good lawdy Miss Claudy. . . .

When that dynamite was detonated, the concussion rocked us backward, and all we could see were branches, limbs, leaves, cornstalks, beaver crap and debris shooting at least fifty to one hundred feet in the air. The concussion of the explosion so stunned my brother and I that we lost our footing and fell over backwards. We were aghast at what was unfolding before us.

I feel certain the "explosives expert" actually was surprised as well, because he quickly ripped off the connecting wire from his generator – turned around and ran for his life. When we looked back in shock, he was already another 50 yards to our rear on higher ground.

I think my father was in almost as much shock as we were. There's just no way to describe the emotions running through one's mind when an explosion of that magnitude occurs for the first time. I would later come to enjoy it with a grenade launcher in the *Army*, but on our farm, it was a whole new experience.

Aside from the abject destruction of the beaver dam – which had completely disappeared by that point – the resulting explosion had also completely removed the beaver lodge as well. Mud, tree branches, pieces of beaver, turtles, fish, and all manner of other "unknown substances" suddenly began raining down upon us.

As if that wasn't enough, another aspect of this little operation which no one seemed to have anticipated suddenly became startlingly evident – the fact that a very large beaver dam at least ten or twelve feet or more in height and perhaps 30 or 40 yards in length – had been retaining quite a bit of impounded water. It, in fact, had created a substantial pond which extended for at least 100 yards or more back upstream and out into at least an acre of my dad's field. We suddenly realized a wall of this formerly impounded water was thundering toward us.

After having observed the fleet-footed retreat of the "explosives expert" – who by then was standing up on the roadway with just a bit of a worried look upon his face – and listening to the roar of the water headed toward us, we didn't require any further encouragement to "run for our lives." All of that impounded water was released in an instant, and it was crashing down toward us at break-neck speed.

Dad suddenly came to his senses and grabbed up my brother in one arm and me in the other, and took off in a sprint. I really don't know how he made it up the incline back up to the road where the explosives expert was standing, because there was a lot of undergrowth between us and the road. Suffice it to say that Dad plowed a trail through the obstructing vines, blackberry bushes and saplings without hesitation.

As we all stood up on the road in semi-shock, it was awesome how the debris had caught in the trees and spattered upon our shoulders and heads. I could see my dad shaking his head, so I know he was both shocked and amused at the same time.

And as for the beaver dam – it had completely disappeared, as also had the beaver lodge. No more toothy pests with which to deal down there anymore. And to my recollection, it was a good 15 or 20 years before any beaver returned to that area, and by that point, my dad had already gone bankrupt, lost the farm (literally) and simply didn't care anymore.

After things settled down just a bit, the "explosives expert" looked at Dad and said, "Anything else?" smiling as he held out his hand for payment. That was pretty much the end of Dad's war against the beaver.

Go-Kart Demon

As one ages, he or she sometimes reflects back upon his or her childhood to enjoy some of the happy – and comical – episodes in his or her life. It troubles me that I have more "years" of these experiences than I like to admit today, but then, that's life. Some of the memories are bittersweet too, particularly the ones that involved my youngest brother – Guy – who was tragically taken from us early in life. On the flip-side, some of my memories of Guy can still make me roar in laughter, and my life will always be richer for having experienced them.

When you were semi-poor and lived out in the "country" as did we in Polk County, Georgia in the 1960s, you many times had to be creative about your "entertainment." One pastime of my adolescence which stands out in particular involved a little item called a "Go-Kart."

When my brother, David, and I were approximately 14 and 15 years of age respectively, and my youngest brother, Guy, was approximately nine, we, to our delight, collectively received a motorized Go-Kart one Christmas. I had been begging and begging my father for a "Mo-Ped," which was a very popular small motorcycle in those days, but he had – for reasons that still escape me – declined, opting instead for the Go-Kart.

Dad's decision couldn't have been based upon safety, because the Go-Kart was imminently more dangerous than the Mo-Ped. Looking back, I'm sure it basically boiled down to cost, since the Go-Kart was somewhat less expensive than the Mo-Ped, and Dad undoubtedly just wanted to get me out of his hair about that Mo-Ped.

I also don't understand my parents' logic in presenting us boys collectively a gift of that nature. Again, it probably had something to do with the money thing. It always boiled down to "money" with dad, and there's just no getting around that fact.

Photographed four or five years prior to receiving the Go-Kart from their father, all three of the Jackson brothers have mischief in their eyes, particularly young Guy (left) with his little tongue stuck out.

In giving us a collective gift that year, Dad and Mother had to have known that it was going to be an object of constant contention between us, and knowing what I now know about their lives at that time, they already had far more "contention" than they could deal with, as their divorce would soon confirm. Ironically, the Go-Kart ultimately became a great gift for us.

This modest motorized vehicle was a great source of entertainment for my brothers and me. After we tired of driving it round and round in our yard, we took it out on the country road fronting our home – and that was truly dangerous. The Go-Kart had no brake lights on it; was not "street-legal"; and the individual driving it was totally unaware of any automobiles approaching from the rear, since the Go-Kart had no rear-view mirror, and the loud rear-mounted three-horsepower *Briggs & Stratton* engine drowned out all sound for the driver.

Nevertheless, we drove and drove and drove that Go-Kart around our yard and on those dirt country roads in the vicinity of our home, exacting maximum pleasure from it. Our front yard eventually was converted from a football playing field to a racetrack.

As indicated above, we three brothers had to "share" the Go-Kart, and that wasn't easy with an item that provided that much pleasure. As a result, we didn't always agree upon whose "turn" it was to drive the little vehicle, or how long that person should be "allowed" to drive it. Conflicts often arose, many times degenerating into a knock-down drag-out fistfight in our front yard.

One day, my youngest brother Guy was driving the Go-Kart and was reluctant to yield it to my brother David or me to ride. Guy was "the baby" in our family, and as a result, he learned early-on that all he had to do to get what he wanted from my parents was to set up a howl. After raising four kids, Mother and Dad had eventually become sensitized to "the howl" from

Photographed circa 1966-'67, the front yard race track had essentially been abandoned as interests turned to other preoccupations. The tall weeds clearly indicate that lawn-care also was no longer a priority with Dad and Mother involved in other pursuits elsewhere as well. Jackson Dairy and some of its pastures and beautiful mountains are visible in the distance.

the fifth child, and they invariably granted him whatever he wanted, just to shut him up.

Guy also learned that anytime he wanted punishment to be exacted upon his siblings, the howl worked wonders in that regard as well. Any conflict with Guy carried with it the imminent threat of the appearance of "the belt" being wielded by my father or mother. . . and, trust me, neither David nor I ever wanted to reach that point. It was just too scary, particularly if the punishment was being doled out by Dad on one of his "angry" days.

As explained above, the marriage between my dad and mother eventually began degenerating over a six- or seven-year period, ultimately culminating in divorce in 1969. In the years just prior to this unfortunate event, we kids were essentially left to fend for ourselves much of the time and to settle our own problems. Sometimes, we were creative about this "settlement."

My brother David and I always had a football handy in the front yard in those years, because we loved throwing it to each other and playing "touch-football" with friends and neighbors. After the acquisition of the Go-Kart, however, with the associated problem of dividing up the usage time between us three brothers, a new game was born. It was known generally as *"whomp the driver monopolizing use of the Go-Kart."* If one of us was driving the Go-Kart without sharing it with the other two, that offender became the target for our football flings.

Invariably, it was my brother Guy who most over-extended his allotted time-limit for usage of the Go-Kart. As a result, he quite often was slated for pigskin punishment. As described above, Guy was accustomed to getting his way, but with Mom and Dad out of the picture, things had changed considerably. Guy could no longer count upon them to provide him with specialized treatment.

Now it wasn't a simple matter for one to hit the driver of the Go-Kart with the football, so the offending driver many times didn't take a lot of abuse. For one thing, he was a constantly-moving target racing around the yard. For another, a part of this game eventually became *"Run down the football-thrower with the Go-Kart"* – an aspect at which Guy excelled.

Looking back, David and I usually were the ones exacting our "pound of flesh" from Guy for monopolizing the Go-Kart, and it resulted many times in a tearful and angry Guy. In our defense, however, the tears weren't necessarily the result of any pain that Guy was suffering. They, to the contrary, were actually from rage. In point of fact, Guy had an exceedingly quick temper *(which he had inherited from my father)*, and he absolutely despised "losing" at anything. *(Many are the checkerboards he flung into the air in frustration.)* He considered being hit by the football to be the equivalent of "losing" on his part, and that was actually the origin of his rage and tears.

Also, Guy wasn't completely weaponless in this little game. That Go-Kart could be a very effective instrument of pain if someone actually "wanted" to run someone else down with it, and Guy eventually had no hesitation whatsoever about using it to inflict maximum pain upon his brothers.

It also wasn't as if Guy couldn't simply relinquish the Go-Kart anytime he preferred and walk away with no further damage. Though he was loathe to admit it, Guy actually "preferred" monopolizing the Go-Kart, no matter that such a practice made him a target of the football. Over time, the fact that he thoroughly enjoyed meting out punishment to David and me with that motorized ankle-breaker was unmistakable.

Since we came to consider it a game – even though it meant Guy rode the Go-Kart most of the time – we eventually gave Guy a football helmet to wear, so that any "strikes" we made with the ball were hard-pressed to even slightly harm him. As he crouched down inside the cockpit of the little kart – wearing the protection of the football helmet – it was virtually impossible

(Illustration courtesy of Tatiana Mack, "YaneyaArt," Alpharetta, GA)

to hit him anywhere but in the head and on the shoulders with the ball. A strike on the shoulders did nothing but sting a few moments, and a strike on the head – due to the protection provided by the helmet – didn't hurt at all. No, Guy retained control of the Go-Kart simply because he enjoyed punishing us. Period. End of story.

Now when I say "punishing us," I'm not talking about "running up to us in the Go-Kart and then 'stopping' before striking us too hard." No. . .No. . . . I'm talking about flat out mercilessly running completely OVER us with that Go-Kart, rendering us prostrate and often injured upon the ground.

The worst part about such a "run-down" was that on the way "down to the ground" as it were, the victim invariably enjoyed the truly horrible experience of falling down in a sitting position upon the spark plug which stuck straight up into the air on top of the Go-Kart's gasoline-powered engine. One has not lived until one has sat down upon an "active" spark plug, particularly a plug in a highly-revved, three-horsepower, third-degree burn rendering *Briggs & Stratton* engine.

It was in the attempted avoidance of the onrushing Go-Kart that one usually was introduced to the spark plug. As Guy was nearing us in that speeding vehicle of vengeance and we could see that a collision was inevitable, we instinctively jumped straight up into the air to avoid the mind-numbing pain of instantly-broken ankles. The frame on the front end of the Go-Kart was made of heavy tubular steel positioned low-down on the ground, and it was extremely unforgiving to ankles. When we jumped up, however, it was rarely high enough to actually clear Guy and the Go-Kart. We'd usually end up "cart-wheeling" over him and then sitting down with a thud upon the terrible spark plug at the rear of the cart.

I can still clearly recall the high cackles of glee that Guy made in his joy of catching David or me out in the middle of the yard, and being able to run us over with that Go-Kart, and then of being able to turn around for a second strike while we lay crumpled and "shocked" upon the hard ground. The concept of "mercy" simply did not reside in the codicils of the heart of my youngest brother, Guy.

Aside from the trauma of being physically run over by a Go-Kart, the act of sitting down upon a live spark plug just scrambles one's brain for a moment or two. The mind goes blank from the voltage, and it's sometimes difficult to immediately regain the ability to walk, let alone "run for one's life" to avoid being decimated all over again. Guy absolutely lived for such glorious moments, and would endure endless torturous taunting and strikes with the football just to be able to experience one such revenge.

Anytime David or I threw the football, we knew we'd have to retrieve it before retreating to the porch or a tree in the yard to avoid Guy's "wheels of justice." And many times, the football would roll out into the middle of our big front yard, setting up a scenario of either "take a chance on retrieving it" or "sit and do nothing." Guy knew we were eventually going to take the bait and sprint out into the yard to retrieve the football. If we didn't chance it immediately, he would taunt us, calling us all sorts of abusive and insulting names and doing anything he could to tempt us into making the mistake of running to retrieve the football.

Though small, that Go-Kart could accelerate up to 10 or 15 miles per hour – more than enough to overtake a runner on foot. When he'd catch us in the open yard, a wide evil grin would inevitably spread across Guy's face signaling that the vengeance of Attila was about to descend upon us. All David or I could see were Guy's two beady eyes inside that football helmet and that widening grin of revenge.

Guy had no compunction about running us down either. If he had broken our leg or arm or ankle, he "might" have been remorseful for a moment

Mary (age 4), David (age 6), Olin (age 7), and Patricia (age 8) pose as instructed for the camera prior to being driven to church in December of 1958, possibly on Christmas morning. Olin and Patricia support young Guy (age 1), who isn't certain what exactly is going on, but is remaining "manageable" nonetheless for the moment. (Photo by Marilyn Jackson)

_____

or two, but it would have rapidly dissipated. Sympathy was in exceedingly short supply from Guy as he exacted a pure old fashioned "butt whooping" upon his older brothers.

Guy used the fear that the Go-Kart engendered to maximum advantage too. After he had run us down and we lay groaning upon the ground – usually with the breath knocked out of us and with aching ankles and a brain scrambled from "electrification" – he'd throw out that high-pitched cackle, then turn the Go-Kart quickly around and start back immediately for another strike.

After the moment or two of recovery on the ground, David or I would just be convincing ourselves that it didn't really hurt quite so bad, when we'd suddenly become acutely aware that Genghis Guy was bearing down on us yet again with the Go-Kart to make yet another strike – that ever-present evil grin spreading widely across his face. That was all it took for fleetness to return to one's battered body.

Somehow, through several years of this "game," we, amazingly, never suffered any broken bones which, to me, is something of a small miracle. I don't know how we were that fortunate, but then, looking back, I don't know how we made it through a lot of the incidents and experiences of those essentially parentless days. It's probably a big part of the reason that I'm pretty much crippled up in my ankles today.

The last time I saw the old Go-Kart, my nephew had laid claim to it. Guy had graduated to a Harley-Davidson "Sportster." I was living far from home by then, and married to my first wife with a whole new set of problems which would soon prove to be much more painful than the old Go-Kart, but that's another story.

Lest you be deceived, however, I still carry to this day a very healthy respect for spark plugs of any type, and due to my experiences with the Go-Kart, I probably always will. I suspect David does too.

—⟫⟪—

Capital Punishment
for a Brother

As the late rock-star George Harrison once quipped, "Forty years passes in a flash," and, indeed, I can confirm from personal experience that it truly does. I, nevertheless, can still see my brothers and sisters so clearly in my memories, recalling our experiences as we grew up "out in the country" of rural Polk County, Georgia. All of my immediate family of seven are now gone with the exception of my sister, Patricia, and brother, David, but my memories of my siblings and parents will live on with me until I take that great final trip myself.

We were a typical lower-middle-class family. We lived reasonably well, but there were no extravagances. As a result, we children had to be creative about our daily "entertainment," and it was often a rough-and-tumble existence that my two brothers and I shared.

The Yard Fights

My brother-in-law still laughs in remembrance of the times in the late 1960s when he visited our home to pick up my sister for a date. We, of course, were oblivious to the fact at that time, but my brothers and I were apparently somewhat entertaining to individuals who happened by our home.

When he drove up into our driveway, my brother-in-law said that almost invariably, David (my younger brother) and I would be rolling around in the yard, pummeling each other in an argument over some issue. We always fought outdoors in the yard, because we knew that Mother and "the belt" awaited us should we dare to undertake such activity indoors. As long as we weren't tearing up the house inside, she didn't seem to care too much if we were tearing up the landscape – and each other – outside.

The fights in which my brother and I engaged weren't the total enter-tainment package either. My youngest brother – Guy – earnestly enjoyed these fisticuffs because they provided him with an excellent opportunity for revenge upon his two older brothers for previous transgressions.

When Guy saw one of these fights flaring up between David and me, he immediately began a search for a hefty stick. David and I both knew that we'd be fighting a war of attrition "on two fronts" from that point forward. Guy would wait until the fight had developed to the point that one of us – either David or myself – was on the ground, then he'd beat the bottom man mercilessly with the stick.

Guy was totally impartial in these affairs too. If I happened to have the upper hand in the fight and David suddenly was able to throw me off and gain the advantage, Guy immediately reversed his allegiance and began tat-tooing me (instead of David) with the stick just as vigorously as possible. He didn't care which one of us he punished, because in his eyes, we deserved whatever he could dole out – and we probably did deserve it too. As long as he was able to beat on one or the other of us, Guy was happy, because somewhere earlier in the day, previous week or month, both David and I had committed any number of offenses to warrant Guy's vengeance.

Through the process of trial and error, Guy had learned over time that he could get away with these vengeful outdoor retaliations too. Neither David nor I dared turn our attention to swatting Guy (who was six years younger and much smaller than us at that time); we were simply too busy pummel-ing each other. The one who turned his attention to Guy would quickly get punched in the nose by the other brother, so we had to focus upon the imme-diate matter at hand – and Guy was abundantly aware of that.

I can still see these incidences in my mind's eye. . . and somewhere in the background, I can hear my brother-in-law mirthfully chuckling to himself, all the while vigorously urging us on. "Kick him in the balls!" he'd shout gleefully.

David and I almost always allowed Guy a measure of latitude in these affairs, because I am more than certain that he was more than justified in the punishment he doled out to us. Over the years, he received an abundance of abuse from his two older brothers.

<u>The Parachute</u>

Take the "parachute incident" for example. In the 1960s, there was an *Army-Navy Surplus* shop downtown in Rockmart where old military cast-off items could be purchased for a song. David and I loved to find interesting oddities there which we could buy for pennies on the dollar and put to adventurous good use.

On one occasion, we bought several small parachutes about the size of a standard umbrella. I have no idea what the original use of those small devices might have been, but we lost no time in finding a form of mischief in which to employ them.

When we had returned home, we began experimenting immediately to see how effective the little chutes were. We first attached small stones to them and dropped them from the tops of trees, the barn – any place that offered "height." Then we graduated to the use of small animals in the chutes. We tied the cat in one and dropped it off the roof. If that cat actually did have nine lives, he used every one of them that day.

We eventually hit upon the idea of using Guy in one of the chutes. Now Guy wasn't a moron by any stretch of the imagination. In fact, all things being equal, he was actually much brighter than David or me, but he was only seven or eight years of age at this time, so after a fair amount of "creative" coaxing, we were able to convince Guy that he could jump off the roof of our home – with the aid of the little parachute – and "gently float" unharmed down to the ground below. *(Yes. I know.)*

Guy had been watching just enough of those old World War II movies which showed U.S. Army paratroopers floating gently down into war zones using the much-larger standard-issue parachutes. As a result, he just didn't grasp the fact that our little parachute was of no more use than those little miniature umbrellas on top of female mixed drinks. To give him confidence, David and I climbed up onto the roof of the house with him, all the while explaining that the little parachute was *"a real U.S. Army parachute – just like the ones you saw on television."*

When Guy jumped off the roof of our house holding onto that little parachute, he, to say the least, dropped like a rock. The little chute provided just enough resistance to keep Guy from being seriously harmed, but not enough to keep him from getting the breath thoroughly knocked out of his lungs.

When Guy bounced off the ground below, both David and I winced. We knew it wouldn't be an easy "flight" to the ground for him, but even we didn't think it would be quite as bad as it was.

Somehow, Guy, who was a tough little booger, miraculously did not break any bones. He, understandably, was quite upset with us. And the fact that we couldn't control our laughter didn't help matters at all. I'm sure Guy filed that one away for future major revenge.

For a good month or so thereafter, both David and I were very careful not to turn our backs on Guy or allow him any opportunity for retribution, because we knew he'd have no mercy on us. And I do mean "no mercy" too. Guy was like that. . . He could be brutal. . . And he had an elephant memory.

The Ear Glue

In looking back, the times that Guy did exact revenge upon us probably were well-deserved . . . . but they absolutely did not warrant the degree of severity my "little" brother Guy often doled out. Take for instance the night of the rubber cement.

Now, for reasons which I have never been able to fathom, Mother and Dad put we three boys in one little room to sleep each night. . . . It was a scenario just begging for trouble. . . . even with the threat of Dad's wrath constantly hanging in the air. Maybe they were cheap. . . Maybe we were just too poor. . . I don't know from whence came their judgment. I just know there are circumstances which parents should not allow if they want to retain "peace in the valley," and the placement of the three of us in one room to sleep was a case in point.

On the night of the rubber cement incident *(sounds like a twisted murder case, doesn't it)*, Guy waited until David was fast asleep. Earlier in the day that day, David had been hard at work in the use of a tube of standard old rubber cement to glue together one of those plastic airplanes that were supposed to be so much fun for little boys back in those days *(What can I say? We didn't have mobile phones or iPads back then. Okay?)*.

When he heard David snoring peacefully that night, Guy knew his moment had arrived. David had made the fatal mistake of not waiting until "Guy" was asleep before going to sleep himself. The first rule of life in our little family was *"Don't turn your back on Guy."* The second rule was *"Don't do anything which warrants the attention of "the belt" from Mom or Dad – especially Dad."* The third rule was (more emphasis): *"Don't ever ever ever turn your back on Guy."*

Anyway, as David snored peacefully, Guy awakened me as he took that big ole tube of rubber cement, placed the tip of it into David's ear canal, then squeezed for all he was worth. He then tossed the glue in my direction and took off to hide.

Now I don't know why Guy was able to get away with such transgressions. Maybe it was because he was the "baby" of our family. Maybe Mother and Dad knew he took a lot of torment from us, so they just gave him a "pass" on a lot of things. I honestly don't know. Whatever the reason, Guy was able to get away with most anything – just short of murder – and was rarely ever punished for misbehaving.

After he had squirted David's ear full of that terrible liquid, it only took a moment or two before it took effect. All of that nasty old benzene, acetone, hexane, heptane and toluene – most all of which are devastating to the soft inner tissue of one's ear – began taking dramatic effect. David literally erupted. I've never seen such flopping around in all my life. David not only was flopping, he set up a howl that would have made *Wolfman Jack* green with envy on even his best night.

I couldn't believe what was going on right before my eyes. David quite simply was scaring me to death. I had never seen such trauma. I didn't know whether to run toward him to help him or to flee for my life.

You see, that's the thing. . . I was well aware that such a commotion in our little home at 10:00 pm on a work-night would never go un-punished. Just doesn't happen. Somebody "had to pay."

As I blinked in shock, I could clearly see that it was only David and me in that little room at that point. Guy had vanished like smoke up the Pope-stack. My life flashed before my eyes, because not only did I hear imminent punishment stomping angrily down the hall from where my parents were "sleeping," I suddenly realized that I was sitting there with the squashed out tube of that nasty ole glue right there on my bed.

Guy could do that when he wanted. He'd commit an unpardonable sin against David or me, and then he'd just disappear. Poof! He had hiding places that we could never find. It was most vexing.

It was at about that time that the angry heavy footsteps coming down the hallway reached and burst through the door to our room. At that point, we always knew that "the belt" was painfully near at hand, and somebody was "about to pay the piper," . . . . and there wasn't anyone in that room at that point except me and the victim.

If you grew up in a home where corporal punishment was standard fare, maybe you know or recall the angst involved in this scenario. . . . In order to exact maximum effect for being disturbed, the parent stomps down the hallway for fully eight or ten seconds before actually reaching the site where the punishment is to be administered. This is intended to (and does) exact maximum horror. By that point, the object of the punishment has been doubly punished, because not only is he terrified crapless, he is still going to actually get the "crap" beat out of him with "the belt." Trust me... It was the epitome of undershorts clean-out time. We never ever wanted to hear those footsteps of doom.

Anyway, there I am, cowering in my bed, with David screaming and flopping in the other bed. My eyes had to have been the size of coffee cup saucers when the door burst open and Dad walked in with – yep, you guessed it – "the belt," and it looked like that big piece of leather stretched for fifteen feet behind him. You think I didn't do some fast talking? A rich Georgia country lawyer had never demonstrated such skill.

When Mom and Dad realized Guy was actually the center of all the commotion, I would swear that they briefly considered using the belt on me just for good measure. However, they simply grabbed David up and took him to the Emergency Room at the local hospital. And once again, Guy never received even a tongue-lashing. He certainly didn't get tattooed by "the belt."

As for me, I was afraid to sleep for weeks after that. If Guy could impose that much torment upon David and me with no punishment whatsoever in the offing, my world was a very, very, dangerous place indeed.

The Lamp Post

A number of years later, after having matured into his early 20s, David was repairing the wiring in the yard lamp post at the end of the walkway to our home. He had been very cautious, determining which circuit breaker supplied current to the light post, and making certain to turn off that breaker before beginning the re-wiring.

David was doing everything "by the book," exactly correctly in order to safely re-wire the lamp post, but he overlooked one small item... He overlooked Rules #1 and #3 of survival in the Jackson household: *"Never ever turn your back on Guy! Never!"*

While David was absorbed with his work, Guy slipped quietly into the house via the back door and, as he watched in delight out the window, flipped the circuit breaker back to the "on" position just as David was splicing together the hot wire.

Now bear in mind, I'm not making light of this incident. It was an extremely dangerous bit of mischief, and I'm going on the record right here and

now to vociferously state: <u>DO NOT EVER ATTEMPT THIS ACTION</u> <u>YOURSELF!</u> <u>IT IS VERY VERY VERY DANGEROUS!</u> <u>PEOPLE</u> <u>HAVE LOST THEIR LIVES WITH SUCH STUPIDITY!</u> <u>OKAY</u>?!

On the other hand, it was a unique opportunity which Guy simply could not allow to pass by. As stated previously, he had no mercy whatsoever when it came to "pay-back" with my brother David and me. That's why we had to watch him so closely.

Also as stated previously, David almost certainly deserved a bit of "pay-back" for some previous transgression against Guy.... No... Let me correct that. He very definitely deserved some pay-back for some previous transgression. He just didn't deserve that severe a level of pay-back.

Thankfully, the ground wire was firmly attached and the ground beneath David's feet apparently was nice and dry that day and the electrical shock – though still severe – was not so strong that it greatly injured David (at least it didn't clean his clock). If you've never received a shock from a standard 110-volt house current or worse, take it from me.... YOU DO NOT WANT TO CROSS THAT THRESHHOLD. OKAY?? No one

– I repeat – no one wants to be lit up by electricity, especially by a current of 110 volts or more. That's one reason it is used as "capital punishment" for criminals. When Guy flipped that breaker, David suddenly was arms and legs akimbo, doing the hokey-pokey.

As he witnessed the spectacle outside, Guy was beside himself with laughter. He was a breath away from rolling around on the floor. Unfortunately, he made the classic mistake of leaning out the front door to taunt and laugh at David – who was still a bit foggy from the voltage – post electrocution.

When he saw Guy, David knew exactly what had happened and, quite frankly, had homicide on his mind had he been able to catch his brother whom he chased around the house with a ball bat. If he had caught Guy that day, a very, very, serious can of "whoop-ass" at the very least would have been opened and administered. As usual, however, fleet-footed Guy was far too swift and agile and he was long gone.

Every time I saw that old light post thereafter in the front yard, I thought of that incident and had to chuckle anew. But then, almost reflexively, I'd also look over my shoulder to make certain the merciless avenger wasn't in the neighborhood too.

And David. . . . well, he simply has never been the same. He doesn't sleep soundly anymore, and he has an exceptionally-healthy respect for electricity - and glue.

The Frog Gig From Hell

My wife, Judy, and I occasioned once to enjoy dinner with a very old friend and his wife. Billy Franks and I have known each other since childhood. We attended school through almost every grade together – all the way to the 12th grade. We worked together at the same cotton mill, and later experienced white-water rafting and other adventures together. As old friends often do, we began re-living some of those adventures during our dinner, recalling some of the "low-lights" of our youth.

"I remember one night I went frog-gigging," Billy began. "Elroy and Buford Lamplighter stopped by the house. *(Note: Buford and Elroy were two of the town "toughs" in those days, known for street-fights and drunken brawls at the local drive-in called 'Gus's' on Friday and Saturday nights. They many times were fine individuals when sober, but when intoxicated, it became a whole different ball game with them. One was well-advised at that point to simply turn around and walk quickly in the opposite direction.)*

"They asked if I wanted to go frog-gigging with them, and before giving it proper thought, I just said 'Sure,'" Billy smiled. "I should have known better, because I could smell the beer on their breath when they walked in the front door. Buford told me I needed a good frog gig, so I started digging around Daddy's garage. I knew there had to be one there someplace, but all I could find was a "fishing gig," which has several more tines *(spears)* in the head of the gig than does a frog gig. It was literally 'the frog gig from Hell.' (Billy had begun smiling in remembrance by this point.)

(For our more refined readers, "frog-gigging" is a time-honored "semi-hunting" activity in which one takes a long pole tipped with a very evil looking gig with which large bullfrogs – of the eating variety – are hunted and "gigged" on a pond, lake, or large creek. The activity is conducted after dark, using not only the evil-looking gig, but a substantial spotlight which the user shines

into the eyes of the frogs to temporarily blind them. Since this hunting endeavor occasionally is also conducted under the influence of a tad of alcohol, some odd adventures have been known to occur from time to time.)

"I was only fifteen at the time," Billy said, smiling even broader now. "Neither Elroy nor Buford appeared to have consumed much beer, but they weren't feeling any pain either. I simply should have known better than to join them, but my immaturity got the better of me.

"Buford, having already been ticketed for DUI several times, asked me if I wanted to drive," Billy said. "I took him up on this offer because my better judgment did forbid me from getting into an automobile with him at that point. Truth be told, though, a little voice in my head was also screaming at me to 'Run like Hell,' but I just didn't want to 'wimp-out' on them.

"Anyway, Buford told me to drive out Morgan Valley Road to the bridge beneath which Euharlee Creek passed. He said there were a lot of frogs along that stretch of the creek.

"When we got to the bridge, Buford – who was the oldest – told me to park beside the road," Billy continued. "He said we'd have to jump off the edge of the bridge down into the creek. Now when he said 'jump off the bridge' down into that dark void, it began to truly dawn upon me that I had entangled myself in something that I was about to regret. It was pitch-dark, and a bat couldn't have known how deep that creek ravine was, let alone a half-crocked Buford Lamplighter, but the big man wasn't taking 'No' for an answer.

"Even though I knew I was a damn fool for doing it, I went ahead and jumped off Morgan Valley Road Bridge into the deep dark recesses of Euharlee Creek and just hoped for the best. And yep... That was a mistake.

"When I hit bottom, I wished to goodness that I *had* just told Buford and Elroy that I was simply scared crap-less and bowed out of this little escapade," Billy grimaced in remembrance. "It still makes me knot up just to remember it. I had to lay there on the ground for several seconds, wheezing and coughing, trying desperately to get breath back into my lungs without letting them know that I couldn't make a little jump like that without showing great pain.

"In the process of my delayed recovery, it suddenly occurred to me that Buford and Elroy quite probably would be jumping right behind me into the same spot, especially since they couldn't 'see' the result of my jump, and were definitely intoxicated. I therefore knew that if I didn't get a move on,

I'd regret this mistake even more. I rolled quickly to my right and dragged myself as best I could out of the way.

"It was a good thing I did too. I could hear Elroy loudly complaining and refusing to jump because he couldn't see what he was jumping into. *(Somehow exercising better judgement, drunk, than I had, sober.)* Four or five seconds later, Elroy bounced off the rocks at almost the exact spot where I had hit, then groaned and rolled over trying to regain **his** breath.

"Judging from his actions at that point, I don't think Elroy actually freely 'jumped' off that bridge. I think Buford 'threw' him off, because as soon as he could breathe again, Elroy uttered a string of obscenities at his brother who by that point was laughing hysterically from back up on the bridge.

"After a few more seconds, Buford himself – who could never be mistaken for being cowardly – jumped and landed right on top of Elroy," Billy chuckled. "I heard a big 'whoosh' and some coughing and then cussing and Elroy came up screaming at his brother even more. Buford, who was distinctly larger and heavier-muscled than Elroy, just grinned and told him to shut up before he scared off all the frogs. Elroy hurled another epithet at his brother before stumbling along up the creek.

"It was at about that point that I realized I had an even bigger problem," Billy added with a flourish. "It was dark as a train tunnel in that creek and, like the idiots we were, we had only one little flashlight. Looking back, I'm surprised they brought any light at all.

"The absence of a good flashlight was bad enough, but the bigger problem was that I couldn't help but notice the multitude of eyes shining back at me from the creek bank," Billy continued. "They probably weren't anything more than bullfrogs, possums, or maybe harmless – but quite large – water snakes, but to an impressionable 15-year-old, they were all the dreaded croco-moccasin rattler. I have to tell you, I was petrified, but, again, the last thing I was going to do was let Buford and Elroy know it.

"We started walking up that dark creek tunnel, and the Lamplighters were making so much noise stumbling and falling as we walked that we never got near enough to a frog to gig it. Hell we never even knew if all those 'eyes' actually *were* frogs. Elroy cussed again as he stumbled along, stumping his toe. After an hour or so of sweating, cursing, and with bleeding toes from the large creek-stones, Buford must have seen a vision of an ice-cold *Blue Ribbon* beer, 'cause he suddenly informed us that we were going back to the truck – and Buford always set the rules.

"I, quite frankly, was relieved that he was calling it 'quit' so soon," Billy chuckled. "I hadn't been this beat-up, bruised, scratched and tired in quite some time.

"Now by this point, we were in a place where the creek banks were very high and steep," Billy smiled again in remembrance. "We had to walk a short distance before we could find a place where we had even *a chance* of climbing out. Unfortunately, Elroy was too fat and Buford was too drunk to climb, so I was 'elected' to climb up first. *(Billy's grin was ear to ear by this point.)*

"I crab-crawled up that bank while they pushed me from below," Billy said. "When I reached the top, Buford held up the handle-end of my fish gig to me – with all those nasty extra tines pointed back down towards him in the creek – and told me to pull him up the bank. I just looked at him for a few seconds trying to make certain he was serious, but he didn't blink. He grabbed hold of the gig just above the gig head and gruffly shouted 'Pull!'

"To this day, I don't know how Buford Lamplighter thought a 15-year-old boy was going to haul his 220-pound carcass outa' that creek-bed," Billy said, shaking his head and still in disbelief. "I gave it my best effort, but I was exhausted, and Buford was about 120 pounds too heavy. I somehow was able to get him about halfway up the side of the creek bank when my sweaty hands suddenly slipped off the handle of the gig. Buford flew – head-over-heels – back down into the creek with a thud.

"The next thing I heard was a very strange kinda' primal scream. *(Billy was giggling mirthfully now.)* It wasn't just a yell. It was a ferocious and pain-filled bellowing – the kind of outburst that tells you in no uncertain terms to run in the opposite direction.

"By this point, my eyes had adjusted some to the darkness, and as I looked cautiously down into the creek-bed, I could see Buford lying on the ground on his back – with that fish gig sticking a good three or four inches into the meaty part of his thigh. He was holding onto that gig for dear life too, trying his best to keep it upright in the air so that it didn't fall sideways and rip at his flesh.

"I said 'Are you okay?' knowing as soon as I said it how stupid a question it was.

"He quickly screamed back 'Hell no I'm not okay you damn lap-eyed lunatic!' He added a few other choice words I can't repeat here in polite company.

"I didn't have a clue what to do next," Billy laughed, holding his sides

uncontrollably by this point, "and Elroy was no help whatsoever. He was standing a few feet away enjoying the situation immensely with a stupid grin on his face. I'm sure he also was very relieved that it wasn't him with that prickly spear sticking out of his leg. He stumbled over to Buford to help right the gig.

"Buford suddenly screamed at Elroy 'Don't touch it! In case you haven't noticed, moron, that's blood comin' outa my leg.'

"Elroy, who was eternally up to mischief of some form or fashion, turned around and looked up at me on the creek bank. With a big grin, he said 'I think I can help him.' When he then winked at me, I remember thinking that I should probably just cut my losses and tactfully try to make my way back to the car. I knew nothing "good" was about to come out of any of this.

"Elroy turned around and gripped the gig near Buford's leg," Billy croaked, laughing almost hysterically by this point. "Buford's eyes widened in disbelief. His lips began quivering, but his voice just wouldn't seem to function. Even though he knew his brother was fully capable of such sincere devilment, he just didn't believe that he'd dare actually attempt anything so foolish as what he appeared to be about to do!

"Never a person to 'beat around the bush,' Elroy suddenly – with all his might – jerked the gig backwards in a ferocious attempt to tear the spiny barbs

Euharlee Creek still enjoys a plethora of wildlife even today, but few, if any, individuals would consider it a viable opportunity for frog gigging anymore.

from Buford's leg," Billy gasped, laughing uncontrollably now. "Even though it was an unbelievably-powerful yank, the gig with all those barbs didn't budge an inch from Buford's leg. . . but it did tear unmercifully at his flesh.

"I guess maybe he actually thought he was helping," Billy said, now with tears running down his cheeks, "but I also couldn't help but believe he was getting in just a little bit of 'pay-back' too for the earlier treatment up on the bridge.

"After Elroy's yank at the gig, Buford didn't react at all for a second or two," Billy croaked. "It was like he was in another world. Then the pain hit him like a south-bound freight train, and he screamed louder than a train-horn.

"When his brother began roaring, Elroy didn't even hesitate. He dropped the fish gig handle and ran for his life. Buford lunged for Elroy with murder in his now deeply blood-shot eyes, but all he got was thin air. He then started running his hands through his pockets searching for a gun, a knife, or a big rock – anything – to use on Elroy, who by this point was floundering down the creek in a mad dash to get as far away from Buford as possible.

"Then Buford screamed at him again," Billy added. 'You son-of-a-bitch!!! I'll kill you if I ever catch you!!' The bushes shook and I guess every animal within five square miles must have run for cover.

"I truly think he meant it too," Billy heehawed again in remembrance. "Buford had an arrest record for several *Assault & Battery* charges, and was known to be brutal on occasion. I think that from experience – up close and personal – Elroy had learned the hard way when to flee his brother's reach.

"By this point," Billy said, "Buford had used up a lot of energy, and I'm sure he wanted nothing more than to just get out of this mess and get to a doctor. He looked up at me desperately and told me to come down and help him back up the creek to the truck.

"I knew it'd take two of us to get Buford's 220 pounds back out of that creek. He was just too heavy and unstable for one person, and the extreme pain from his wound had made him woozy. Someone would have to hold the gig and keep the handle from getting snagged in the undergrowth to avoid causing more hysterics and murder attempts.

"I called to Elroy to come back and help us, but he instantly refused," Billy continued. "He was nobody's fool. After much coaxing and knowing that he was going to have to walk home if he didn't help, Elroy finally relented, but he wouldn't get any nearer to Buford than the far end of the gig handle. I guess he knew better than to get within arm's reach.

"By this point, Buford was willing to agree to anything. So here we went, three men stumbling back down the creek-bed, with a long-poled fish gig sticking out of the leg of one participant.

"Elroy still wasn't really helping matters any either," Billy intoned. "I could hear him giggling about his earlier 'clean & jerk' effort with the gig, and he was only half-heartedly trying to keep the long pole from getting tangled in the weeds and vines, and every time it snagged, Buford had another conniption fit.

"And I was amazed," Billy moaned. "Elroy seemed to be thoroughly enjoying tormenting Buford! Every so often, he'd let the end of the gig-pole snag in some bushes or brush or something, and when he did, Buford screamed so loud that I was terrified all over again, and then he'd start running back through his pockets yet again searching for something to use to punish Elroy. At that point, Elroy would just drop the gig-pole and dash back down the creek to safety once again, cackling insanely.

"I really don't know how we did it, but we finally got Buford back out to the truck," Billy sighed. "We had to load him really carefully into the back bed of the pick-up in order to accommodate that long gig-pole.

"I finally got back behind the wheel to drive, and Elroy hopped into the front seat. As soon as we reached downtown, though, Elroy just bailed out of the front seat without a word into the street and hit the ground running.

I guess he had made up his mind that it was just too chancy to be in the same zip code with his older brother once that gig had been removed. I heard later that he had actually left the state.

"I finally got Buford to the emergency room at the hospital," Billy added, "but our problems were far from over. In fact, the emergency room created a whole new set of problems. Anyone getting even near to that gig in Buford's leg was taking his or her life in their hands.

"One doctor finally convinced Buford that he could relieve most of the pain if he would just allow a local anesthetic injection around the barbs, but Buford hated needles, so he was having none of that. He swatted the first doctor who advanced on him with a syringe, bouncing him off the wall. He then warned them all that the next one who tried that would wake up on the floor.

"One thing led to another, and I guess that by then, the pain must have been really building in Buford's leg," Billy smiled ruefully, "cause when the doctors were about to discharge him to do whatever he pleased about the gig, Buford got hysterical. When he realized he had no choice, he finally relented and allowed the injections. I thought he was going to pass out before they finished.

"Every time that doctor injected the anesthetic around a barb, Buford flinched and the doctor reflexively jumped back. Buford's first swat had gotten his attention.

"I guess it took an hour or so to cut all of those fish barbs on the gig out of Buford's leg, and every time one was removed and Buford could feel the slightest tug on that ragged bloody flesh in his leg, he'd lift that big arm to swat someone else, and each time, the doctors would jump back and threaten to leave again. Even with the anesthesia, I can still hear Buford screaming threats. It was nightmarish.

"I don't know where Elroy lived after that," Billy stated matter-of-factly. "That was the last time I heard of him or his brother going frog-gigging – or, for that matter, doing anything together. In fact, after that night, I heard Elroy not only had left the state, but had actually changed his name.

"And God forbid," Billy laughed one last time, "since that time, I don't think anyone has ever dared to mention anything about frog-gigging again in Buford's presence."

—•❧ ❧•—

Memories of the 1960s
And a Place Called Gus's

I occasionally return to my hometown in northwest Georgia where I grew up in the 1950s and '60s, more often than not to attend the funeral of an old classmate or family-member. Often as I pass through the town of my birth, I can't help reflecting upon the many changes which have occurred since my childhood days there, and my mind often wanders to memories of my experiences in those days of my youth.

I don't know how many of you have ever had the good fortune to enjoy the movie *American Graffiti (Universal, 1973)*, but when I saw it the first time, it galvanized me, because it almost perfectly captured a slice of Americana (now long gone) which accurately depicted a very similar storyline in my own life. The movie, in fact, almost seemed to have been made *about* my hometown.

Of course, that was the very intention of famed filmmaker George Lucas who created the celluloid classic. That is often the hallmark of a great movie: art accurately imitating actual life. It is the very essence of great theatrics.

Now there were many, many aspects of *American Graffiti* which reflected the youth and innocence of 1960s small-town America, and there were many, many characters in that movie that residents of small towns all across our great nation undoubtedly felt they knew personally. In my own hometown, it was equally-simple to associate many of the characters portrayed in *American Graffiti* with individuals I had known as I was growing up:

The eternally-cool drag-racer, *John*, (portrayed by Paul Lemat); the hopeless nerd (portrayed by Charles Martin Smith); the inimitable *Curt*, who is slated for college but just can't make up his mind about his future (portrayed by Richard Dreyfus); and the ultimately intelligent never-does-anything-wrong *Steve* (portrayed so poignantly by Ron Howard); were all very characteristic

Gus Weaver, owner/operator of Gus's Drive-In in Rockmart rings up another sale at his cash register. Bins of candy and other delights are visible in the background.

of some of my own friends and acquaintances from the early 1960s.

I think, however, that it was the fast-food drive-in hang-out in the movie – *Mel's Diner* – that most captured my attention. In my youthful days, a little drive-in at the edge of my hometown was the epitome of all that *American Graffiti* sought to portray and embrace – and much more.

Gus's Drive-In

Throughout the 1950s and '60s, *Gus's* drive-in in fact was much more akin to *Mel's Diner* than would seem humanly possible. Now I know that perhaps sounds like an exaggeration, but had you been there yourself, or able to ask some long-time resident about it who had been there, I'm sure my contention would be confirmed.

Gus's was built sometime in the late 1940s by a businessman named Gus Weaver. He and his wife – "Miss Jessie" (or "Miss Jeffie." I never really knew which) – owned and operated the establishment for the duration of its existence. Throughout the years, *Gus's* wasn't necessarily the place where the "proper" kids collected, but most of the Rockmart teenagers nevertheless met their friends there at least occasionally, and Gus and Miss Jessie kept it clean and respectable for most of its 20- or 30-year lifespan, so it wasn't a "dive" by any stretch of the imagination.

As I matured into my junior high and high school years from 1963 to 1969, *Gus's* was still *the place* where teenagers congregated, but by 1969, it also had become a much less "tame" diversion. It was still the place where the players on successful *Little League* baseball teams often gathered for free milkshakes and post-game celebrations; and still the place to occasionally take a date, or to "hook-up" with friends vying to meet that special young lady, etc. Beyond all this, however, in its later days, *Gus's* also had become a place where young "toughs" went to make a reputation for themselves.

It was at about this same time that old Gus Weaver finally passed away, so the "law-enforcement" aspect of this venerated landmark ceased to exist.

Miss Jessie took over full operation of the business and did her best to continue her husband's traditions, but by this point, she was somewhat elderly herself. "Law-and-order" at *Gus's* therefore pretty much ceased to exist.

Part of the problem lay in the fact that old Gus had chosen – probably for tax reasons – to build his drive-in approximately 20 yards from the Rockmart City Limits. This meant that the local city police did not patrol or respond to any law enforcement needs at *Gus's*. That was the domain of the county police, and at that time, the county had only a sheriff and one deputy and their office was located at the county seat of government in Cedartown, which was eleven miles away. So anything which necessitated law enforcement at *Gus's* was "done and gone" by the time the county police finally arrived on the scene.

Nevertheless, Miss Jessie did an adequate job of management at *Gus's*. And as long as you were a respectful paying customer, Miss Jessie was your friend. If, however, one was intoxicated or otherwise causing trouble at *Gus's* (which had become standard fare on Friday and Saturday nights by the late-1960s), Miss Jessie was not a person with whom one wanted to trifle. She had a *Smith & Wesson .38-Special* which she carried around in her pocket, and she wouldn't hesitate to "pull it" if necessary.

"Mr. T" and the "T-Burger"

In addition to the camaraderie and *joi de vivre* (as the French put it) which drew high school students to *Gus's*, another attraction was the delicious food. There is no way today to describe the mouth-watering hot dogs and hamburgers and fried onion rings and delicious milkshakes for which *Gus's* had become famous, and the individual responsible for a big part of that preparation and cooking was a fellow called simply "T." Don't ask me from whence came the name "T." I simply do not know.

I can still smell the delicious aroma of the chili-dogs, onion rings and hamburgers which T made famous, and which one immediately encountered as soon as he or she entered the parking lot at *Gus's*. The chili-dogs and hamburgers cost 35 cents and 45 cents respectively, and they, and most of the rest of the delicious fare at this illustrious drive-in were made famous by T.

When Miss Jessie wasn't available, T also became the on-site "enforcer," especially if someone placed an order for food and then failed to make payment. Under those circumstances, T was just as unpredictable and dangerous as was Miss Jessie.

Photographed in 1950, Gus's was a landmark for at least two decades, patronized by teenagers and occasional adults from all over the area. It still lives in the memories of a few Polk County old-timers as a place of high adventure and delicious food. The notorious jukebox which sat unmolested for some fifteen years, stood in the center of the substantial parking lot (not visible, far right).

T knew that the *Gus's* parking lot was filled with a bunch of rowdy "white boys" looking for an opportunity to establish a reputation. When T marched out the kitchen door to collect for an unpaid hotdog or hamburger, he always – always – carried a butcher knife that was almost as big as he was. He didn't work six days a week from noon till 11:00 pm to cook up food for free, and he "took no prisoners" when someone attempted to leave without paying.

Like I said, *Gus's* was that kind of place – lively. There was a line-up of "curb-boys" to take food orders and then serve it on the trays which the patron hung on his or her half-rolled-up window – just like at the drive-in movies (which also are now just as extinct) – and also just as portrayed in *American Graffiti*.

There was also a big "jukebox" in a little wooden weatherized shack – all alone no less – in the middle of the parking lot. It too was much the same as the jukebox portrayed inside *Mel's Diner* in *American Graffiti*. Someone could always plug in a dime (later a quarter) and enjoy the latest tunes from all the rock & roll stars of that era.... if that patron wished to chance the huge rats who lived beneath the shack and survived on the scraps of food left in the parking lot at the conclusion of each night's festivities.

In the back room of *Gus's*, a professional billiards table was often abuzz with activity and high-stakes gambling on Friday and Saturday nights. Disagreements in some of these games also were the instigation of some of the knock-down-drag-out fisticuffs which routinely proliferated in the parking lot.

"Young Toughs"

As stated above, in the mid- to late-1960s, *Gus's* was also the place where young "toughs" – usually of the "predator" variety – congregated to establish the local "pecking order." Just as is so often the case today, there were a lot of roughnecks back in those days, and if you hung out at *Gus's*, you had to be prepared to deal with that scenario. If you weren't prepared and didn't deal with it, well – you were just another Charles Martin Smith. Know what I mean?

In those days, "drag-racing" was also a regular pastime "near" *Gus's* out on "Prospect Road" and elsewhere. Prospect bisected old U.S. 278 right at the parking lot at *Gus's* and was the site of quite a bit of action. Racers would sometimes line up approximately halfway out Prospect and race back toward *Gus's*, and I have to confess right here and now that it took some "brass ones" to be involved in that action.

One individual, "Spider" Thompson, was running neck-and-neck with a competitor one evening and was so determined to win that he never let up on the accelerator as he thundered down Prospect and approached the intersection of U.S. 278. So intent was Spider upon winning the race that he never attempted to apply the brakes at 278, sailing through the air right down into the parking lot at *Gus's*. Several parked vehicles became drag-racing casualties that night, but miraculously, no one was killed.

Action was always the name of the game at *Gus's*. I remember an occasion when a young roughneck named "Bubba" Hines followed his usual routine of intimidation. He, however, made the mistake of humiliating a fellow named "Hooty" Reeves on this night. As usual, Bubba felt certain he could perform a "ground and pound" (and thus further enhance his reputation) on this presumed victim.

As was the case with most of his targets, Bubba outweighed Hooty by at least 50 or 60 pounds, and that extra bulk was solid muscle too. Fat tissue need not apply to Polk County plowboys. Bubba was accustomed to "having it his way" long before *Burger King* came to town too.

On this occasion, however, old Bubba's luck had simply run out. He made the classic mistake of coming to a knife fight *(in those days, it was almost always "knives," not guns)* with only his fists. When Hooty finished slicing and dicing old Bubba and then hammering him senseless, he was left lying on his back in shock in the parking lot, blood streaming from multiple wounds across his body, rain falling upon his face and washing the blood into the gravel, waiting for someone to rescue him and take him to the Emergency Room at the local hospital.

Needless to say, old Bubba was considerably more cautious after that little tragic episode, and he most certainly never crossed Hooty Reeves ever again. Bubba, if nothing else, was a quick-study on those types of matters.

That was the way it was at *Gus's*. If one was seeking a "rep," that was the place to go get it in the 1960s. Another regular denizen of the *Gus's* chronicles was Buford Lamplighter. Now Buford was even larger than Bubba Hines, and ate nails for breakfast. Bubba, as a matter of pure self-preservation, always kept a low profile when Big Buford was in the parking lot. Interestingly, no matter how big a "bad-ass" one thought one was at *Gus's*, there almost always seemed to be someone bigger and badder.

"Crusher" Stephens

On one memorable evening, even Big Buford met his match. That night, he had consumed his usual two six packs of canned courage and had stepped out of his car, loudly challenging anyone within earshot in the parking lot (which meant everyone). To emphasize his presumed dominance, Mr. Lamplighter began slamming his fist into the hoods of the cars in his vicinity, just daring someone to exit one of the cars to take issue with him and the large dents he was placing in their cars. When Buford appeared on the scene, one could hear engines cranking all over the parking lot as patrons eased out onto U.S. 278, abandoning the field.

These proceedings almost always occurred near or after 11:00 pm, after *Gus's* had closed for the night and Miss Jessie's .38 and T's butcher knife and any form of law enforcement were all far removed from the scene. With the beer doing his talking, all Buford wanted was a challenger so that he could pound out an even-greater reputation.

Interestingly, despite his demeanor when intoxicated, when he was sober, Buford actually was a reasonably likeable human being. The arrogance and bullying nature "pretty much" receded from the picture.

Just as had many in Polk County, Buford had grown up hard. He had dropped out of school at an early age to work in a local cotton mill to support his invalid father (who actually was laid up with a bottle of moonshine most of the time), and the only way he knew to acquire the respect to which he felt he was entitled was to dominate his peers physically.

Well, every dog has his day, though. After he had pounded on a number of car hoods within 40 or 50 feet of his own car, Buford finally made the mistake of assaulting the hood of a car owned by one "Crusher" (another of the bullish monikers all the local toughs seemed to acquire) Stephens who happened to be visiting from Cedartown. Now Crusher had gone unnoticed by Buford, right up until the big man (and I mean big) unfolded himself to step out of his car.

When Buford had slammed his fist into the hood of Crusher's car, it had left a sizeable dent, and it was a dent Buford Lamplighter lived to regret. When he saw Crusher emerging angrily from his vehicle, tire tool in hand, Buford became acutely aware of his mistake. This was a whole new experience for him and Buford had that look on his face that indicated he needed to check his pants. You know the look.

In order to avoid an immediate loss of face, Buford nonchalantly turned his back on Crusher and retreated to the far side of his own car where he began berating another unfortunate individual, no doubt silently praying that Crusher was simply headed for the restroom. The tire-tool, however, should have been a dead-giveaway, as it was to most of the knuckle-draggers at *Gus's*.

Crusher never even hesitated. He began tattooing the hood of Buford's car with a vengeance, giving a whole new meaning to the term "textured surface." He next moved to the windshield, creating nice spider-web patterns all across it, working his way across the top of the car and ending with the trunk.

Despite his better judgment to the contrary, Big Buford screamed an epithet in rage at Crusher from the edge of the parking lot to which he had retreated. He, nevertheless, had sized up the situation with Crusher and decided that, under the circumstances, his car would just have to be expendable.

What Buford didn't know was that Crusher had only just begun to retaliate. He meant to exact maximum retribution to make certain Buford didn't ever make this mistake again.

After he had tired of abusing Buford's car, Crusher suddenly bolted for the big man himself, but the lesser bully was way ahead of him. That night, Buford Lamplighter became a champion sprinter unsurpassed in Polk County history. He cut a trail across the back side of the parking lot at *Gus's*, hotfooting it up into the tenements beyond on the hillside, ultimately disappearing into the distance. Crusher never even came close to catching him, but he did finish off Big Buford's car with a devastating battering after he returned to the parking lot.

Juke Box Heaven

Now lest you think all of the action at *Gus's* was violent – it wasn't. It had its comic light moments as well – if nevertheless sometimes still a bit destructive. Take for example the forays of one Lester Hurt.

As a result of the high thievery condoned in present-day society of the 21st century, a valuable item such as a jukebox could never be left completely unattended these days in a parking lot, especially during off-hours, and it certainly couldn't be left completely unguarded in a drive-in parking lot over-night. It would simply be loaded onto a trailer and hauled away by thieves in the night.

Back in the 1960s, however, such a crime was not much of a consideration. In those days, even the town outlaws had their limitations as far as lawlessness was concerned. The little jukebox at *Gus's* therefore sat unmolested out in the parking lot in its jukebox shack hour after hour, day after day, year after year with never the slightest attempt ever made to vandalize or steal it. . . . That is, until the night of Lester Hurt and the haughty lady.

Lester's grudge against the little jukebox began innocently enough. It all started one evening when a female kept playing the same record in the jukebox over and over again. *(This of course was in the days when a jukebox physically played records called "45s" instead of a digital file. These round vinyl disks were often referred to as a "45" because that was the number of revolutions per minute necessary for them to spin in order to produce music.)*

Finally, by the 15th or 20th play of this one particular 45, Lester hit upon the idea that it might serve as a good "intro" to strike up a conversation with the lovely young thing who kept playing the song. He stepped out of his car and casually walked over to the young beauty and inquired as to whether or not she liked the record. The beauty took one look at Lester before dismissively and sarcastically replying "Of course stupid. What do you think?" Bad mistake.

Lester never missed a beat. He turned, walked over to the jukebox, smashed the glass window on the device behind which the records were playing; grabbed the offending disk, then flung it at the by-now totally shocked debutante and yelled "There! Go play it someplace else!"

This act of retribution gave Lester a measure of the satisfaction he had sought, but it also meant the end of the jukebox and its beloved music thereafter for everyone at *Gus's*, because Miss Jessie simply didn't put up with that kind of behavior. She didn't even bother to have the damaged jukebox repaired. She just loaded it up into a truck, hauled it away, locked up the little jukebox shack, and that was that. No more music at *Gus's*.

For reasons unknown, this enraged Lester. Maybe it was the abuse he received from his friends for being responsible for the removal of their music at

Gus's. Maybe it was the thought that the sassy female had now permanently denied him access to music at *Gus's*. I really don't know.

What I do know, is that from that point forward, Lester made it his mission in life to abuse the little jukebox shack at any and every opportunity. He tried setting it on fire. He tried ripping it down. . .He tried most every conceivable method known to man to take his anger out on that shack – but it was one tough little structure.

Finally, Lester must have reached the end of his rope, because one Saturday night, *Gus's* was hopping with action as usual – despite the absence of the rock & roll music everyone had enjoyed. Lester wheeled into the parking lot, backed his car up to the jukebox-less shack, threw a chain around it, quickly harnessed it to the bumper of his car, and then with tires a'smokin' and gravel a'flyin' went sailing up the highway dragging the shack behind him, shooting sparks all across the highway.

That was the last anyone ever saw of the jukebox shack – or the jukebox for that matter. Nothing was left behind except the little concrete pad upon which the jukebox and shack had once sat.

Rev. Weinstein

Above and beyond those already mentioned, there were many other "characters" at *Gus's* over the years. Another of the town characters – Bruce Weinstein – enjoyed "preaching" in the parking lot in his youthful days, doing his best to stir up trouble by mimicking one of the more colorful radio evangelists of that day from the back of Lester Hurt's pickup truck.

On one noteworthy night, Miss Jessie finally had endured all she could handle. She emerged red-faced from the warm confines of *Gus's*, .38 in hand, and ordered Bruce off her property. "I won't listen to anyone mocking (evangelist) Lawrence Stanley that way," she loudly admonished.

Interestingly, having just returned from Vietnam where he had been involved in some heavy firefights, that little *.38 Special* didn't much disturb Bruce, but it apparently upset Lester quite a bit. The last thing he wanted to do was to stop one of the slugs meant for Bruce. So, without a word to his friend, Lester stomped on the gas, somersaulting Bruce out into the parking lot on his back, knocking the breath completely out of his lungs. As he turned to rise slowly, Bruce watched as Lester faded quickly up the highway into the distance.

Miss Jessie must have let Bruce off with a stern warning, because he was still alive the following day. Chastened, but alive. I never heard of him doing any more "preaching" at *Gus's*.

Last Days

I don't know what transpired at *Gus's* in its final days. Just as portrayed in **American Graffiti**, I departed for the University of Georgia in 1969, never again to reside in my hometown. Following college and a three-year stint in the Army, I returned to attend graduate school, moving on to various professional endeavors in public relations and journalism, my career taking me farther and farther away from *Gus's*.

When I returned to my hometown briefly in the mid-1970s, the little drive-in was only a memory and an era had been lost forever. Miss Jessie had passed away – her .38 quietly retired to a dusty drawer no doubt.

I suppose that *Gus's* eventually had garnered such a bad reputation that teenagers had ceased passing their weekends there altogether, and the little drive-in ultimately had had no choice but to shutter its windows and lock its doors. The old building stood vacant for a number of years, and then one sad day, it just disappeared entirely.

I was later told that "T" had found a new location across the street at a convenience store where he still occasionally served up his patented "T-burgers." Nothing, however, could replace *Gus's*.

Today, another building occupies the sacred space where the venerable drive-in building once stood, and a package store was built nearby on the old parking lot.

If you look through some of the old *Rockmart High School* yearbooks of the 1950s and 1960s, you will occasionally see a scene photographed at *Gus's*. Many old friends and acquaintances in those photos no longer even walk this earth, but the memories of this *"Happy Days"* drive-in from yesteryear will undoubtedly survive until the last of the children of the 1950s and '60s have all gone to that big drive-in in the sky.

—❧ ❧—

Darker Days

The early years of my parents' marriage (the late 1940s to the early 1960s) seem, for the most part, to have been happy times. Dad had established his own independent dairy business on a farm he had purchased in 1950. By 1961, Dad's business was thriving. I clearly recall that in those days, his wallet literally bulged with currency.

It was also in those days that Dad seemed almost care-free, and, in most ways I suppose he was. He had no significant debts to speak of. He had few if any enemies. At that point in time, life was a breeze for Dad. Somewhere along the way, however, Dad seemed to lose his way. He gradually reverted from being an enthusiastic "capitalist" to something bordering upon a "socialistic" mentality, and his professional career suffered greatly from this handicap.

I also recall as a child that Dad routinely addressed my mother as "Petunia." That was his loving – and humorous – "pet-name" for her, since he knew she loved that particular flower, but her "kill-record" in growing them was pretty-much 100%.

In 1957, after our family (five children) had outgrown the old farmhouse in which we were living, Dad contracted for the construction of a new home across the pasture upon a knoll in the distance. Work progressed on this home and it was completed in 1958, and we moved excitedly into these new quarters that summer.

For the first few years in this new home, our family continued to live happily, but storm-clouds were gathering on the horizon. Poor life-decisions, pathetic money-management, and growing selfishness were teaming up to destroy us.

Looking back from a mature perspective today, Dad's decision to build the type of new home into which we moved mystifies me. He borrowed approximately $20,000.00 (equivalent to approximately $224,671.00 in 2025

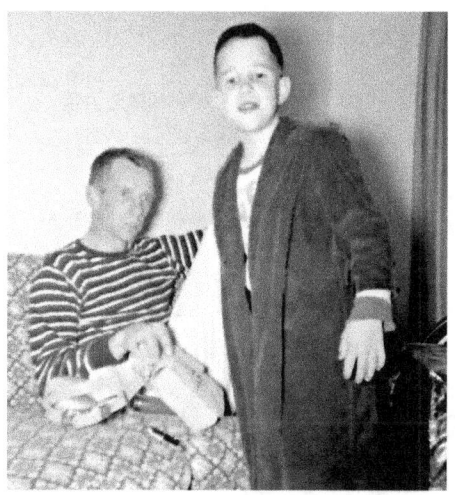

Photographed on Christmas morning, 1959, the author is oblivious to his father's darkened mood (rear). By the early 1960s, Mom and Dad's marriage was in serious trouble. (Photo by Marilyn Jackson)

dollars) to build that home, and it accomplished very little for our family logistically.

For instance, my two brothers and sisters and I were all still crammed into one small room; Mother and Dad were still sleeping on a hide-a-bed couch in the living room; we had but one bathroom over which we all fought, and in which the hot water was exhausted after the first bather each evening; and the newest arrival in our family – Guy – was still consigned to separate quarters in the tiny utility room where he might be more likely to sleep in peace.

(That, of course, was what's known as "pissing into the wind" in a family of five children in one small house. There was no such thing as a quiet household for a sleeping baby when four young siblings are boxed up in a room just up the hall. As a result, Guy wailed in despair for what seemed like hours on end before Mother or Dad would free him from his imprisonment.)

About the only thing of significance which that new house accomplished for us was that it provided a warmer "insulated" environment in the winter and a cooler "air-conditioned" environment in the summer. As cold as our former home had been in the frigid months, maybe the expenditure of funds for the new abode made sense solely for that reason. I just don't know. I think the jury is still out on that one, particularly from a financial perspective.

By 1963, it had become clear to me – and no doubt to my younger brother and older sister – that something was seriously amiss in our family. Even on Christmas mornings sometimes, before we were allowed to enter the living room to see what "Santa" had brought us, my parents could be heard in angry arguments. There obviously were some terrible issues afoot which were fracturing our family, and these would become much more pronounced in a year or two.

A New Life

It was sometime around 1964, that my father apparently had the first inklings that his "future" lay someplace beyond the confines of our home in northwest Georgia – and the dairy business in which

GEORGIA MILK PRODUCERS, INC.
ROOM 207-208
33 HUNTER STREET, S.W.
ATLANTA 3, GEORGIA

523 6071

RALPH O. JACKSON, JR.   TELEPHONE
FIELD REPRESENTATIVE   JA 3-5522

he had invested so much time, money and energy. That year, Dad purchased (to accompany the 1963 Chevrolet station-wagon we already owned) a small new olive-green six-cylinder, "straight-shift-on-the-column" *Ford Falcon* sedan, and he suddenly was free to pursue a livelihood beyond the parameters of our little town.

Now at the time, my brothers and sisters and I were told simply that Dad was seeking employment elsewhere because the income from the dairy had decreased dramatically. This was partially true, but in reality, Dad and Mother were also arriving at what's known as "a fork in the road, with each taking a separate fork."

The first year or so, Dad passed off his newly-found professional pursuit as "insurance sales," and I think he did in fact make an effort to sell the *Farm Bureau Insurance* he purported to offer. In point of fact however, any "sales" Dad made were very few and far between, because he simply was not a determined salesman, and after a year or so, he gave up on this venture.

Dad next became captivated by a whole new professional trajectory. He had decided that the price of dairy milk – which had plunged of late – could somehow be controlled if the state's dairymen banded together and functioned collectively. The new concept was what came to be known as the *Georgia Milk Producers (GMP)* – and Dad had a big part in the founding of that endeavor.

GMP sought to organize all the dairies in Georgia and to strategically set and control the pricing of Georgia dairy products, so that the market could no longer be readily flooded with underpriced milk. It was an idea which actually had a lot of merit, and eventually grew into a viable enterprise which is still in successful existence today.

In those early days, however, *GMP* paid no salaries to its founder(s) and/or management, and Dad labored along strictly in a volunteer capacity in a free room at the *Georgia Department of Agriculture* at the state capitol complex in Atlanta. I still have one of his early *Georgia Milk Producers* business cards

Photographed on Easter morning (April 21, 1960), the Jackson family was the picture of happiness and prosperity. In four short years, however, a variety of factors would begin tearing the family apart. (Photo courtesy of Dean's Studio, Rockmart, GA)

which he proudly carried with him as he "politicked" for this new endeavor.

Dad had completed a little over one year of law school at the University of Georgia when he dropped out to marry my mother in 1948, and I suspect he envisioned himself as assisting with the legal and political aspects of *GMP*, drawing upon his legal training. Though politics and the legal profession were the career fields for which Dad yearned the most, they simply were not to be a part of his "paid" career trajectory until many hard years later.

Dad continued to survive off a limited income from our dairy back in Rockmart, but it was a livelihood of progressively diminishing returns. He kept a hired laborer who, during weekdays, milked and "managed" the cows and supposedly "farmed" the acreage for Dad to provide forage for the cattle. Due to the very limited income offered in return for this labor, however, these workers often were woefully inept and came and went freely over the years.

Some of Dad's laborers were very honest and well-intentioned individuals, but some others not so much so. And even the honest and well-intentioned ones sometimes made glaring expensive mistakes in Dad's absence.

Some of these workers also invariably did very little in the way of actual farming and/or dairying, because they were completely unsupervised. After all, by the mid-1960s, Dad was absent from the premises Monday thru Friday, being 60 or 70 miles away in Atlanta, and he paid these laborers very minimal wages for their "services." Dad did, however, provide free housing and utilities (in the old farmhouse in which we had originally lived) as well as free weekends as minor incentives for these laborers.

Sometime around 1965 or '66, Dad unfortunately "took up with" another woman in the Atlanta area. By late 1966, with the dairy operations

71

failing, Dad very obviously had pretty much written off our farm and his life with us. He was spending more and more time away from us, and appeared to have firmly decided that his future lay beyond the horizons of our family and town. The love which once had existed between our parents was dying a painful death.

Hard Times

By 1967, my brothers, sisters and I were seeing very little of dad. He would usually appear back at our home on Friday afternoons in order to take care of the dairy operations over the weekend (as agreed with the hired hand), but on Sunday evenings, he would light out again for his Atlanta life. It seemed almost like he couldn't leave quickly enough.

By the time we reached our teen-age years, my brothers and I were required to help Dad with the dairy operations. We eventually were involved in so much of the labor that he began paying us $5.00 each per week. *(And to emphasize, that payment was "per week," not "per hour.")* And sometimes – when Dad was "preoccupied" elsewhere, my brother and I were required to solely handle *all* the dairy operations, right down to milking the cows, plowing the fields, harvesting forage for the cows, and many other responsibilities of dairy operations in Dad's absence.

We eventually learned that Dad had a nice poolside apartment in Buckhead (an affluent Atlanta suburb) where, from 1964 to 1966, he had been living during any non-working hours in Atlanta. We, his children back at his former home received progressively-less supervision and parenting.

Dad continued to blame our problems on the fact that the dairy was failing, and he steadfastly maintained that he was searching for work elsewhere in Atlanta during the week. Mother, however, apparently was suspicious, because she arranged on occasion for my brother and me to accompany Dad to stay at his apartment on weekends, and on at least one of these occasions, Dad spent the night elsewhere. In fairness, Mother had also found someone else to whom she had turned her attentions, so the problems within our home were not all one-sided.

As his financial circumstances steadily worsened, Dad was forced to give up his Buckhead accommodations. In the days and weeks ahead, he became more distant and his life progressively more dissolute.

Maternal Retribution

Amazingly, despite the many ways that he failed us, I still loved my father. And I always dreaded Sunday afternoons, because I knew he would again be leaving us to return to Atlanta. On one such sad occasion, I hurried out to the front drive at our home to hug my father and bid him a tearful "goodbye." That little demonstration of loyalty became very costly to me once Dad was gone. From that day forward, my mother no longer treated me the same as she did my siblings. I was relegated to status as an "outsider."

By that point, my brothers and sisters had quickly learned to demonstrate total allegiance to my mother since she was the managing adult and breadwinner. She had made it abundantly-clear that anything less than total loyalty to her (rather than to my father) would result in circumstances which were very unpleasant. I just hadn't caught on to this situation quite as quickly as had my siblings.

In the days ahead, unless I wished to do something outdoors or away from home, I was essentially banished to the cold basement bedroom of our home where my brother and I slept. I was not allowed to visit my youngest brother's newly-constructed upstairs quarters nor those of either of my sisters. In the summers, in order to get me "out from under-foot," I, as a youngster of barely 11, 12 or 13 years of age, was routinely shipped out to a subsidized summer camp someplace for several weeks - much against my will - usually in the lowlands of south Georgia or the uplands of North Carolina.

Because of my loyalty to my father, my mother made sure I was also placed "in harness" almost any time there was a chore to be completed, or grass to be mown, or tasks at my grandmother's home. My relationship with my mother went steadily downhill.

In fairness, I, to some degree, do not blame my mother for her actions. She truly had her hands full managing our household in Dad's growing absence – cooking meals, cleaning the house, washing clothes, buying what little groceries we could afford, and making certain things remained at least semi-operational in the face of our growing poverty. And when my dad ceased the provision of financial support to us entirely, I don't know how my mother got us through that stretch. Those truly were hard times.

My mother, however, was the direct opposite of my father when it came to money-management. She could squeeze a nickel until Thomas Jefferson screamed. She found a way to return to school so that she could become a

73

high school home economics teacher, and, in the meantime, was able to get an attorney to put the squeeze on Dad.

Paternal Retribution

Ironically, I soon learned that my costly loyalty to my father was actually sorely misplaced. He ultimately made it clear that we were a burden which he no longer chose to bear.

My feelings of love for my father quite shortly began to be converted into fear. Dad's income had nose-dived and he began taking his bitterness out on his family. Looking back, I can understand a certain amount of his torment too, and can forgive a certain amount of his absentee parentage.

Dad's financial acumen (or lack thereof) continued on a steady downward trajectory. As an example, in 1964, just prior to giving up on us and departing for "greener pastures," he borrowed $15,000 *(the equivalent of slightly more than $141,000 in 2025 dollars)* a portion of which he immediately used to build a large addition to our home. I don't know if he did this as a last-ditch effort toward placating my mother or what.

The $15,000.00 had been borrowed against the dairy under the auspices of having those funds to *enlarge the milking operations and herd,* allowing repayment of the note from the increased income from the dairy. It doesn't take a rocket scientist to understand the illogical nature of this scenario, but that's how my father managed money in those days as he sank deeper and deeper into debt.

There are, in fact, a number of things from my childhood which still stand out starkly in my memory, one of which is my father's vicious temper. When he was in one of his depressed and potentially-violent moods, I as a child, was terrified of him.

By 1965, Dad had sunk into a sea of alcoholism, and it would continue to be a major problem for him long years into the future until he finally sought professional treatment at Brawner Psychiatric Institute in Atlanta in 1982. By the mid-1960s, his relationship with my mother had become nonexistent, and the only reason she still allowed him in our home was that he was returning each weekend to milk the cows at our dairy to generate a bit of income which he shared with us to buy groceries and other meager supplies each week.

As a result of dad's alcoholism, it soon became obvious to my older sister, younger brother and me that what once had been a safe home had evolved into a very irresponsible – and even somewhat dangerous – environment. By the late-1960s, there was virtually no parental supervision at all in our household.

On one occasion sometime around 1965, I recall waking up one morning to the heavy smell of smoke in our home. When I ran upstairs, I discovered that one end of the couch in our den – to which my father had been consigned to sleep by my mother – had been completely destroyed by a fire which fortunately had been extinguished before it could spread further. Dad had been smoking a cigarette in a drunken stupor the previous night and had dropped it between the cushions of the couch when he fell asleep. If my sister had not been awakened by the smoke, our entire home could easily have been burned. It is a small miracle that Dad did not die from smoke inhalation as he lay sleeping on the couch.

By 1969, my parents had filed for divorce. It was finalized in November of that year, and Dad married someone else almost immediately that December.

On September 14, 1970, auctioneers disposed of Dad's entire 500-acre farm for pennies on the dollar. He might just as well have given the property away to charity. The funds from the sale came nowhere near to covering Dad's indebtedness, because he had mortgaged everything we had: our home, the dairy, the acreage, the tools, machinery and farm equipment – everything – to the hilt.

Our life as we knew it, had simply vanished. By that point, however, my older sister had married and moved away; my younger brother and I had moved away to struggle a year or so in college; and my younger sister had opted to live with dad in Atlanta. Only my youngest brother Guy, remained at home with mother. My other brother, David, and I were desperate to leave our steadily-degenerating life behind, and Dad somehow set it up so that still more money was borrowed in order for us to go away to college, only this time, he set it up so that the funds were borrowed in "our" name, since his credit by then was nonexistent.

Maternal Determination

It wasn't long after that that Dad's creditors came a'callin' to remove the contents of our home – including my mother and youngest brother Guy – so that they could repossess the structure. After starving and failing in college, my brother and I had, in desperation, joined the *United States Army*, so Mother was left to deal with the problem alone.

Workers hired by the bank which held the mortgage on our home were in the process of stacking our furniture at the end of our driveway when Mother's attorney suddenly enlightened the bank's loan officer. Dad's creditors couldn't legally touch "our" residence when foreclosing upon "Dad's" property, because our home had been awarded to Mother in the divorce decree. If she could get it re-financed at a rate at which she could afford the monthly payments, she could retain possession of our home. And just like the "Scarlett O'Hara" that she was, that's exactly what Mother did.

Mother had also begun focusing upon the completion of her undergraduate degree in Home Economics and then upon a six-year certification in that degree field. With those credentials, she sought – and eventually obtained – stable employment in a local high school.

In the years ahead, Mother worked steadily and devotedly upon her teaching career, eventually earning a full retirement pension. During her teaching career, she had also taken advantage of several other investment opportunities, including a 401K, and had steadily invested her meager income in a very wise manner.

Life can be cruel, however, and Mother's life continued to be devastated by tragedy. Just a few years after her retirement and the peace which came with it, she was informed somewhat coldly and clinically by her doctor that she had terminal leukemia. Though she fought on bravely for seven or eight years, she eventually succumbed to the deadly disease.

When she passed away in the summer of 2008, Mother owned – outright – our home which she had filled with valuable antiques. She also owned a nice automobile, and a number of acres of property surrounding the home. Additionally, her 401K and other investments had grown very nicely as well. As a result, she left a tidy inheritance from these holdings and investments to her four surviving children. Mother definitely had a way with money-management of which my father had not a clue.

In contrast, when Dad passed away in 2011, he owned his home, but not much else. He left what little he owned to his second wife, and absolutely nothing to his children.

—•❫❪•—

College Days Shenanigans

Many of us have memories of foolishness as adolescents. We simply did things of which we possibly aren't necessarily proud today when examined from a mature perspective. Some of it was idiotic, but some of it was just down-right fun too... incidents which will stick with us until the day we die. Memories for the ages.

Take for instance my first days at the University of Georgia... I had left a lot of sadness and despair back at my home in northwest Georgia, and, in all honesty, I was just unprepared for higher learning.

On my first trip to "my new home" at UGA, my father actually deigned to give me a ride to Athens (since I had no automobile or transportation of my own). I think, in all honesty, that he was just glad to get me "out from under foot."

It was my first day in the dormitory to which I had been assigned – Clark Howell Hall – right there next to immense and historic Sanford Stadium.

Last time I checked in 2024, this old dormitory somehow still existed, but I think it is used for other things these days.

In earlier days – 1947-'48 – my dad (who is a 1945 graduate of Georgia Tech in Atlanta) had also attended the University of Georgia *(after returning from service in the U.S. Navy in the South Pacific during the closing days of World War II)* having been accepted into the University's Law School. It was here that he gained his initial designs upon a legal career in some form or fashion. He didn't know exactly what form – just "some form."

Dad never finished Law School (at least not at the University of Georgia) because my mother said "Yes" when he proposed to her one day early in 1948. They were married later that same year. *(He did however – many years later - obtain a Juris Doctorate Degree and gain election to a county judgeship, so I guess he ultimately achieved at least a portion of his life goals.)*

In his brief sojourn at the University, Dad told me that he had lived in the very same dormitory – Clark Howell Hall – in which I was assigned quarters in 1969. Amazingly, he also informed me that he had actually lived *in the exact same room* to which I had been assigned. The odds of that happening in a setting as large as the University of Georgia are obviously somewhat infinitesimal – but so also were the odds of a lot of strange things in our family.

<u>Thanksgiving</u>

In 1969-'70, there were often surprising little side-adventures among our crew in Clark Howell Hall. That Thanksgiving, several individuals in addition to me were without transportation (or money) to return home to our families for the holiday. *(As explained earlier, Dad had declared bankruptcy in 1968-'69, and remarried in 1970. My family was in a distinctly-desperate status, so I really had no desire to return home then anyway.)* We "hold-overs" decided to have our own little "thanksgiving" right there in the dorm.

For reasons unknown today, back in those days (in the late 1960s), there were a number of "turkey" farms on the outskirts of Athens. Perhaps there still are today. . . I just don't know. Someone came up with the bright idea of stealing a turkey, then slaughtering it and cooking it in the little kitchen downstairs in the laundry room at Clark Howell where a stove also existed. Sounded like an adventure.

Now how we thought that 1/ ponying up a portion of the cost of gasoline to drive to Jefferson, Georgia, then 2/ running around in turkey do-do for an hour trying to catch a live turkey to steal, then 3/ somehow subduing and transporting that live turkey back to the dormitory, then 4/ slaughtering, gutting and cleaning it, then 5/buying the necessary items with which to cook it, then 6/ actually cooking the darn thing, were easier and less expensive than just pooling our scant resources to go "buy" an already "cooked" and "prepared" turkey, is beyond me. It defies logic. And we were "college kids" too, supposedly at least with a modicum of intelligence. I have no excuse to offer.

None of the logic in this matter deterred us in the slightest from making utter fools of ourselves, and we did it quite well. Late at night a couple of days prior to Thanksgiving, we loaded up a car and headed out to the nearest turkey farm. I don't even remember where it was, but I'm pretty sure it was on the outskirts of Jefferson, Georgia. I do recall there were a lot of very "big turkeys" there and that they were reasonably fleet of foot in a large containment compound full of turkey do-do.

Well we chased and we chased, running around in all that turkey crap; falling down in that mess and generally getting all that turkey do-do all over us, doing disgusting things that I don't even want to discuss today. Despite its drawbacks, this little adventure was not without its measure of fun.

Eventually, someone somehow actually caught one of the big birds. In the midst of our efforts to subdue the gobler, we made a bit too much noise, and the turkey farm owner (or manager or night guard – I don't know which) came running out to the turkey corral to see about all the commotion.

Well, we had just managed to tie that big turkey's legs, and two of us were dragging it to the car as the owner/manager reached the other side of the corral. "What the hell is going on out here!" he yelled at us.

By this time, the hilarity of all the turkey poop covering us from head to foot, coupled with the turkey which was still flopping and jumping all around, began getting the best of us. Someone started cackling and that set off all the rest of us.

It was also at about this time that we heard a huge "booommm!" as the owner/manager fired a shotgun into the air, to get our attention. If he thought that was actually going to slow us down, he missed his guess, because it instead (very understandably) shifted us into "high gear." We threw that gobbler into the back seat (yeah. . . the back seat – turkey crap and all), piled in on top of it and sped away as quickly as the wheels of that car would take us.

As we were driving away, we heard yet another "boommm!" from the man's shotgun, except this time, we both heard and felt the pellets hitting the car. Luckily, we were just cresting a hill and headed down on the other side, and were far enough away that the damage was minimal. I don't know how the owner of that car later explained all the shotgun pellet holes and dents in it. I'm just glad I didn't have to participate in that little bit of sleight of hand.

Anyway, at that point, despite all the turkey poop covering us and all the energy we had expended and danger we had faced in this little episode in hilarity, we actually debated throwing the big bird out on the side of the road. "Suppose we get stopped by the police," one of our party squawked. "What do we do then? Play like the turkey is our pet?"

I really don't recall what made us hang onto that turkey. We knew we still had to clean it and cook it – and it was a really big bird. Maybe we just didn't want to be facing a Thanksgiving with no memories and nothing but *Coke* and peanut-butter crackers to eat. Whatever the circumstances, about 45 minutes later, we were in the back parking lot of Clark Howell Hall dormitory, where we assassinated and gutted that Thanksgiving dinner. Those woods back there stank to high Heaven for a week or more, and we'd just smile whenever some unknowing soul mentioned it.

After we had killed and gutted it, we pulled feathers and then more feathers off that bird for what seemed like hours (Even after we had pulled what we thought were "all the feathers" off it, it still had these little mini-featherettes on it which we had to work on still longer. In the end, we never got all those tiny feathers off that bird, but we didn't care.)

We next washed off the finished product as best we could in the big laundry sink downstairs (which also subsequently stank for a week or more); seasoned it, then put it in a huge pan to cook, and popped it in the oven. And we cooked; and we cooked; and we cooked.

That big bird ultimately took what seemed like a day or two to cook, but it finally reached the point that it smelled pretty "edible." The only problem was that by the time the cooking was complete, Thanksgiving was almost gone. Late at night on Thanksgiving evening – along with a loaf of bread and a few other "side dishes," we sat down to eat it. And we not only ate on it that night, we ate on it for days thereafter, cutting portions and storing them in the refrigerator.

Looking back today, I'm still amazed that one or more of us didn't die from ptomaine poisoning or some other drastic illness. But like I said, it was more the adventure – than the bird – that counted with us.

It seemed like there was constant foolishness such as this afoot. Some adolescents get away with it, and some – like my youngest brother – don't. But that's another story.

Immortal Jake Scott

During Winter Quarter, 1969 student registration at the *University of Georgia*, I was at *Stegeman Coliseum*. At that time, that was where they conducted student registration. I don't know where or how they do it today, but I'm certain it's much more "digitally" oriented today.

Anyway, I was standing in a line that stretched outside this somewhat unique building which has huge arches that put the golden arches of *McDonald's* to shame. The huge curving structures stretch from the ground on one side, up over the huge building, then down to the ground on the opposite side.

The guy in front of me was making conversation as we stood in line and waited. I was cold and wasn't really paying attention to what he was saying. At one point, he stated somewhat matter-of-factly that "I saw Jake Scott ride his motorcycle from this arch right here all the way over the top of *Stegeman* and then back down to the ground on the other side."

"Uh huh" I responded absentmindedly, not taking the guy serious for a moment. I later discovered in shocked disbelief, however, that he had actually been telling the truth.

Pictured is Stegeman Coliseum at the University of Georgia with its unusual parabolic arches across which former University of Georgia standout safety Jake Scott gained immortal fame.

One has to see those arches over *Stegeman* up close and personal to get an idea of just how amazing a stunt that was. But Jake Scott was an amazing individual, and, in my modestly-learned opinion, didn't get anywhere near the credit he was due for his athletic feats.

Jake only played football at the *University of Georgia* for two seasons. In those days, freshmen weren't allowed to play on the Varsity team, and, such was his prowess on the gridiron, that Mr. Scott didn't even play his final year of eligibility in 1968-'69, opting instead to "Go-Pro."

During his two varsity seasons at *Georgia*, Jake led the *SEC* in punt returns and punt-return yardage and his 440 yards on 35 returns and interceptions set school records in both categories in 1968. Such were his skills that Jake also is still tied for the school record for career interceptions with 16 and is second in interception return yards with 315. He shares that record with Bacarri Rambo (2009) and Dominick Sanders (2014), but his (Scott's) numbers came in only 21 games, while it took Rambo and Sanders more than twice that many (55 games each) to achieve the mark. One could therefore reasonably claim that Jake Scott owns those records outright.

In the 1970 *National Football League (NFL)* draft, Jake was taken in the 7th Round – a 159th overall pick – by the *Miami Dolphins*, and never looked back. And the *Miami Dolphins* soon learned what a wonderful investment they had made too.

It wasn't long before the *NFL* at large also realized just how special this dude from the *University of Georgia* actually was. He was named to the *Pro*

Bowl five consecutive times between 1971 and 1975. He recorded 35 interceptions in his six seasons as a *Dolphin*, a mark which stakes his claim to being the *Dolphins'* all-time leader in interceptions. He recorded another 14 interceptions in his three years with the *Washington Redskins*.

Jake was a leader on the back-to-back *Dolphins Super Bowl Championship* teams in 1972 and 1973 too, where he was named the *"Most Valuable Player" (MVP)* of *Super Bowl VII*. He intercepted two passes that day with his biggest "pick" coming in the fourth quarter. With Miami clinging to a 14-0 lead, *Washington* drove 79 yards to reach the *Dolphins'* 10-yard line. Scott ended the drive with an interception in the end zone.

In an **Atlanta Constitution** newspaper interview in 2020, Mike Cavan, quarterback of the *Bulldogs* during the years Jake was with the team confirms that Scott was quite the character. Cavan also confirmed as fact the legendary story of Scott driving his motorcycle over the breadth of *Stegeman Coliseum's* concrete parabolas while attending UGA.

"No question," Cavan stated. *"It happened."*

Following the end of his professional football career, Jake Scott moved to Hawaii where he, surprisingly, became somewhat of a recluse. He simply didn't enjoy anything associated with glitz and drama, and completely eliminated it from his life.

Jake Scott essentially lived a quiet life following the conclusion of his professional football days. He wasn't a big-time sports analyst or "color commentator," or "play-by-play announcer." He shunned anything to do with that life.

Jake Scott died tragically in an Atlanta hospital in 2020, ironically following, of all things, an accidental head injury he suffered while visiting his mother. After all those head collisions and feats of prowess performed by Scott, his life was ended by a simple fall in which he struck his head.

Today, if one travels to the *University of Georgia's Stegeman Coliseum*, there is a reason that they have those heavy-duty iron obstruction bars blocking ground-level access to the now-famous arches (though one has to concede the likelihood of a student attempting to match Jake's daredevil feat is fairly remote). In fairness, at the very least, the arches at *Stegeman* should have a historic sign on them which reads: *"Jake Scott Was Here."*

—❧ ❧—

The Great Divide in Social Acceptance

W hen I look back today at my life in adolescence, I have to confess it is a painful undertaking. Only those who have experienced "being on the outside looking in" socially, know what I'm talking about. As "country folk," my brothers and I were definitely "on the outside" regarding our city friends with whom we interacted socially. In the early years we never realized it, but as we matured into our junior high and high school years, it became painfully obvious.

It wasn't that my parents or forebears were "backward" or uneducated. Quite the contrary. Dad was a 1944 graduate of Georgia Tech in Atlanta, and ultimately earned a Juris Doctorate degree in law, and Mother attended the University of North Carolina. And my grandparents were very prominent in town, my grandfather being a stockholder in several banks and my mother's mother being a prominent high school chemistry teacher. My two brothers and younger sister and I, nevertheless, simply were never really included in the little cliques and adolescent social circles enjoyed by our friends.

Exclusion Beginnings

Sometime around the 7th or 8th grade in school, young boys begin to realize just how desperate their circumstances are becoming if they are not maturing as swiftly as are their contemporaries. Most of those with muscular physiques and agile well-proportioned bodies were immediately ranked above those who were skinny or overweight and less-talented at sports. For these and other reasons, it is also at about this time that the separation between the "athletes" and the "non-athletically-inclined" begins to take place in junior high and high school..

I have always loved sports – particularly baseball and football – but excellence in sports was an uphill grind for me. Oh sure, I played *Little League* baseball every summer until my 13th birthday, and on the junior varsity football, basketball and track & field teams at my junior high and high school, but I *excelled* at very little. My strength, reflexes and agility simply had not developed to the point of allowing me to be competitive in sports – and they never did until I was well beyond high school.

Looking back, despite the fact that none of us excelled in sports, all of my younger siblings and I might have had a much better chance with just a modicum of parental support and encouragement. My parents, however, simply placed their priorities elsewhere.

When I look back at the photos of my grandfather Jordan – so confident and smiling in his athletic uniforms at Stanford University in California from 1910 to 1913 – I can't help but be proud. He was a starter on the Stanford track and field and baseball teams, and a champion in pole vaulting, and this was at a time when track & field events far exceeded football in prominence and importance at most institutions of higher learning. Very little of that Jordan athletic prowess, however, had trickled down to me.

As previously explained, we lived in a very rural setting where my father owned a dairy farm. We walked in cow manure, plowed the fields, and punched cows when we weren't at school, church, or otherwise preoccupied, and we (except for my older sister) almost always were "on the outside looking in." My brothers and I certainly weren't socially prominent.

If that sounds like "poor-mouthing," well, I suppose that's just what it is, but it, nonetheless, is the honest truth, and it was a fact of life we could not avoid. My younger brother and I somehow made it through this maze of non-acceptance, but my youngest brother, Guy, did not. He ultimately succumbed to the pressures of being excluded and, in the absence of parental supervision, simply dropped out of high school. His subsequent lifestyle eventually cost him his life.

Following my high school years, my lackluster personality bled over into my initial college years as well. I continued to struggle, both scholastically and socially.

Being All I Could Be

One day, I just decided I needed a dramatic change in my life. I was tired of a lackluster life of introversion. I walked to the local Armed Forces recruiting office just down the street in Athens, Georgia, and signed up for a tour of duty in the *United States Army* at the height of the Vietnam conflict in Southeast Asia. I just didn't care.

Instead of sending me to Vietnam, however, the Army trained me as a military policeman and sent me to Europe to serve on the security detail of the Army Commander of *NATO*. I didn't know it at the time, but things were about to change for me in a big way, and I was about to leave my previous life far behind.

My initial duty was of course the least-desirable – that of "gate-guard" at the sprawling *United States Army Europe (USAREUR)* complex headquartered at Campbell Barracks in Heidelberg, Germany. For approximately a year, I stood guard at one of several gated entrances to Campbell or nearby Patton Barracks, controlling traffic, checking identifications, and carefully inspecting automobiles for explosive devices.

In the performance of this duty, we invariably wore a Class-A dark-green uniform which included an array of Army brass insignia and what little qualification medals and service ribbons, etc. which we had earned at that early stage in our military careers. All of the brass items had to be shined and polished, our uniforms sharply pressed, and our boots spit-shined each evening in preparation of the following day's duty. Our .45 caliber side-arms were maintained for us, so we thankfully avoided that responsibility. Interestingly, this uniform preparation was actually something at which I found I excelled.

Every day at "Guard Mount," the individual with the sharpest uniform was granted a reprieve from duty that day, and I quite often was so honored. Eventually, a lucky-few of those individuals with a continual record of "sharpest uniform," and with the most time-in-service, and who were deemed to be in the best physical condition and with a reasonably-high intelligence quotient, were assigned duty at the highly-sensitive U.S. Army "Command Building" at which the *Commander-in-Chief* ("CINC") and the *Deputy-CINC*, along with a host of other general-grade officers congregated for duty each day. Aside from the above-described necessary qualifications, the military policemen on duty in this complex were also required to have a *Top Secret* security clearance for obvious reasons.

The author at the highly-sensitive United States Army Europe Command Building in Heidelberg, Germany in 1974.

Approximately halfway through my tour of duty in the Army, I was selected for one of the top security assignments in Europe, much to my delight. No more standing at a gate in freezing rain or in 90-degree heat for hours on end, inspecting vehicles for hidden improvised explosive devices for me. No, from that day forward, I was permanently-assigned to the group of individuals responsible for the security of the *USAREUR* Command Building during the days and evenings, a job which I held until my tour of duty had expired.

One of the other "perks" of this duty, was that it often included service in the *USAREUR "Color Guard"* detachment anytime the CINC traveled around Europe and during official functions. We were the riflemen and flag-bearers representing *USAREUR* and the *United States Army*.

By this point in time, I had put on extra muscle, and I was tall and dark-haired with a high level of confidence in my capabilities. I had been trained in the use of a variety of weapons, qualifying as an expert in the use of the standard sidearm (Colt .45), the M-16 automatic rifle, and even with the M-79 grenade launcher (which is somewhat unusual). And at 22 years of age I could finally "turn a head or two" when it came to the fairer sex, and I took full advantage of this.

When my tour of duty had expired, I thought very seriously about signing up for another tour, but then I reminded myself that things can quickly and easily change from better to worse in military duty stations. Our circumstances in Germany were also becoming increasingly dangerous with terrorist activities.

I therefore decided that it would be in my best interest to "cut my losses" before I became a victim of a terrorist's improvised explosive device. When my tour of duty was complete, I returned stateside and reentered the University of Georgia to finish my college degree under the G.I. Bill, and to continue my diligent pursuit of the fairer sex.

I eventually married, but I didn't get it right until my second wife. (*More about that later.*) I subsequently founded a successful publishing company from which I retired at the age of 51. My sweet wife and I live a happy life today in retirement. We thank the good Lord each day for the many blessings he has bestowed upon us.

—⊹⟩ ⟨⊹—

The 1972 Terrorist Attack On the U.S. Army in Heidelberg, Germany

The year 1972 would usher in one of the most momentous events since World War II in Germany, setting the stage for emergency circumstances within the *529ᵗʰ* for years into the future. However, in May of 1972 when I arrived "in-country," I, for all intents and purposes, was oblivious to the growing storm-clouds, as were most of the United States Army personnel in Germany at that time. I was just another young man from the southern United States who was glad to have a place to sleep and be provided with three square meals a day.

Flawed Security Policy

On May 24th, 1972, two female German nationals drove two vehicles with stolen *USAREUR* license plates through the front gate of the *USAREUR* complex at Campbell Barracks for which the *529th* provided security. In those days – which of course were considered "peace-time" in Europe – the fact that the vehicles had *USAREUR* license plates provided them with an automatic "entre'" into the otherwise secure facility.

That was the security policy at that time. As things turned out, it was a flaw in the system, but as far as the official U.S. military security staff at Heidelberg were concerned, there simply was no need for excessively-strict security measures on *USAREUR*-tagged vehicles. And there were hundreds of officers who worked daily at the *USAREUR* headquarters offices who were apoplectically-indignant at having their credentials checked, regardless of the circumstances, fully believing they were "above" any such security checks.

They would all shortly be rudely awakened to the deadly reality of a growing menace.

The decade of the 1970s in Germany witnessed the most dangerous period for the United States Army in Germany since the mid-1940s. In the four years from 1970 to 1974 alone, 129 deadly acts of terrorism against the Army occurred in Germany. From 1970 to 1980, there were 312 acts of terrorism committed against the Army. Though little-known at the time and little-realized by most Americans today, a native element in Germany – muchly composed of the children of former *NAZI* Germany military officials – had made it their goal in life to uproot the American military presence in their country – no matter what the cost.

It would later be learned that both of the falsely-authorized vehicles allowed into Campbell Barracks in Heidelberg on May 24, 1972, contained immense improvised explosive devices (IEDs). One of the vehicles was driven back to the vicinity of the ivy-covered officers' club in the rear of Campbell and parked next to a yellow Ford Capri in the large parking area. The other vehicle was parked a short distance away beside the *USAREUR Command & Control Center* known in Army parlance as *"the war room,"* the site at which any Soviet incursion into Western Europe at the beginning of World War III would initially be monitored and prosecuted.

The adjacent Campbell Barracks officers' club at that time was a very popular area in which officers and their families often converged in the evenings and on weekends for meals and light-hearted family gatherings. A movie theater next door provided further incentive for military personnel and their families to visit this area. I often took in a movie there myself, particularly to enjoy the latest first-run features.

Later investigations by the *U.S. Army Criminal Investigation Division (CID)* would reveal that at about 6:00 pm, Capt. Clyde Bonner, a twenty-nine years-old officer in the Army who was married with two children, invited his friend – Ronald Woodward who was also married with three children – to come see his brand-new yellow Ford Capri out in the parking lot. Bonner's pride in the vehicle that day was understandable, but the decision of the two men to go examine it was a fateful one.

Woodward & Bonner Deaths

At two minutes past 6:00 pm, as the two men were admiring the bright yellow sports car, the IED hidden in the vehicle parked immediately beside

The aftermath of the terrorist bombing at Campbell Barracks in Heidelberg, Germany on May 24, 1972. (AP Photo)

Bonner's Capri detonated. The resulting explosion was absolutely devastating and horrifying. It tossed vehicles and their contents like matchsticks around the parking lot and turned an otherwise organized group of vehicles into a large expanse of absolutely twisted chaos.

According to the official *Army Criminal Investigation Division (CID)* report, the detonation instantly ripped all the clothing – including boots – from Bonner's body, and dismembered it into numerous portions, all of which were strewn throughout the parking lot. Boots, clothing, and various and sundry other small items from the blast victims were discovered hanging from nearby trees for weeks thereafter.

Woodward was killed just as instantly, and though the blast tore off and scattered his clothing as well, his body was somehow shielded to some degree so that, according to the report, the blast did not destroy his corpse. I can vouch for that, having seen autopsy photos of the body.

Approximately 15 seconds later, a second detonation – equally horrendous – occurred in the other vehicle across the parking lot, doubling the chaos now filling the vicinity around the Officers' Club. The *War Room* was an ultra-high security complex, the existence of which was not supposed to have been common knowledge. Interior security for these offices was also provided by contingents of the *529th MP Company* all of whom had no less than a *"Secret Intelligence"* security clearance – the highest security protocol available at that time.

As a result, it is still debated today how the terrorists were able to gain knowledge of the existence of the *War Room* complex. Perhaps they did not even know of it at all and the placement of the IED in that vicinity was pure happenstance. The answer to that – as well as many other questions concerning this terrible incident – will probably never be known, since none of the perpetrators chose to reveal any details of their nefarious activities, and within a few years, most all of the perpetrators were deceased themselves from various causes.

Charles Peck Death

Inside the *Command and Control Facility*, further *CID* investigative reports indicated Charles Peck died when a soft-drink dispenser – driven by the force of the blast from the terrorists' car parked outside – slammed into him, crushing him against an adjacent wall. I will never forget the bloody handprints Peck left upon that wall where he apparently had attempted either to rise following the blast or, perhaps, simply to brace himself after being flung against the wall and crushed by the soft-drink container.

Whatever the circumstances, Peck was fatally injured, and the two bloody smears from his hands sliding down the wall to the floor where he had collapsed and died clearly indicated the story of his demise. His death had been quick and bloody, just as had those of Bonner and Woodward.

Aside from the fact that they wreaked havoc with the automobiles in the parking lot, the bomb blasts – despite the fact that they exploded in vehicles parked outside in the parking lot – were unbelievably devastating to the interior of the buildings near which they were detonated.

Aside from those in the parking lot, any other vehicles in the vicinity of the two IED-laden automobiles were tossed and crushed as well. The lot had essentially been converted into a virtual jungle of twisted and destroyed vehicles – some lying atop others – whose contents had been obliterated and strewn as well across the cobble-stoned expanses throughout Campbell Barracks, some as far away as the interior parade ground of the complex.

The explosives were later determined to have been in the 50 to 60-pound bomb range. They had been planted where they of course would render maximum damage, killing not only United States military personnel, but the wives and children of these personnel, the German workers inside the compound, and anyone else unfortunate enough to be within range of the explosives. One can only consider it an act of God that no more than three individuals died from their injuries in this wanton criminal act. Numerous other persons were injured by flying glass and debris, but none of their wounds proved fatal.

Had the second detonation been timed to explode 15 or 20 minutes (instead of only 2 or 3 minutes) after the first explosion when crowds of the survivors had begun emerging from the Officers' Club and theater and running and staggering across the parking lot, there undoubtedly would have been far more deaths. Again, there but for the grace of God were many further casualties not suffered.

When the detonations occurred, the front gate-guard at Campbell reportedly was shocked beyond description at the horrendous blasts. When the initial explosion was triggered, the guard reportedly leapt in shock before running into the *529th Operations Center* 45 to 50 feet away to seek instruction from the *529th* desk sergeant. As both men no doubt ran back out into the street to look across the Campbell Parade Field toward the source of the blasts at the rear of the complex, a large cloud of debris was gathering over the parade field.

Though the horrendous concussive effect of the blasts was more than enough evidence of an emergency situation, when soldiers and civilians in the vicinity witnessed the smoke, dust and debris filling the air above and raining down upon the compound, they knew the circumstances were indeed dire.

Emergency Response

Emergency medical technicians, personnel from the *Army CID*, the *529th* and *536th Military Police* units, as well as contingents of the German civilian police began arriving quite quickly at the scene of what most everyone now was certain was an intentional terrorist attack. Some shocked and injured civilians and U.S. Army personnel began streaming toward the *529th Operations Center* at the front gate, many of them in shock and explaining that huge explosions had occurred.

Meanwhile, back at Patton Barracks approximately one-half mile away (as the crow flies across country), the men of the *529th* were well aware that an emergency situation now existed. The shock-wave of the blasts rattled and shook the buildings and sent some of the older experienced veterans at Patton immediately to the *Orderly Room* for further instruction.

Patrol units from the *529th* were quickly dispatched to Campbell. All existing NCOs and officers living off-post were immediately summoned, and additional emergency personnel were organized.

Since many civilians and *Army* personnel were injured, confused, and now stranded without vehicles at the Officers' Club and theater – though the situation warranted an initial examination by explosives experts – emergency personnel nevertheless advanced immediately into the area of the blasts. As previously-stated, the devastation of the attack would have been immensely greater had any additional explosives been set to detonate during this time of rescue, but luckily, no such delayed explosives had existed.

Once it was determined that it was safe to examine the scene, a massive investigation was organized. The perimeter of the large parking lot was roped and sealed off by *CID* and *MPs* from the *529th* and *536th MP* companies, and the task of an extensive forensics investigation and the identification and removal of the bodies, began in earnest. Injured personnel were removed to the *Army's 130th Station Hospital* just up Romerstrasse.

The Heidelberg terrorist attack was only one of numerous similar bombings in the early 1970s which targeted U.S. military installations. Other attack sites included Augsburg, Munich, Karlsruhe, Hamburg, Berlin, and Frankfurt just to name a few. It had suddenly become exceedingly dangerous to be located on a U.S. Army base in Germany. Some of the major incidents during this time included:

Attack on the Munich Airport, February 10, 1970: Three terrorists attacked El Al passengers in a bus at the Munich Airport with guns and grenades. One passenger was killed and 11 were injured. All three terrorists were captured by airport police. The *Action Organization for the Liberation of Palestine* and the *Democratic Front for the Liberation of Palestine* claimed responsibility for this attack.

Attack on the Frankfurt U.S. Army Officers Club, May 11, 1972: An Army lieutenant colonel was killed and 13 persons injured when three bombs shattered a *Fifth Corps* headquarters officers' club in Frankfurt, Germany.

Massacre at the Munich Olympic Village, September 5, 1972: Eight Palestinian *"Black September"* terrorists seized eleven Israeli athletes in the *Olympic Village* in Munich, West Germany. In a bungled rescue attempt by West German authorities, nine of the hostages and five terrorists were subsequently killed.

Terrorist Culprits

In the months over the next two years, it was discovered from investigations that a majority of the attacks inside Germany were being committed by a group of extreme radical socialist leftists known as the *"Red Army Faction,"* or *"Baader-Meinhof Terrorists."* As it turned out, most of the individuals involved in these acts of terrorism, interestingly, were, as explained above, the children or grandchildren of former *NAZI Army* officials who had made it their mission in life to oust the American military from Germany by force, using fear as a motivational factor.

The *Baader-Meinhof* terrorist group included many different individuals, but the primary leaders were later revealed to be Gudrun Ensslin, Andreas Baader, Ulrike Meinhoff, Irene Goergens, Ingrid Schubert, Angela Luther, Irmgard Moeller and Holger Meins among others.

Luther and Moeller were ultimately determined to have been the individuals heartless enough to plant the explosives inside Campbell Barracks. They were not captured that day, remaining at large for a number of weeks. They, however, had been described to *Army CID* officials by several individuals who had witnessed their suspicious behavior following the parking of their bomb-laden vehicles inside Campbell.

Both Moeller and Luther were ultimately captured by German law enforcement personnel and paid for their crimes. That, however, did nothing for the loved ones of their victims – Bonner, Woodward, and Peck.

Following the May 24, 1972 incident, the men of the *529th* took pride in the fact that Gen. Michael S. Davison, the *CINC* at that time and his staff had not been endangered on that day, nor was he ever endangered prior to his retirement from the Army in 1975. His successor, however, was not so fortunate.

After being placed on "alert status," the *529th Military Police Company* was fully mobilized. No one was granted leave of any type, nor any type of absence whatsoever.

In the hours, days and weeks thereafter, there would be no such thing as a vehicle passing into Patton or Campbell Barracks without an intense examination not only of the identity of the individual(s) in the vehicle, but also of the vehicle itself for explosives. Anyone not in possession of the proper identity credentials not only were barred from the compounds, but were detained for further investigation. This procedure was set into motion on all the other U.S. Army bases in Germany as well.

For a young man from the southern United States freshly assigned to his first duty station in the United States Army, this incident was quite an experience. I, however, had been carefully trained in military police work, and was now getting a chance to use that training first-hand.

— •❯❯ ❮❮• —

Moments of Military Mirth

T he late Jerry Clower, a hilarious stand-up comic from the 1980s-1990s, was immensely popular on the comedy club circuit back in the day, and reminded me somewhat of the dark humor which often prevailed within the ranks of the *529th Military Police Company* in Heidelberg, Germany in which I served in the *United States Army* from 1972 to 1975.

One of Clower's skits involved two hunters, one of whom had wounded a large bobcat which had escaped into the brushy confines of a tall pine tree in northern Alabama late one night. According to Clower's skit, one of the hunters ascended the tree to run the wounded animal back to ground, but ran into a bit more resistance than he had anticipated.

Long story short, after the tree's branches had shaken violently for several minutes and howls of pain had erupted on and off from the shadowy confines of the treetop, and after the hunting partner still on the ground had been unable to see the bobcat to shoot it, the climbing hunter up in the tree eventually yelled quite desperately down to the ground with the urgent plea to *"Just shoot up here amongst us and give one of us some relief!"*

It was dark humor such as this which sometimes prevailed in the *529th Military Police Company*. Despite the intense security mission of this unit – particularly in the months following the May 24, 1972 terrorist incident at the *U.S. Army's* Campbell Barracks in Heidelberg, Germany – things began returning to a semblance of normalcy in six or seven months, but the times remained tense, nonetheless.

In an environment such as this, young men – even military policemen charged with the security of such sensitive areas as the *United States Army in Europe (USAREUR)* headquarters and the commander-in-chief therein in Heidelberg – often pursue light-hearted amusement just to keep their sanity.

As talented, dedicated, and duty-bound as were the men of the *529th* under normal circumstances during the decade of the 1970s, there were also simply a number of "characters" there who were overly adept sometimes at seeking amusement through a measure of foolishness – sometimes even to the detriment of their own safety.

"I.Q. Deficient"

The late Specialist Fourth-Class I.Q. Deficient was one such unusual soul. Blessed with movie-star good looks – great hair, an ever-present bright smile, tall broad shoulders and a naturally muscular physique – I.Q. also had a gift for gab that just wouldn't quit. Women drooled over him, but Albert Einstein he wasn't.

According to his story, I.Q. had "washed out" of *Airborne Infantry School* due to "bad knees," and had somehow wound up in the *529th*. It wasn't unusual for guys from non-military police units to occasionally appear within our ranks. The *529th,* however, only retained the best. If one had flaws, he or she usually was eventually "weeded out" and transferred to another duty station.

By and large in the early 1970s, GIs had a difficult, at best, time acquiring female companionship, particularly that of an attractive German fraulein. These ladies, in general, simply snubbed most GIs. I suppose that "turn-about is fair play." After all, it had been barely a generation (25 years or so) since these GIs' fathers had subdued and imprisoned many of these "ladies'" *NAZI* fathers and grandfathers – some for *"Crimes Against Humanity."* So I suppose a little animosity toward American soldiers could be understood.

The mistake Americans seem to make time and time again, however, is the expenditure of the treasure of our country and the blood of our men to conquer an evil rogue empire, only to turn right around and not only give the country right back to the vestiges of those rogues, but to spend our treasure yet again to *re-build* their devastated country. The logic just defeats me... What happened to "taking over" and permanently "occupying" a conquered nation? But I digress...

When it came to attracting German fraulein companionship, I.Q. Deficient was an exception to the rule. He always had an attractive German lady on his arm, and something just didn't seem right about it, because, to put it bluntly, despite all his admirable qualities, even I.Q. knew that he wasn't "the sharpest knife in the drawer."

A view from the vicinity of Bismarkplatz looking down the entrance to the Hauptstrasse in the old main street of Heidelberg near the famous castle. (Photo by R. Olin Jackson)

Specialist Deficient also was forever bringing his female companionship into the barracks late at night, and forcing the rookie GIs to listen to those ladies cooing and moaning in delight in the dark corner where he bunked. The fact that females were strictly forbidden in the barracks was beside the point as far as I.Q. was concerned. The rules more often than not simply did not apply to him.

At least a portion of I.Q.'s popularity within the ranks of the *529th* stemmed from the fact that he never knew an enemy or a stranger within our ranks. That big smile rarely left his face and he incessantly circulated among all the troops, never favoring anyone and befriending almost everyone.

I.Q. often drew duty on the front gate at Patton Barracks. Pulling security on the gates was not the most inspirational or rewarding of jobs, and due to the drudgery of that task and Specialist Deficient's nevertheless happy-go-lucky nature, he was constantly in pursuit of the previously-described amusements to pass the time.

One of I.Q.'s most favorite "diversions" was right around the corner from the Patton Barracks front gate at a little Italian restaurant called *San Remo* (*The restaurant and even the building have sadly disappeared completely from the landscape since the departure of USAREUR from Heidelberg in 2013*). At the time, *San Remo* had some of the best cold beer in town. *(Though they were probably brewing it in an old car radiator out back. . .)*

This was the thing about the Patton gate gig. It offered several "options," if you will, to the enlisted men manning that post that the other duty stations simply could not provide. It therefore was I.Q.'s favorite post.

First of all, it offered *"the San Remo boogey."* No other *529th MP* duty station had a restaurant with delightfully-cold German beer a mere 50 feet away. There simply were no "San Remos" (or any other such distractions) anywhere near any of the other ten or twelve duty-posts. All of the MPs at those other sites were either isolated in their work or else working at *Top Secret* posts which brooked not even an infinitesimal bit of dereliction of duty.

The Patton Barracks gate-post boasted another distinction which Deficient enjoyed, that being that it sometimes included a "non-NCO" (read Spec-4 rank) as the "desk sergeant," opening up the possibility of even more foolishness at this duty-post. This isn't to say that the Spec-4s assigned as desk sergeant there were unqualified or derelict in their duty. Not by a long shot. *(I occupied this seat of responsibility myself many times.)* It's just that they sometimes perhaps didn't run quite as "tight a ship" as a hard NCO would have run, because they (the Spec-4 desk sergeants) had to actually "live" with the men they were supervising, and "hard-case" Spec-4 desk sergeants invariably were ostracized by their enlisted compatriots. *(This obviously is the very reason that NCOs who live in the barracks are almost always isolated from the enlisted men.)*

The desk sergeant on duty at the Patton gate also simply took it for granted that no one would ever be so brazen as to pull a *San Remo* beer-a-thon while on duty. Things such as that just didn't happen in the *529th* – that is, until I.Q. hit town. He was just a different breed of cat. He "dared to go where others feared to tread" – or some such nonsense.

As a result of all of the above, I.Q. Deficient – on his fateful final day of duty in the *529th* – was slipping back and forth – undeterred – to *San Remo* for cold beer during his Patton gate-guard duty breaks. By 2:00 or 3:00 pm that afternoon, though he was still able to manage his gate-guard duty, Specialist Deficient should have been relieved from duty – mainly because he was "snockered" – not "hammered" – but snockered nonetheless. And I'm sure he would have been removed from duty if anyone had been aware of his shenanigans – but at that time, there simply wasn't any "hard and fast rule" against taking one's hourly breaks in the cool inviting confines of *San Remo*, and who knew what he was doing while he was over there. Right?

Now in his "de-natured" condition and while standing in the traffic intersection supposedly checking identifications and controlling the traffic into Patton on a lazy summer Sunday afternoon when that traffic was virtually nonexistent, I.Q. had dangerously decided he was going to practice "quick-jack-a-round-into-the-chamber" of his Colt .45 sidearm. *(A perfectly good example of the reason inebriated soldiers are immediately removed from duty and disciplined – but, again, I.Q. was an exception to the rule.)*

Somewhere along the line, someone had demonstrated to I.Q. that if he grasped the heavy .45 sidearm and pulled it partially up out of the holster and then – pressing it firmly (friction-wise) against the front of the holster – jammed the weapon back down inside the holster, he could jack a round into the chamber with only one hand.

I don't know the name of the MP who demonstrated this little bit of foolishness to I.Q., but he should have been disciplined as well. I.Q. nevertheless, had actually become quite adept at this dangerous bit of gunplay, and was understandably proud of his achievement.

As the hours passed and I.Q. went back and forth from *San Remo* to his gate guard gig, he continued practicing. He'd jack a round then look up and smile. . . Jack a round, look up and smile.

After each one of these little "jack-a-round" sequences, I.Q. was having to drop the .45's magazine, eject the live round, and then re-load it back into the magazine. In each instance, that round kept getting more and more difficult to load back into that magazine, and it eventually became comical to watch, as did much of I.Q.'s other actions at this point. Meanwhile, no one of a supervisory capacity had yet noticed or realized what was going on.

With something this dangerous, I.Q. Deficient's luck was bound to run out – and it eventually did. During one of his jack-a-thons, his index finger apparently inevitably curled inside the trigger guard, causing him to accidentally pull the trigger as he jammed the weapon back down into his holster. *(Note: In case you, the readers are wondering, I was off-duty on this day. I observed some of the above for a short period of time from the second floor window on the north end of the Deuce-Nine barracks, but I wasn't really aware of what I.Q. was doing until the hammer actually fell on this little incident. I was provided with the rest of the details from I.Q.'s gate-guard partner later that afternoon after all the excitement had died down.)*

The favorite haunt of I.Q. Deficit was photographed in 1974. It was here that he passed the hours enjoying cold German beer prior to his disastrous front gate duty. (Photo by Bob Walls. Reprinted with Permission)

One can only imagine Specialist Deficient's unmitigated shock when a huge resounding "boom" suddenly rocked the usual silence in the courtyard area at the Patton gate. Timed almost perfectly with this discharge was a substantial hop which I.Q. almost comically and spasmodically performed in his shocked reflexive response to the big .45's loud discharge. *(I did observe this portion of the incident.)*

Looking down quickly, I.Q. suddenly grasped the fact that blood was spurting out of his leg. The heavy .45 slug had entered his upper thigh, and, almost inexplicably, had traveled down through his knee – blowing it out – and then had exited from his lower leg. It's a minor miracle that the round did not sever his femoral artery and quickly result in his death. I'm certain I.Q. never walked on that leg thereafter without a substantial limp.

After he realized what had happened, I.Q. immediately hit the ground and began drawing quite a bit of attention. Troops began running to his aid and EMTs were quickly summoned.

As a tourniquet was being applied to his leg to shut off the blood pooling at his feet, I.Q. began lapsing into incoherency and shock. As the EMTs were loading him onto a gurney and into a waiting ambulance, he began screaming at the top of his lungs – *"I'm off the gates! I'm off the gates! I'm off the gates forever! Ah Ha! Ha! Ha!"*

And you know what? As things turned out, this was one of I.Q.'s statements which turned out to be exactly accurate. After they drove away with him in the ambulance that day, I never again saw nor heard from I.Q. Deficient. He simply vanished from the public record, and faded into history.

Knowing him, he probably was honorably discharged after being awarded a *Purple Heart* and *Good Conduct Ribbon*, and lived the remainder of his life on a fat monthly medical disability check, but that's just this present-day layman's assessment.

Later that same day, it was decided that the round which had passed through I.Q.'s leg needed to be located if possible. I suspect this was desired for the incident report. I went down to help search, and won the lottery when, approximately 100 feet from where I.Q. had been standing, I discovered the still-bloody slug on the cobblestones in the street. It apparently had exited I.Q.'s leg, bounced skyward off the cobblestones, and then fallen back onto the ground.

Some 30 or 40 years later, when a roster of the *529th Military Police Company* veterans began circulating, I noticed that the ever-colorful I.Q. Deficient unfortunately was listed as "deceased." As sad as was that discovery, I have to admit that it didn't surprise me in the least. I, nevertheless, salute your eternal happiness and always effervescent personality I.Q. You generated constant goodwill among the enlisted personnel of the *529th,* and will be remembered fondly as long as the veterans who served with you still exist.

"Ewer Dirtnap"

Another of the incidents which went down in the lore of the *529th* for a number of years occurred one evening at one of the favorite watering holes of *Deuce-Niners* in downtown Heidelberg. It quite possibly would never have occurred without the influence of German beer. No. . . . Actually, that's just not true. I'm sure it would inevitably have occurred regardless of the circumstances.

Zillertal's was a small bar and pub near the historic Hauptstrasse *(main street of old-town Heidelberg)* which had been patronized consistently by the troops of the *529th* for a number of years prior to the early 1970s. It fell out of favor sometime in the mid- to late-1970s with the advent of the discos and other more-popular clubs such as *"Shepherd's"* downtown, but for a while, *"Zill's"* was riding high – literally. I'm certain it is long-gone today.

At any rate, on a warm summer evening in 1974, a group of us had gathered there as we occasionally still did. One of the guys who participated on this evening – Specialist Paine Innaass – was your proto-typical bully, who enjoyed humiliating others for reasons I still don't understand. I mean this guy was blessed with good looks and intelligence and a great job within the *Deuce-Nine*, yet spent untold hours constantly abusing the lower-level enlisted men around him.

As stated, Paine had a cushy job on the administrative side of the *529th*, and, as such, was never exposed to the rigors, boredom, - and, yes, dangers – of "gate-guard" or *"Top Secret* post" duty. In fact, he was never required to pull any MP duty at all, and, in general, just lived *"the life of Riley."* He was another of those who were simply blessed with good fortune and widely envied by the line troops.

Despite all his blessings, though, it was just never enough for Specialist Innaass. On this night at *Zillertals,* Paine was more abusive than normal (if that was even possible). The guy he had targeted for abuse that evening – we'll call him "Bill," – was relatively new in the *529th* and unaware of Paine's penchant for doling out abuse.

The further Specialist Innaass got into his mugs of beer, the more abusive he became too. Bill was one of Paine's typical victims. He was somewhat reserved; intelligent; and a pretty sharp dude overall, and Paine was just naturally antagonistic to those types. Maybe it was petty jealousy. Who knows? And the longer Bill simply good-naturedly endured Paine's torment, the nastier Innaass became.

Yet another guy in our group – Sgt. Ewer Dirtnap – was a beefy, ham-fisted, happy-go-lucky guy from the mid-western United States. Virtually everyone liked Ewer. He was the polar-opposite of Paine – always with a wide friendly smile, just like a big friendly puppy.

As the evening wore on, Innaass's taunts eventually began taking a toll on Bill, and most everyone in the group sympathized with him, but, as was usually the case, everyone just let Paine rant on. After listening to his abusiveness for an hour or two, many of us – Sgt. Dirtnap in particular – truly wanted to shut him up.

Finally, totally exasperated, Bill got up to leave when he could tolerate Innaass's insults no longer. Sgt. Dirtnap, with a heart the size of Manhattan and the courage of a lion, stopped the young man and calmly said, "Hang on. Don't leave. Let me handle this. Exchange seats with me."

When this happened, we all just thought that Ewer was going to pull Paine aside and give him a good tongue-lashing. News flash . . . That option wasn't even remotely on Sgt. Dirtnap's radar. He had bigger plans.

To the eternal appreciation of those of us present, Ewer didn't waste any time whatsoever with words. Mr. Innaass was still yammering on incessantly when the good sergeant drew that big ham-fisted right arm of his wayyyyyy back – oh, I'd say back down somewhere around Africa – and when it shot forward like a howitzer round, it caught Innaass flush on the left eye with a punch his great-grandfather felt. When Paine stood up quickly to en-gage Ewer, Dirtnap delivered one of the most memorable left upper-cuts I have ever seen. It would have brought a smile even to former Heavyweight Champ Mike Tyson's face. It sent Paine ass over elbows backwards out of his chair and onto the floor.

Sgt. Dirtnap wasn't done yet either. He calmly rose from his seat at the table and walked around to stand over Paine (who by then was waving away the stars floating around his head) and got right down in his face and said, "If you ever open your mouth to abuse anyone in this unit like that ever again, I'll give you double what you just got. You hear me soldier??!!"

I don't know if Specialist Paine Innaass actually heard Ewer or not. He was still shaking out the cobwebs and trying to figure out where he was. After a few moments, he recovered a bit and, without a word, got up and staggered off back to the barracks.

The next morning – whoa baby! It was "shiner city" for Paine. The entire area around and within his left eye socket was dark black, blue and bloody, and remained that way for well over a week.

And, to the surprise of many, Paine had suddenly become a walking road-sign for humility too. From that point forward, every time he was about to meet someone from our group on the street or in a hallway or any-where else, Innaass immediately turned and walked in another direction. His abusive nature had evaporated, and his personality had changed 180 degrees – literally. Sgt. Ewer Dirtnap had gotten Paine's attention big-time.

I'll never forget Dirtnap's big smiling face and one resoundingly impres-sive night at *Zillertal's* way back in 1974, when he entered the folklore of the *Deuce-Nine*.

Stan and the English Chicks

One of the truly amazing mysteries of life is the almost magical and many times inexplicable attraction of a particular female to a particular male. What one female finds attractive in a male may be truly repugnant to another of the fairer sex. I learned early-on that there simply is no rhyme or reason to this often paradoxical situation. It sometimes is just beyond explanation.

I was exposed to a particularly impressive example of this while in the *529th* in 1973. On a day of "off-duty" one afternoon, several of us dropped by an apartment rented by Specialist Stan K. Fingers and several other *Deuce-Niners*. We often got together to play poker and pass the hours.

Now Stan was not one of the line-MPs at the *529th*. To the contrary, he was a mechanic who worked in the motor pool, keeping our Jeeps, patrol sedans, and three-quarter-ton vehicles, etc. serviced and in good running condition.

Specialist Fingers was also another of those guys who was popular around the company almost from Day 1. He was friendly to a fault and usually conversational with most people, invariably with some humorous story to relate. He always seemed to have a smile on his face and a song in his heart. *(Funny how those attributes win friends, huh?)*

Now due simply to the nature of his job, Stan almost always had a sloppy uniform, scuffed-up, un-shined, oil-soaked boots, and, more often than not, just a generally "greasy" unkempt appearance – inevitably with dark caked grease beneath his fingernails. *(Hey. . . What can I say? It's the mechanic's calling card. Always has been and always will be.)*

To put it bluntly, Stan K. Fingers simply had motor oil running through his veins. Automotive mechanical work was his life. If he'd had manicured nails, a neat hair-cut, and tidy neat clothing, we very definitely would have wondered about him in the opposite direction. . . Ya know ??

Anyway, despite his unattractive features, Stan – just like I.Q. *(see above)* – was surprisingly popular among the ladies. Also as explained above, in the early days when most *U.S. Army* GIs were getting snubbed by the German ladies, Mr. Fingers – grubby fingernails, greasy uniform and all – invariably was stylin' with a foxy lady in tow. Sometimes the breath-taking quality of these ladies could be shocking too.

One incident in particular involving Stan stands out in my memory – that of "the English chicks." Heidelberg quite often was frequented by attractive females from "across the pond" in England. At that time, our historic little burg was a popular and inexpensive tourism destination for the British ladies. It also attracted the females because it had two major institutions of higher learning – *Schiller College* and the historic *University of Heidelberg* – both of which had a high percentage of female enrollment. For whatever reason, there frequently were attractive ladies from the United Kingdom for our viewing pleasure, but just like all the other females, they almost invariably were simply "out of reach" for GIs unless one's name was "Elvis."

On the particular occasion in question, I have to admit I was stunned to discover that Stan had not "one," but "two" of these ladies, and not only was he squiring them around town, they had even decided to take up temporary residence at his apartment. And these females weren't just attractive, sports fans. . . . these ladies were "drop-dead gorgeous."

Stan never attempted to do a thing about his appearance for these ladies either, yet they seemed to be absolutely crazy about him. And when I say "crazy," I mean "sex-thang" crazy. Stan K. Fingers had it going on. . . You know?

On the morning that we had dropped by his apartment, we actually had a motive other than friendly visitation. We wanted to snag a bit of exposure to these gorgeous "ladies." One of Stan's roommates who also worked in the motor pool was sitting at the kitchen table on this morning wolfing down some warm buttered toast with jelly when we came rolling in. *(He didn't offer us any of the toast, gobbling it down himself. We, however, shortly were greatly relieved that he hadn't.)*

Stan soon joined us from the bedroom, explaining the "ladies" were still "sleeping it off" from the previous night's festivities downtown. "Yeah, we got up for a little while early this morning to eat some breakfast," he snorted, chest puffed out. . . "but then couldn't resist a little wild stuff on the kitchen table, ya know? Used the butter-stick on 'em," he added with a wolfish grin on his face, snorting again and nodding toward the now mostly-depleted stick of margarine his roommate had been scarfing down.

Those words had scarcely left Stan's mouth before his roommate began choking and sputtering, hopping over to the kitchen sink to croak up his buttered toast. When he had recovered, he turned red-faced to Stan, steam shooting from his ears, and bellowed "You did whattttt!!!!????"

At this point, Specialist Fingers – immensely enjoying the mounting humor in this situation – was overcome with mirth. "Yeah!" he croaked. . . "Both of 'em!"

"I'll kill you" his roommate bellowed, lunging at Stan who quickly retreated back into the bedroom where he slammed and locked the door behind him, breathless from laughter as his roomie pounded upon the door in rage.

"Absolutely amazing," was all we could say or think as we left that day. Yep. . . Stan K. Fingers had it going on. . . . And it was a good long while before any of us could once again eat "hot buttered toast."

Riot on the Riviera

I don't know who came up with the idea. My three room-mates and I were sitting around our apartment off-post one day when we decided we should take a trip to some exotic location we had not yet visited in our travels. After all, we were in "Europe." We had ample time on our hands and it might be a long, long, time – if ever – that we passed this way again *(I can almost hear peals of **Seals & Crofts** in the background.).*

One of the guys eventually came up with the idea of taking a trip to Spain. I had already been to France several times, as well as Belgium, Holland, Austria, Scotland, and a number of other places, but never to Spain, so that choice suited me just fine. Our "travel planner" got to work on the logistics.

By that point in our lives, many of us had our own transportation. One of the great things about Germany is that even a poor GI can obtain quite a nice "ride" there for considerably less than that vehicle would cost in the United States. And if one had a "connection" – for instance a German "used car" dealer who eagerly sought "American cigarettes" as most Germans did since they were unable to obtain them on the open market without paying exorbitant prices, then one quite possibly could obtain a really nice German-made vehicle at even less cost.

As had my other friends with "transportation," I had opted for a moderate vehicle – the *Volkswagen* – because it was so prevalent in Germany, and the prices therefore were extremely reasonable for a "used *Volkswagen*." I also didn't want to spend a lot of money, because I had heard from other GIs that the cost of shipping a vehicle back home was prohibitive for lowly enlisted personnel.

I think I wound up spending in the neighborhood of $300.00 on the *Volkswagen* I ultimately purchased. Now I know that almost sounds like pocket change today, but adjusting for inflation, $300.00 in 1972 was the rough equivalent of approximately $1,950.00 today (2025), so it wasn't dirt-cheap. Nevertheless, it was still a bargain.

Despite the fact that it in effect was a "used car," the *Volkswagen* I had selected was virtually new except that it had a door on one side which had been crumpled in and replaced. And when I say "new," I mean almost "brand new." I had gotten quite the deal because, as explained earlier, I was not a tobacco user, so I had saved up "black-market" cigarettes equaling approximately $125.00 in 1972 dollars.

When the day came to pick up my new car, I was thrilled. And needless to say, when the day that my tour of duty in the Army was complete and I had to return to "the world," I examined every possible way to get that vehicle back to the States affordably, but nothing worked. I wound up donating it to a good friend – who was as thrilled as I had been when I had purchased it a year earlier. But I digress. . . .

We set out driving across Belgium, then France, and eventually down the Mediterranean Coast to the Spanish Riviera. The destination we had chosen was Barcelona and "Casa del Sol" on the Mediterranean. We'd be able not only to enjoy the Riviera, but also the delights of one of the larger cities in Spain.

One of the "sights" we wanted to see was a bull-fight. Barcelona has a huge bull-fighting arena. I'd never previously been to such an event, so this was going to be a totally new experience for me.

After we arrived in the city and had gotten set up in our hotel room, we set out for the beach. We purchased leather "bota-bags" – a Spanish invention of a large pouch into which one can pour a bottle of wine through one end which was then corked up, and then squirt the liquid through a much smaller opening into one's mouth as one desired.

After a day of wine, sun and fun in the Mediterranean, we decided that the bull-fights were next on our agenda. When we arrived at the arena, I couldn't help but notice that all around the exterior there were numerous shops selling all manner of leather goods and fresh beef. It seemed a bit strange to me at the time, but I was still suffering from the effects of the bota-bag and a bit of sun-stroke.

At any rate, I wasn't the only one of us who hadn't previously been to a bull-fight. None of us in our group had. We knew only that there was a matador who "teased" a huge bull with his cape back and forth in the arena until the bull was worn out. We didn't know much more than that – at least I didn't.

As GIs are often want to do, we started on our bota-bags again that day, so we each were essentially half-way through a bottle of wine before the first bull even entered the arena. Looking back, we were pretty-inexperienced young men – barely 20 years old each. We had no idea that a matador in Spain is the equivalent stature-wise of the heavyweight boxing champion in the United States.

I also didn't know that there is a "toreador" and there is a "matador" – two entirely different "animals" if you will. The toreador comes out first and does the hard work, tempting the huge bull, running him back and forth and stabbing him each time he passed with these short little barbed spears known as "banderillas" which caused a massive loss of blood from the animal, eventually exhausting him. After the toreador has completed his torments of the beast, the matador then makes his appearance.

When the first toreador was introduced in the ring, we noticed that an unusual amount of cheering and respect was directed his way. I don't recall the exact circumstances, but I'm sure we were a little surprised that so much adulation was being heaped upon what appeared to us to be a sissy-looking little man in tights with a little cape – but what did we know??

With each pass, the toreador stabbed more and more of these banderillas into the bull until he soon was simply a bloody mess with the blood pooling up at his feet on the dirt base of the bull-ring. Soon, the exhausted animal was able to do nothing but stand and stare dumbly at the toreador, obviously totally befuddled at how he could keep failing to eliminate his tormentor.

We of course were watching this in awe. When the bull could move no more, the matador strutted out and applied the coup de gras to the bull, driving a long sword between his shoulder blades down into his heart, causing him to collapse in death on the spot. We were aghast.

After this first bull was dispatched, we kinda just looked at each other. "Do they actually consider this a sport?" we inquired among ourselves. There was no "sport" to this. The bull essentially has no chance whatsoever. To our way of thinking, the bull just set himself up for failure while the prissy little toreadors and matadors strutted and preened for the audience's loud cheers as they dispatched the huge animal. We were disgusted.

We watched several more of these "fights" – all with the same results. Finally, however, something unusual happened. One of the bulls – to the unmitigated shock of most everyone present – broke with the normal routine of charging the bright cape and missing the toreador, and chose instead to charge directly at the man himself, much to his horror. The results were stunning. The rampaging bull caught that toreador on his horns and, in his rage, flung him like a rag-doll several rows up into the seats. When he fell quickly back down to earth and landed with a loud bang in the seats, that poor toreador didn't move an inch. When they carried him off on a stretcher, he was still unconscious and the onlookers were aghast.

Well... This was obviously a tragic occurrence, but for some strange reason, we four GIs simply felt that, in an unusual sort of way, justice had prevailed. Americans are like that.... quite often pulling for the underdog in a fight – even if it's a bull. And if ever there was a true facsimile of an underdog in this contest, it was definitely these bulls who were so easily being dispatched and then dragged unceremoniously from the ring.

Now when the toreador was flung up into the stands, a total hush came over the thousands in the crowded arena. As far as they were concerned, their "hero" had been totally unexpectedly crushed. They were devastated.

We Americans, on the other hand, responded quite differently. One can only imagine the surprise and outrage of the Spaniards when, about two-thirds of the way up in the huge Barcelona arena, four Americans are loudly cheering and clapping in acclamation for the bull. I'm sure they were thinking *"What in the hell is going on? Keel those gringos! Keel them!"*

It was at about this time that five or six young "toughs" sitting up behind us began throwing half-filled containers at us and openly challenging us to fight. By this point, we had all run through the contents of our bota-bags, so we were pretty-well hammered, and unaware of the growing danger around us.

One of the Spaniards pulled what looked to be about a two or three-foot-long knife from his belt and held it threateningly in his hand. *(No metal detectors or contraband seizure in their arenas.)* In reality, that knife was probably only about a 10 or 12-inch blade, but still a very, very dangerous weapon in the hands of someone who knew how to use it.

The knife-wielding Spaniard and his friends began slowly advancing on us and we began to take up drunken defensive poses. Even though we'd been taught in Basic Training how to disarm a knife-wielding opponent, that training was little more than a distant memory at that moment. We, for the most part, were in La La Land.

At about this same time, one of our group, Leeroy, staggering a bit, held up his hand to halt the Spaniards' advance by saying "Wait!! Wait!! Wait!!... I'm not ready!"

I don't know if our opponents had any idea what he was saying (probably not), but they almost certainly could understand the universal language of the raised hand signaling one to "Wait," so they paused, smiling to themselves. Leeroy then reached into his pocket, pulled out a tiny *(and I do mean "tiny")* little one-inch pen-knife, and, taking his time, very methodically opened it up with two daintily-extended fingers, then held it up and very drunkenly assumed a defensive stance, then motioned the Spaniards to come get us.

This obviously seemed so absurdly ridiculous to our challengers that they all suddenly burst out laughing – great big belly-laughs. I'm certain they had to have been thinking *"Crazy Americans. Maybe we won't keel them? Nah! Keel them anyway!"* This kept up for several minutes.

As the Spaniards continued to hoot and roll, those around them began laughing as well. Luckily for us, at about this same time, a pair of attentive Spanish *Federales* (police) came strolling up and we at least had the good sense to tactfully leave under their escort.

Needless to say, our impression of a Spanish bull-fight took a noticeable "hit" that day, falling to the absolute bottom of our list as far as righteous "sports" were concerned. We left shortly thereafter to return to Germany – a little older, and a little wiser. We also threw away those damn bota-bags.

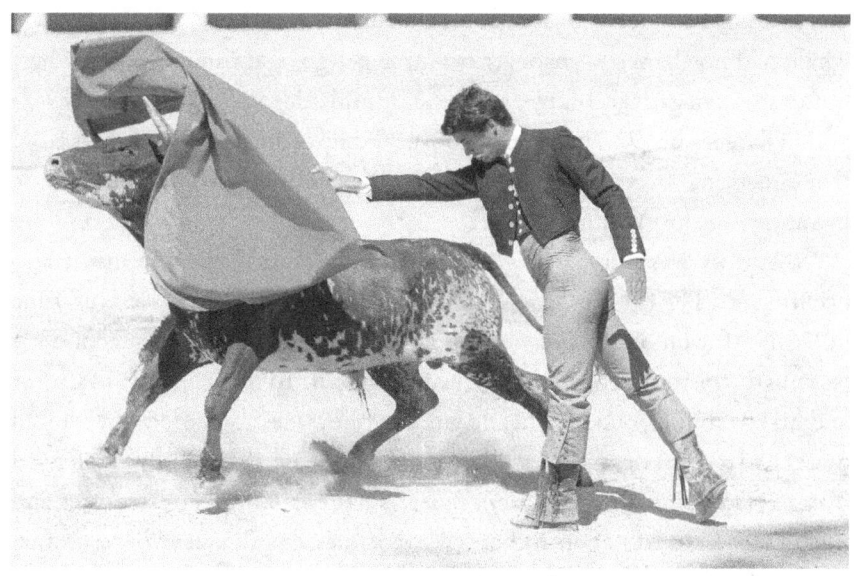

The Devastations of 1980

Shortly after returning stateside from my military duty in Europe, I made the classic mistake of a lot of enlistees – that of marrying too quickly. I had "played the field" for a couple of years before being cornered one evening by a tall bleached-blonde female who quickly became a fixture in my life. I simply didn't understand what was going on at the time, but it later became painfully clear. Today, I refer to her simply as "Plaintiff."

Six or seven months after meeting her, Plaintiff turned up pregnant. Though my better judgement was screaming at me to run as fast as I could from this female and never look back, I didn't do it.

Instead, I entered the "bonds" of matrimony with her. It was a marriage which had no chance whatsoever from the get-go, and though I do my best not to speak negatively of my ex today, it is difficult to avoid.

In January of 1977, my son was born, and he is the only bright spot from that situation. Everything else involving that union is, well, one of those memories one just wishes to forget.

Not only was our marriage fated for failure on its own terms, it also occurred during the ill-fated Jimmy Carter years. That period of time (1976-1980) would ultimately be categorized as some of the worst economic years in the history of our nation, due in large part to the ineptness of Carter and his economic policies. Oil and gasoline shortages abounded; the United States had a pathetic military which daily was being successfully challenged overseas *(Remember the American hostages crisis in Iran?)*; interest rates and inflation soared out of control; people were out of work everywhere; and on and on. *(Old-timers may also recall that during these years, the economic and prevailing circumstances were so bad that even the news media carried a special barometer of the circumstances of that day - each day - which they called "The Misery Index.")*

112

Plaintiff and I struggled along for several years. We were both eventually employed in pathetically-low-paying entry-level state jobs. Due to the breathtakingly excessive cost of gasoline and other necessities required just to "reach" our sites of employment, our salaries did not begin to cover our expenses. . . yet we persisted. We had no other choice. We tried to "look on the bright side," but we found nothing but a perpetual storm.

I finally obtained an opportunity for an interview for a job with the *Georgia Department of Agriculture* (in the winter of either in 1978 or '79; I don't remember exactly.). And wouldn't you know it, on the day of my interview which might offer me employment with a little bit of "sunshine," the Atlanta (and much of Georgia) traffic was paralyzed by a rather severe snow storm. I drove as far as I could get, and when I could get no further, I simply got out and walked as were some other "strandees."

When I got to the Agriculture Building, there were very few people there – only those with 4-wheel-drive vehicles. Fortunately for me, none of the other job applicants that day showed up either. "If you'll come to work in this kind of weather, I know we can depend upon you. You've got the job," said the assistant commissioner who interviewed me that day.. She just had no idea how desperate I actually was. If Hell had yawned before me on that street that day, I would still have abandoned my car and walked to that interview.

I won't go into any further traumatic details of my marriage to Plaintiff, other than to describe one or two significant aspects. After all, it did produce my son, and, subsequently, my grandchildren, all of whom I dearly love.

Sometime in 1979, in yet another desperate situation, I was searching for a vehicle which I could purchase with our meager dollars and for which the gasoline it used would not reduce me to pauper status at the gas pump. I purchased a shiny-bright orange 1974 *Volkswagen Beetle* (Yes. Another Volkswagen.) which turned out to be one of the better decisions I made in this ill-fated marriage.

I had located the *Beetle* through a newspaper advertisement. It had only 38,000 miles on the odometer, but had been wrecked on the right-front corner. It also had a carburation problem of some sort, and, for those reasons, was inoperable. The owner – who had a number of other vehicles at his disposal – had simply towed it to his front yard and forgotten it.

As explained above, I had spent three years in Germany from whence the *Volkswagen* originates and in which they still proliferate today. I had carefully researched and purchased a *Volkswagen* there in 1973 when I was stationed in Heidelberg in the U.S. military. I had selected my 1967 Heidelberg *Volks* from a number of other choices owned by a very talented and shrewd German mechanic who I had befriended and who subsequently advised me on the various important aspects of determining the health of the *VW* engine and transmission.

I therefore knew the little orange version I had located for Plaintiff and myself in the newspaper advertisement in 1979 was anything but a "lemon." I had listened to the engine run briefly before the carburation failed, and I had felt and listened to the transmission as it shifted smoothly into gear. All that vehicle needed was a replacement of the right-front wheel assembly and a clean-out of the gas tank, fuel line, and carburetor (all of which had become clogged by a fine silt of red clay, apparently from tainted gasoline), and it would then be the virtual equivalent of a new vehicle. After completion of these repairs, I had a smoothly-running and dependable automobile for which I had paid a very small sum.

That little *Volkswagen* became a short-term life-saver for us. Plaintiff and I could drive it all week on one tank of gas back and forth to our jobs downtown in Atlanta, and it was extremely dependable. As a result, I, in turn, was extremely fond of that vehicle.

We had only been in our marriage perhaps a year before it became abundantly clear to me that Plaintiff had an entirely different agenda from my own. She also had apparently married me because she believed that with a college education, I would easily land a well-paying job – something everyone especially craved in those days. I guess that after a year of my futile job search, reality had begun to set in with her.

Anyway, the day before Christmas of 1979, we set out for Plaintiff's parents' home in Birmingham, Alabama. We had spent the last Christmas or two with them since our circumstances at home were so bleak. Now as I said, I was really fond of our little *Volkswagen*. I had labored long and hard to remove the gas tank and clean it thoroughly; remove and replace the gas-line; and remove and take the carburetor to be rebuilt. I was proud of it.

As a result, I babied that little *Volks*. Following any substantial trip anyplace, I enjoyed taking a hose and soapy water to it and cleaning it up. I did this following each trip to Birmingham to visit Plaintiff's parents.

Plaintiff's father, however, apparently took umbrage at my use of his water. Perhaps I should have been more judicious. I don't know. We were poor as church-mice and one would presume that he would have been a bit more compassionate and charitable.

That Christmas Eve, I received – strangely – a packaged gift from Plaintiff's father beneath the Christmas tree, and I could see that Plaintiff and her family looked like the cat that had swallowed the canary. I, however, being accustomed to receiving little or nothing for Christmas since I was a child, was pleasantly and stupidly pleased just to be receiving anything at all.

Imagine my surprise on Christmas morning, when everyone was opening their gifts and I opened mine to discover a used garden hose. I have to confess right here that I truly did not know how to respond as Plaintiff, her father and mother and others turned away with smirks on their faces. They thought it was funny. To me, it was just short of cruel.

Plaintiff's father had never been positively-disposed toward me. His disdain was rooted in my inability to find employment in those hard times. Yes, I struggled to find a job in 1977-'78 during the first years of our marriage, but it's not like I wasn't desperately-searching for employment, just like millions of other out-of-work Americans during the Jimmy Carter years. The U.S. unemployment rate in 1979 was almost 8%, which is just short of catastrophic.

Just as with Plaintiff, I think her father thought that, since I had finished college, that my diploma was an automatic entre' into a well-paying job, and when that didn't happen, he became embittered by our poverty. As I said, our marriage was doomed almost from the outset.

We returned home the day after Christmas, and I quickly sensed a definite "alteration" in Plaintiff's personality. She was much more aloof, uncooperative, and defiant. I, however, was oblivious to what was actually going on. My "radar" simply didn't work in those days, and I paid dearly for it.

Several weeks later in the dawning of 1980, we set out for our jobs in Atlanta as usual – with the exception that Plaintiff demanded to drive us to work that day. That was not normal by any stretch of the imagination. She drove like ABFD (that's Greek for former NASCAR legend *"Awesome Bill From Dawsonville"*), and quite frankly, I was a nervous wreck after arriving at any destination to which she had driven us.

Nevertheless, I also hated fighting the Atlanta traffic, so I relented. I let her play "dueling-vehicles" down Georgia-400 Highway and Interstates 285 and 75 to our jobs.

When we reached my employer – the *Georgia Department of Agriculture* – at which I had gained a pitifully-paying employment the previous year,

Plaintiff stated stiffly "I'll keep the car today and I'll be by to pick you up after work." R-i-g-h-t-t-t-t...

I passed the day as usual in my entry-level position at the Ag Department. At approximately 4:30 that afternoon, I received a phone call. It was Plaintiff. "Well.... I'm gone," she stated matter-of-factly. *(I could almost hear her picking her teeth with a toothpick.)*

"Oh? On your way to pick me up?" I responded stupidly.

"No. I'm gone," she repeated harshly. "You'll have to find some other way home."

"G-Gone? Gone where?" I stammered, now growing really uneasy.

"I'm leaving, and I'm filing for divorce," she replied, with utter finality in her voice.

The next thing I heard was a click as she hung up the phone. I'd like to somehow make this humorous, but that's just not possible. It was just so .... cold. Indescribably "cold."

To say I was shocked doesn't do justice to the word "shocked." There I was, an hour away from home. No way to return, and, though I didn't realize it at the time... no way to even get to work anymore either. My little orange *Volkswagen* was gone forever. Never saw it again, but I would have given up a hundred of them to retain possession of my son, who also was now gone.

I sat – totally stunned – at my desk for a few minutes. Was this yet another of her cruel family jokes? I couldn't believe that I had been that "out to lunch" on the circumstances. I simply did not see this one coming at all.

Anyway, long story short, I called my brother-in-law who was a division director at the *Georgia State Merit System* right down the street. He wouldn't even have considered denying me a ride home – particularly under the circumstances – though it was a bit out of his way.

When I got back to our tiny abode outside Roswell, Georgia, I was honestly afraid to walk inside. When I finally summoned the courage to open the door and enter our living room, it was as I had feared. The room was totally empty, as were the other six rooms in the modest structure we had called "home."

Plaintiff, in fact, had left me an old mattress upon which to sleep. Everything else – and I mean everything – had been cleaned out. No dishes. No curtains. No bed-sheets or blankets. I didn't even have a fork or spoon with which to eat – even if I had had something to eat, which I did not, since she had also cleaned out what little food had resided in our cupboard and refrigerator. I have to give her credit in that realm. When it came to "clean-ing out" a house, she was thorough.

Interestingly, she did not take the refrigerator, but that wasn't an act of compassion. I have no doubt in my mind that in actuality, whomever she had recruited to load up *our* furniture into a *U-Haul* almost certainly had drawn the line at the weighty food cooler.

Plaintiff even took my record albums, but left me a big stack of bills. As the late famed Southern humorist and best-selling author Lewis Grizzard once amusingly quipped in one of his books describing his divorce, *"A woman who will do that will cut you."*

As bad as it was, though, things, amazingly, were about to become even worse for me – much worse.

—⊹⟫ ⟪⊹—

Guy

My brother Guy was the youngest of my four siblings. He was born in 1957, the year my father decided to contract for the construction of a new home for us on our farm in northwest Georgia.

From the outset, we knew Guy was special. Since he was the youngest, he, understandably, received an overwhelming amount of latitude from my parents for any transgressions, an overwhelming amount of personal attention, and an equally overwhelming amount of abuse from his two older brothers. *(At least for the first ten or twelve years of his life. . .)*

Guy quickly learned, however, that if anything displeased him, he had several "weapons" in his arsenal: He could utilize a loud squawk or screech, and Mother or Dad would shortly arrive on the scene – usually with "the belt" – to punish my brother David or me – usually me. It didn't matter if David or I were not at fault, either. Anyone messing with Guy received either a screaming vocal threat of butt annihilation, or the immediate application of "the belt" for said purpose. Guy also had a set of very effective dental weapons in his mouth which he didn't hesitate to use to great effect.

My father was a "no nonsense" type of individual, particularly in the last years of his marriage to my mother. He brooked no disturbances or problems within our family circle. Anyone who dared any transgressions – and by anyone, I basically mean my younger brother (not Guy) and me – earned a beating with "the belt." It was just that simple.

My brother and I lived in a certain amount of fear, but Guy flourished in this environment, receiving quite a bit of special treatment. He was the only one of us to ever receive a beautiful house-trained Labrador puppy; the only one of us to receive a motorcycle (though actually a "mini-motorcycle" known as a "mini-bike"); the only one of us boys to be given his own private

Guy Jordan Jackson is pictured at his graduation from kindergarten in 1962. His calm demeanor in this photo belies his precocious nature.

room in our home; the only one who never had to worry about "hand-me-down" clothing; and the list went on and on.

During Guy's short life, Dad was present in our family on a full-time basis for perhaps seven years or so. So not only was Guy spoiled with special treatment, he also received swiftly-decreasing parental governance. He therefore came to believe he could "get away with" almost anything – and for a while, he did.

In 1964, however, with Dad's departure "for work in Atlanta," and Mother's attentions turned elsewhere with involvement away from home with another individual, Guy eventually reached the point at which he was completely unsupervised. His mindset involving preparation for a future professional career and the course of his life eventually became somewhat contrary to that of the norm of society, and certainly to that of his four siblings. Rather than studying and earning good grades in preparation for college, a professional career, and a stable law-abiding future life, Guy simply chose a different career path.

In 1969, my mother and father were divorced and my father declared bankruptcy – a victim of unbelievably inept money-management and inexplicably-poor decisions in his professional life. My brothers and sisters and I became the flotsam in this disaster – destitute and desperate. Guy, meanwhile, floated in the middle of this vortex of desperation.

As a result, in 1973, when he was sixteen years of age, Guy did the unthinkable in our family. He quit school in the 10th grade. To my knowledge, the only other member of our family to pull such a stunt was our grandfather, but that had been in 1905, when educational morays were patently different in America. In the 1970s, no one serious about a successful professional career in life, "quit school." It just didn't happen.

Guy, however, was anything but devoid of positive attributes. To the contrary, he was exceedingly intelligent and talented. Between his thirteenth and fifteenth years of age, he was a member of Troop 14 of the *Boy Scouts of America* where he excelled in rank. He also ultimately was awarded the coveted *"Order of the Arrow"* designation, one of the highest awards/recognitions available in the *Scouts*. My brother still has Guy's cloth *"Order of the Arrow"* sash.

In 1974 at seventeen years of age, Guy began taking flying lessons. I don't know how he wrangled it, but he somehow was able to essentially obtain free instruction from a local resident who had taken Guy "under his wing" as it were, due in no small measure, I'm certain, to the family's desperate financial plight.

I still have Guy's private pilot flight manual and logbook. In his simple, almost child-like style of printing, Guy has written his name and address proudly inside the logbook. On the pages which follow, a flight instructor with the initials "JEM" has dutifully recorded and graded Guy's *"Familiarization Flight,"* his testing on *"Turns, Climbs and Glides," "Climbing and Gliding Turns," "Emergency Procedures," "Slow Flight & Stalls," "Rectangular Patterns,"* and *"Slow Flight & Landing Stalls"* in a Cessna 150. Guy eventually completed his training and *"Soloed"* later that summer. He had to have been proud of this achievement.

Guy also seemingly had friends everywhere. He became the "go-to Guy," literally when someone needed help with something, because there seemed to be few things for which Guy did not have a solution, particularly as involved the mechanical and construction worlds.

In the summer of 1974, Guy, with no income of which to speak, somehow also convinced the owner of a worn-out inoperable 1950s-era *Willys Jeep* to either "donate," or, perhaps, to sell him this relic "on time." Guy set up a block-and-tackle from the limb of a tree in the front yard of our home. He lifted the engine out of the *Willys* and rebuilt it over several weeks. He eventually had a semi-workable vehicle which he enjoyed for a short while. He was very mechanically-gifted.

Sometime around November or December of 1974 – again, when Guy was barely 17 years of age – he set out on what literally was an innocent prank which would ultimately prove to be a terribly life-altering incident. I was in Europe in the Army at this time, and learned about these details through letters and later communications.

Guy and a friend apparently decided that, on a lark, they were going to abscond with what was described as an old, worn-out horse saddle, which reportedly had been thrown into a corner in a derelict barn on what formerly had been my father's farm (auctioned off in September of 1970 for pennies on the dollar to the highest bidder after my father had declared bankruptcy).

To this day, I can't imagine Guy would have had any motive for such a petty theft other than the commission of a prank. It could not have been financial, because the derelict saddle had been dumped in the manure and mud in the old barn, and very obviously just abandoned by its owner as a worthless item. I know the circumstances that existed in that old barn, and anything left there was left to rot.

In all likelihood, Guy's actions in this matter represented little more than a childish vindictive effort to prickle the new owner of our father's farm. Over the years, my entire family had developed a distinct distaste for this individual for various reasons because he clearly held a harsh grudge against my father.

On the day of the incident, Guy had an accomplice who shall remain nameless. He was the son of a fairly-prominent businessman in our little town.

Guy and his accomplice set out that winter afternoon – some say walking, others claim they were driving the old *Willys Jeep* – across the pastures between our home and the aged barns on my father's old farm. Under any other circumstances, the "theft" of what was left of the dilapidated saddle would have been considered fortuitous by the owner. It would have been considered the easy disposal of a worthless item. The owner of that saddle, however – as stated above – carried a grudge against my father – and, indirectly, Guy – and had no intention of just overlooking the incident.

According to some sources, it had snowed a day or two prior to the two boys' grand caper, and so whether they were walking or driving the *Jeep*, they left a clear trail of either tire tracks or foot-prints in the mud and snow. If they were walking, perhaps that is the reason Guy had recruited an accomplice, because a horse saddle such as that used in the American West is just too heavy for one person alone to haul across several cow pastures, especially on a frigid day in snow.

The story that was passed down to me maintains that they drove the old *Willys* across the pastures and it was the tire tracks of that vehicle which left such a clear trail back to my mother's home. Whatever the circumstances,

The glint of mischief was always in Guy's eyes. He was the proto-typical "good old boy" Southerner, and is pictured here in the summer of 1979, with his beloved Jeep CJ-5, one year prior to his tragic death.

the prank was pulled off without a hitch – all except for the tracks through the snow to which the two obviously-inexperienced pranksters did not give any consideration. It then became quite easy for anyone to follow the "perps" right to my mother's house.

Once he realized the circumstances, the owner of the saddle contacted the Polk County Sheriff's Office to file a stolen property report. I do not know what transpired at this point, but my little brother – having never previously done anything even remotely "illegal" in his life – apparently confessed on the spot to sheriff's deputies, explaining almost certainly that he intended nothing more than a prank in the incident.

Under normal circumstances, that would have been the end of this situation. The saddle would simply have been returned to the owner (or to the city dump as it were) and a stiff warning would have been issued to my brother (and normally to his accomplice as well). The owner of the saddle, however, as stated, proceeded to press full charges against Guy for "larceny," somehow attaching significant "value" to the old saddle.

Guy's accomplice in this matter was never approached, nor questioned, nor charged in any manner. I suspect the saddle owner simply refused to press charges against this accomplice since no vendetta existed between them. My brother Guy took the full brunt of the punishment, which, no doubt, was exactly what the saddle-owner intended.

So here we have a 17-year-old adolescent being taken away in handcuffs and incarcerated like a common criminal in the Polk County Jail – where he sat for days with the other prisoners until he could be arraigned for his terrible little crime. As a military policeman in the U.S. Army in Europe from 1972-'75, I drew the duty once or twice of transporting convicted first-time actual felons to prison and witnessing their fear upon reaching the lock-up. I know the fear my little brother must have experienced at this point, and it is unforgiveable that he should have been exposed to such an ordeal.

My father, to his everlasting discredit, refused to provide bail money for Guy. Dad, who had always yearned for a career in the legal arena, apparently was embarrassed by his son being charged with petty larceny – no matter the circumstances. He stated simply that Guy deserved whatever punishment would be meted out to him. He (my father) sat at home while his youngest son bravely faced circumstances in the county lock-up with other common criminals of all make and description.

At this point in his life, my father was bankrupt and married to another woman, and essentially just seemed to wish to "wash his hands" of my family and his son's plight. Despite his financial circumstances, Dad, at the very least, should have approached a bail bondsman to relieve Guy of the agony of his incarceration. Guy was a juvenile, and certainly wasn't what is known in criminal justice circles as a "flight risk" for his "horrible crime," so there was very little if any risk to Dad for such a kindness. I am ashamed to say, however, that he, nevertheless, just left his teen-aged son to fend for himself.

Worse yet, having freely admitted to "the crime," and with no serious legal defense provided for him at that time, Guy was easily convicted of this "theft" and required to serve what, to my memory, was at least a year or two for his actions. One can only imagine the effect this had upon an adolescent who had no "criminal" nature whatsoever and who was yet only a minor.

Guy eventually was sent to a detention center – better known as a "halfway house" – which existed at that time at *Northwest Georgia Regional Hospital* in Rome, Georgia. It wasn't actually a "prison," per se, and, if my memory serves me correctly, the inmates there were even allowed a limited (very limited) amount of supervised time outside the halfway house, but they all were well aware that they now "had a record," and all were mandated to be present

After dropping out of high school, Guy (rear, leaning against the truck door) watched his friends move on to college and professional pursuits while he remained behind. In social situations, he was often excluded. The real tragedy lay in the fact that he was an exceptionally-gifted and intelligent individual who quite likely would have had a bright future had proper guidance been available earlier in his young life.

in this facility unless they had special permission to be with authorized family members. If they dared to violate any aspect of the judicial requirements of this confinement, they would immediately be returned to the main prison population of the Polk County Prison System.

After a year or two, Guy earned his release. I don't know the full circumstances, because he was a juvenile and convicted under "First Offender" circumstances, so no records exist for him today in the Polk judicial or law enforcement system.

Guy eventually realized that with a reputation for having been in the Polk County prison system, no employer in his home county would risk hiring him for anything other than manual labor, and with no education credentials (not even high school) to his credit, he was virtually unemployable elsewhere as well. To his credit, Guy did obtain a General Education Diploma (GED) in order to at least be able to carry that credential.

If he was not already aware of it, Guy soon learned the true extent of his devastating circumstances. By then, he, for all intents and purposes, was a social pariah; a 19- or 20-year-old who qualified for no employment other than manual labor.

I'll never forget the autumn of 1979 when Guy visited me at my home in Mountain Park, Georgia. We searched and searched through the want-ads and employment announcements throughout the Atlanta area for an employment opportunity for him. When he was turned down for a janitorial position at *Northside Hospital,* Guy saw the handwriting on the wall.

To his credit, he proved resilient, rocking along in construction jobs and manual labor positions without complaint, earning what little he could, but it was precious little. He essentially was forced to live at home with my mother in the late 1970s, and began using "recreational drugs" to escape his demoralizing reality.

It was sometime around this point that Guy somehow convinced my mother to co-sign a note with him so that he could purchase a late-1970s *Jeep CJ-5.* He went to a discount tire manufacturer and purchased big "off-road" tires. He also purchased a CB radio, but for the duration of his brief two- or three-year ownership of that vehicle, I don't believe he was ever able to make more than a couple of payments on it, and he still had it when he passed away.

On a rainy summer afternoon on May 19th, 1980, after learning of an opportunity to purchase yet another "escape from reality drug," Guy traveled to a site at which the medication, wrapped in a plastic baggy container, had simply been left by the dope dealer at a gate where Guy was to collect it and then leave his payment. It was raining that day, and the drug had become wet.

Guy nevertheless quickly ingested the deadly chemical before driving away. It is unknown today whether the drug was poisoned, or contaminated, or what, but instead of the temporary release from reality that he sought, Guy instead reportedly found himself wracked with pain – almost as if he had eaten some form of corrosive acid.

Although he almost certainly was terribly nauseated and distressed at this point, Guy motored on, no doubt thinking the ill effects would eventually subside. He had traveled only a couple of miles when he began losing his eyesight. *(I know these things because I later interviewed the two female passengers who were with him that night.)*

At this point, Guy obviously knew he was in serious trouble, but, being one of the braver individuals I have ever known, he did not panic. He drove up into the yard of an individual with whom he was familiar (near what then was a very small *Polk County Airfield),* and explained to him exactly what he had taken so that he could be treated more quickly, then told the individual to quickly drive him to the local hospital. *(The individuals in the Jeep with*

Guy were as sick as was he, and in no shape to drive.)

By the time they reached the hospital, Guy was unconscious. He was taken inside to the emergency room facilities, but the attending physician – rather than treat him immediately – decided instead, amazingly, to just have Guy transported for detoxification at Floyd Medical Center in Rome, Georgia, some 30 or 40 miles distant.

So here Guy was, unconscious, in great need of treatment and no doubt suffering immensely, and this physician chose – for reasons unknown today – to treat the two poisoned females himself, but to have Guy transported to a site 30 miles distant for detoxification. Worse than that, the ambulance transported him under non-emergency circumstances (with no siren).

According to the official toxicology report from Floyd Medical Center, Guy Jordan Jackson died from "an overdose of MDA (amphetamine, 1.6 mg)." It remains a mystery today how anyone could die from a dosage this small. The hour of his injury was recorded as "10:30 p.m. on May 19, 1980." He was pronounced dead at "12:30 a.m. on May 20."

Today, the hospital, its physicians, staff and everything associated with it in Rockmart, Georgia no longer exist. The hospital went out of business more than 30 years ago – along with all records – and the physicians from the 1980s era are now all deceased.

It was sometime around 3:00 am early on the morning of May 30, 1980 that my telephone rang on the floor of my now-vacant home (since "Plaintiff" had removed everything else in January of that year). As soon as I picked up the phone and determined in my groggy capacity that it was my father, I knew it couldn't be good news. In fact, I knew it had to be something truly horrible… and it was.

"Guy is dead," Dad said in a choked strangled voice.

"W-what???!!" I stammered.

"He died from a drug overdose a few hours ago," Dad said painfully and mournfully.

My world came crashing down around me. I was just recovering from an ultra-painful divorce from my ex-wife, and word of Guy's passing was just too painful to consider.

The weeks following Guy's death are now just a blur in my memory. Today, he sleeps peacefully in the Jordan family plot of Rose Hill Cemetery in Rockmart, along with my mother, my sister's ashes, my grandmother, my grandfather, my grandmother's two still-borne twins, and possibly others.

Mary

In 1969, with my parents divorced and my father relocated to Atlanta, my youngest sister Mary – at 15 years of age – apparently decided she'd rather live with my father than my mother. Mary caught a ride to downtown Rockmart to the bus stop where she boarded a *Trailways* bus to Atlanta. Like me, she also never looked back, and never returned to her hometown either, except for an "occasional" brief holiday family gathering.

The bus-ride took her to the old *Trailways* bus terminal not far from *Rich's* (later *Macy's*) department store in downtown Atlanta near Spring Street. I presume from that point that she contacted either my aunt or my Dad to come pick her up. Regardless, from that day forward for the next several years, she took up residence with my father and his second wife, and attended Henderson High School from which she, to her credit, was eventually graduated.

Following her graduation from Henderson High, I suppose Mary's presence either became a threat or a burden to my father's new wife, because she (the wife) reportedly (according to my father) adopted a habit of making derogatory comments about Mary, and making life uncomfortable for her. I later learned through the grapevine that one such comment had quickly earned the new wife a quick sharp smack across the chops equivalent to a similar blow which I myself had received years earlier as a thirteen-year-old adolescent at my Dad's hand. *(He, for reasons unknown, had cultivated a habit of that action with individuals he felt certain he could dominate.)*

Whatever the circumstances, Mary eventually either left of her own free will or was banished by Dad's wife sometime around 1971. I'm not certain of the actual circumstances, because I was at the *University of Georgia* at the time, and volunteered for service in the *United States Army* in December of that same year.

Death for a Dealer

Mary was always exceptionally independent and out-going. In the late 1960s and early 1970s, the area between 10th and 14th streets and up Spring and Peachtree streets to downtown Atlanta had become a "hippie" mecca. Attracted by the cheap housing in the 10th and 14th streets areas, that section of town had become filled with the city's "flower children." Brightly-painted signage and businesses had sprung up from what had previously been abandoned and derelict small office buildings and homes.

I don't know when it was exactly that Mary took up residence on 14th Street. I just know she lived there circa 1971-1973. It was also where she met and began living with a local "experimental/recreational drugs dealer" whose first name was "Larry" (last name now unknown) and who no doubt haunted her dreams for many years thereafter.

Larry must have been involved with the sale of drugs further along on the power spectrum than the recreational level too, because he reportedly had a big-time supplier who took no excuses for non-payment to him by his dealers. When Larry eventually "crossed" his supplier, and failed to make payment for one of his consignments of drugs for street-sale, he (Larry) became a marked man.

The exact circumstances of his death are unknown today – at least by this writer. Suffice it to say that I do recall from the news reports that his body was later discovered in an abandoned well south of Atlanta, and he had been brutally tortured before being murdered, and that was the end of that. Mary lived through all of this.

Sometime shortly after Larry's death, Mary's vulnerability must have been noticed in what was quickly becoming a high-crime area around 14th Street. She sadly and tragically was savagely beaten and robbed by an individual (or individuals) who was/were never identified. Mary quickly abandoned

Mary pauses for a photo with renowned singer/ songwriter/entertainer Tony Bennett at the Fairmont in Atlanta where he was performing, circa 1975.

her life in that section of Atlanta and moved to a new apartment out on Roswell Road near Interstate 285.

Marriages

Mary was anything if not resilient. She soon found employment at what then was one of the South's (and certainly Atlanta's) most popular entertainment complexes – the *Fairmont Hotel*. Some of the hottest acts in the United States performed there, and Mary eventually rubbed shoulders with some of them. I still have a photo of her with several celebrities, including entertainer/singer Tony Bennett back when he was a big star in the early 1970s.

Mary, however, was never able to escape the darkness. She began dating a man considerably older than her who she had met at the *Fairmont*. He was quite wealthy and lived in what then was considered to be the ritzy side of Atlanta on exclusive Riverside Drive.

For the next year or so Mary steadfastly resisted offers of matrimony from this individual, but in 1976, after he had showered her with expensive gifts (including a substantial two or three carat diamond ring), she relented and married him. For the next several years, they lived a blissful existence, attending prominent social gatherings and marquis events. They even had Hollywood entertainer Flip Wilson as a long-term guest in their home while he was engaged in performances in Atlanta.

As the years passed, however, the blissfulness eventually turned ugly. Her husband became abusive. He beat her on a number of occasions, but Mary was loath to end the relationship and struggled on. Sadly, she also placed too high a priority on the money and ritzy lifestyle.

The marriage eventually ended itself. Following a final particularly-protracted and vicious fight while on vacation in 1980 in Rome, Italy, Mary's husband abandoned her with no funds or manner to return home. This was well prior to the advent of mobile phones, and he had taken her cash and credit cards. Mary somehow was able to telephone Mother to get her to wire her the funds for a flight back to Atlanta.

Upon her return, Mary asked a friend to drive her out to the Riverside Drive home just long enough to grab a handful of possessions. She then left in their Mercedes 400 SEL convertible, never to return. She moved into an apartment in Dunwoody, Georgia, and quickly filed for divorce (1980) from her husband.

For the next six or eight months, Mary slept with a loaded .38-Special beside her bed. Knowing her, I don't have any doubt she would have used it too, had the need arisen. Her former husband, however, was soon discovered dead in his home – with a .38 caliber bullet wound in his head. The official cause of death was listed as "suicide."

Mary's life continued on a roller-coaster basis for a number of years. She was never able to escape tragedy. She married a second time and had two children, one of whom died very young from a drug overdose. Shortly after this point, she also divorced this husband as well.

An Incurable Disease

Some years later, when she was in her early 60s, Mary learned that she had contracted the terrible and incurable disease *MSA (Multiple Systems Atrophy)*. The average survival rate upon diagnosis of this affliction is six to ten years. Mary struggled on for several years, becoming weaker and weaker and less able to care for herself.

Ultimately, rather than become a totally-helpless invalid dependent upon others for even the most basic of necessities for life before dying a painful death, Mary chose to take her own life through physician-assisted suicide (euthanasia). She was living on an island off the coast of Washington at the time, where euthanasia was legal, and died peacefully on the beach.

Today, Mary's ashes rest in a grave in the Jordan family plot in Rose Hill Cemetery in Rockmart, with many other members of my family.

—◦⟩⟩ ⟨⟨◦—

"Kids and Life"

As the late television personality Art Linkletter once quipped, *"Kids say the darndest things."* . . . and I can confirm that statement from first-hand experience.

My brother-in-law – Jimmy – was once directed by his wife – my sister – to set up the frame, headboard and mattress, etc. for a cherished antique cherry bed in a guestroom in their home. Though he gives it his best effort, projects such as this were - and still are - simply beyond Jimmy's handyman pay-grade.

Now don't get me wrong. Jimmy is no slouch – not by a long shot. He was an honor graduate from the University of Georgia in Journalism and earned a graduate degree in Public Administration, and was in the process of pursuing a doctorate. He also was a high-level executive in Georgia state government for his entire career, earning a tidy pension. Prior to all of this, Jimmy was a decorated infantry sergeant with the United States Army in Vietnam, where he was involved in some of the most intense firefights of that conflict. No. Jimmy's no flake. Not by a long shot. He just falls short in handyman city.

Rather than pursue handyman projects, Jimmy would much rather be watching his beloved *Braves* or *Georgia Bulldogs* on television. In order to preserve the matrimonial peace, however, one must often tread troubled waters – and try to do it without sinking.

Headboard Trauma

On one of his cherished *"Georgia Bulldogs"* game days, my sister requested (read "instructed") that Jimmy cut a section of three-quarter-inch ply-board to use as a foundation – in lieu of slats – for support beneath the box-springs in the bed. Jimmy of course complied (again, "preserving the matrimonial peace").

Despite his God-given inadequacies in this realm, Jimmy was putting forth his best effort to assemble the bed. His nine-year-old son, however, now fully aware (from past unpleasant experiences of this nature) of his father's limitations and inadequacies, watched from a distance with what can only be described as a bemused look upon his face.

Jimmy carefully measured and then cut, somewhat impatiently, the piece of ply-board. Kick-off for the *Georgia-Clemson* game had already begun. Meanwhile, sawdust was flying everywhere in Jimmy's haste. With sweat dripping from his brow, his hair in complete disarray and with a wild and desperate look in his eyes, the *Bulldogs* fanatic finally managed to get the plywood cut to what he felt were the correct dimensions. Meanwhile, Lindsey Scott had just caught a dramatic pass for a *Georgia* touchdown. The crowd was going wild.

Somehow in the somewhat frantic process of his plywood cutting, Jimmy of course had managed to mismeasure the size for the board, and when the time came to position it down upon the frame, it simply wouldn't fit. No matter what Jimmy tried, the board stubbornly resisted his efforts, and eventually became dangerously wedged against the cherished antique cherry headboard.

Meanwhile, *Clemson* had scored and had taken the lead, but the Dogs were driving yet again and Jimmy was missing it. Short on patience, the Saturday-afternoon carpenter committed the fatal error. He tried to *force* the stubborn piece of ply-board into place. In matters involving wood – especially "antique" wood – the strategy of attempting to "force" anything into place against finely-finished hardwood is just never a good idea. Never.

You can probably guess the rest. The cherished headboard received an ugly gashed scar about six or eight inches in length. . . . the type of ugly gashed scar that no amount of frantic secret polishing or application of mismatched wood stain is going to disguise. Jimmy suddenly saw his life flash before his eyes. He nevertheless continued listening as Buck Belue ran for another touchdown to tie the game, but somehow, the gridiron contest had suddenly lost its luster.

By this point (and from unpleasant past experiences) Jimmy now knew that he was going to be dealing with every married man's nightmare. There was just no getting around it. The sergeant-major of the household would shortly come to make her inspection and Jimmy was preparing himself for the gallows.

Having been in this position on occasion myself, I know that the mind suddenly goes into "survival mode" in these situations. The guilty party begins a last-minute desperate search for a solution – any solution – which will pass the sergeant-major's inspection. Nothing, however, was going to even faintly diminish, let alone repair, Jimmy's terrible faux pas.

In the end, one usually just has to resign himself to "facing the music" under these circumstances – and it's always painful, and Jimmy, having been in this position before, was well aware of this. He also knew that it would not only be painful, but excruciatingly so. That antique cherry headboard was a treasured item.

In Jimmy's case, however, a totally unexpected possible reprieve suddenly presented itself. His opportunistic son – again observing all of the foregoing with delight from the shadows – suddenly seemed to materialize from out of nowhere. Holding out his hand, the budding little entrepreneur stated matter-of-factly, "If you pay me $25.00, you can tell Momma that I did it," a big confident smile spreading across his capitalistic little face.

Now as a child, myself, I personally would never have even considered such a tactic with my father. He would simply have back-handed me into the corner; ripped the headboard apart, and that would have been the end of it – but that's another story which isn't nearly as funny.

Jimmy just blinked in disbelief at his son. "Why in the world would I do that?" he fumed, still irritated as he listened to Clemson threatening to score and ruin Georgia's undefeated season. He also was apoplectic with himself for making such a blunder and certainly did not wish to part so easily with his hard-earned $25.00.

"Well," the adolescent responded, "I'm her 'son,' and if I confess to it, she can't get rid of me, but if *you* confess to it, you'll be 'out the door.'" The youngster then shrugged in feigned resignation for effect.

Choking back the hilarity of his son's statement, Jimmy had been around long enough to know the youngster ironically had a creative – though unrealistic – grasp of the circumstances. He, nevertheless, admonished his son with "hit the bricks while you can still walk," and prepared himself to go "face the music" with the ball-and-chain.

As anticipated, my sister was outraged beyond belief, and she had a knack – no doubt learned at our mother's knee during her menopausal years – for imparting maximum punishment for transgressions of this nature. Jimmy was banished to a chair in the backyard where his cherished *Georgia Bulldogs* not only could not be heard on the radio, but certainly not watched on television either.

In the end, my sister eventually forgave Jimmy, well-aware by now of his genetic limitations in matters of this nature. The treasured bed still has the long ugly scar on it to this day, but in the "memory lane" department, that large scratch ironically is now treasured *almost* as much as the bed itself - *almost*. And *the Georgia Bulldogs* went on to win the game, and, ultimately, a national championship later that season. Jimmy's world was complete.

"The Roof Caved-In"

My own son – Burke – could come up with some real gems from time to time too as a child. One of the more remarkable of these occurred in the early 1980s, shortly after my divorce from his mother, for whom I shall continue to use the famed Lewis Grizzard descriptor of "plaintiff."

At the time, I was living in Dahlonega, Georgia, where I was employed in the *College Relations Office* of the *University of North Georgia (UNG)*. I was dating the wonderful individual to whom I am still so fortunately married today – 40 years and counting as of 2025.

During the last week of December, 1982, I picked up Burke – who was all of five years of age at the time – to stay with me for two weeks. Plaintiff was more than fair in that regard, though I was on the hook for all the costs of airfare, etc. Burke was at that very impressionable age in life when small details could take on immense proportions in his little mind as I was about to discover.

In those days, the late December and early January stretch was a very slow period at *UNG* (which was actually called *"North Georgia College"* at that time, with a much lesser student enrollment). During lengthy holidays such as Christmas, the students – for the most part – returned to their homes and elsewhere for the Christmas break and the college campus was basically deserted. That December, however, turned out to be anything but subdued.

My office at *UNG* was located in the lower level of historic *Price Memorial Hall (the large brick building with the impressive gold-covered steeple that immediately captures the eye as one drives over Crown Mountain toward Dahlonega)*. Price had been constructed in 1878 at a time when exceedingly-rare large buildings of that nature out in the wilds of the Blue Ridge Mountains were often made from immense "heart pine" timbers to protect them from termites and other decay.

The author with his son, Burke, in the summer of 1982 at North Georgia College (present-day University of North Georgia) in Dahlonega, Georgia. (Photo by Gail Dalton)

Over the years, the big resin-saturated wood has performed magnificently in deterring insect pests, but that protection came at a price. The resin-soaked wood was/is also extremely flammable. As a result, preservationists in more recent times had installed a very substantial fire-protection sprinkler system high up in the attic space in case flames ever did/do become a problem in Price. Since there was limited to no heat in the attic space in those days, the maintenance crew simply turned off the water to the sprinklers in the wintertime to prevent the pipes from freezing, bursting, and flooding the building disastrously.

The December of 1982, however, was a bit different weather-wise. It included an early freeze which came in advance of the maintenance crew's annual sprinkler system shut-down. Well... You can probably guess the rest... or perhaps you can't. Regardless, those pipes froze and burst in the dead of night, sending a cascade of water down through the building and filling the lower level with almost a foot of wetness. By the time anyone realized there was a problem, the entire building had been soaked with water; the particle-board ceiling tiles had all been saturated and collapsed into a million bits and pieces throughout all the offices of Price – including mine – and everything in every office looked like someone had set off a bomb. It was quite the disaster scene.

The pipe which had burst up in the attic of Price was in the northeast corner of the building – directly above my office. All of my books, photography equipment, lamps, and other possessions – which I had stored inside what I thought was an exceptionally-safe sanctuary – were ruined. The liquefied particle-board drop ceiling material covered everything. The floor was an amalgam of muddy, debris-filled yuk that one just didn't even want to walk through without water-proof boots.

I had been alerted to the disaster and told that I needed to reclaim whatever of my possessions were "reclaimable" because everything else was going to be shoveled and swept and sucked out and thrown away as soon as possible to try to mitigate the potential for mold damage. Unwilling to be separated from my son who I had not seen in quite a while, I took him along with me to the office, explaining to him what had happened as we drove.

When we walked into what formerly had been my very orderly work space which Burke

An artificial intelligence rendering depicts the author with his son walking to inspect the flooded office space of Price Memorial Hall at North Georgia College in December of 1983.

and I had visited the previous day, his little eyes widened immediately as he surveyed the now totally-destroyed room. It was obvious that his impressionable mind was registering substantial surprise with the disaster which lay before him.

I collected a few possessions which had not been ruined by the water, mud and drop-ceiling debris, and we piled back into my car. All the way home, Burke peppered me with question after question about the flooded offices.

"Where did all the water come from, Daddy?" he queried. "Why did tha roof cave in? Is tha roof gonna cave in at your house? Who were all those men with tha big boots? Do you still have a job?"

"Too Many Pills"

After arriving back home, we unloaded my salvaged possessions at my apartment and then drove to the apartment of the lady who was soon to be my wife - Judy Grizzle - where we were going to eat lunch that day. Judy was busily preparing a meal as we walked in, but only a few minutes after we

The author is pictured with his future wife, Judy Grizzle, at graduation ceremonies at North Georgia College in July of 1983 where he was awarded a Master of Education degree. (Photo by Ralph Jackson, Jr.)

arrived, she surprisingly literally fainted into a heap on the floor. I knew she was glad to see me, but I had no idea that my presence was faint-worthy.

Burke's eyes were now the size of little saucers, so I was keeping an eye on him as I quickly picked Judy up off the floor and placed her gently on the couch, elevating her feet. I had no idea why she had fainted, but she soon recovered consciousness. As I prepared to dial 911, Judy had a conniption fit, insisting there was nothing wrong with her. I wasn't having any of that though, and since I could see that the idea of calling 911 was too upsetting to her, I simply packed her and Burke into the car and drove her to the Emergency Room at the local hospital.

After they had examined her at the hospital, they discovered that she apparently had a very low tolerance for any pharmaceuticals, and that she had accidentally overdosed herself on an over-the-counter cold medication which had also reacted with another medication she was taking.

Meanwhile, Judy's fainting incident, coupled with the disaster at my office, had made quite the impression on my observant son. Had I known how his little mind was working, I would have exercised a bit more caution, but by the time I realized it, it was simply too late.

For reasons unknown to me at the time, Burke had decided that he wanted to call his mother (who lived in Louisiana) that night. He had not spoken to her in almost a week, and I guess the day's events had unsettled him and he wanted to hear her reassuring voice over the telephone. I, of course, had no problem with his wish, so I dialed the number and handed him the telephone – with not the slightest inkling of what was about to happen next.

"Mom!" Burke immediately croaked into the telephone somewhat breathlessly. "I have two big newses. The roof caved in and Judy took too many pills and had to be taken to the hospital!"

The next thing I heard was "Daddy Momma wants to speak to you."

Kids. As a parent, you can never take your eyes off of them, especially if there is a "plaintiff" waiting in the wings.

Fear at the Falls

I look back at some of the things I did when I was young and less cautious, and sometimes I just have to shake my head in amazement. I often wonder just how I was able to make it through some of those days. A camping trip I took with my son back in the summer of 1989 is a case in point.

"Daddy!" my son, Burke, called to me excitedly as he ran to the car to load all his "equipment." "We're going 'white-water rafting,'" he added with a flourish.

When I turned around, I could see he and his cousin, Jack, were dragging a floppy, uninflated two-man raft, which they unceremoniously dumped into the bed of my pick-up truck. I had a bit of trouble concealing my amusement at their thoughts of "white-water" at our camping site, but I didn't have the heart to tell them how far "off base" they actually were. *They'll find out soon enough*, I thought to myself. Our destination was Simpson Falls Creek on my grandfather's old farm, and it (the creek) was rarely beyond a small brook only inches deep in the summertime.

"How are you going to inflate it?" I inquired.

"It has an automatic inflator," Jack, the older of the two responded confidently.

I was glad to see them take any "safe" opportunity at adventure in "the great outdoors." I had done a lot of that in my youth, but it wasn't always "safe." In fact, much of it was downright dangerous.

We were out to do nothing but have a good time, and if their fun meant imagined adventures of white-water rafting, who was I to "pop their bubble." I had no idea just how wrong my thoughts soon would prove to have been.

We were returning to a campsite at which I and members of my family had periodically camped for several generations. It is in northwest Georgia in the foothills ranging down from the Blue Ridge Mountains. It is also the site of a picture-perfect waterfall, and the former site of a historic pioneer-era gristmill.

Simpson Falls Creek winds down through a very steep and narrow mountain chasm and into a cleft where it tumbles over a waterfall before proceeding on down the mountains and into the pastureland below. It is a beautiful spot, but it certainly offers no "white-water" rafting opportunities – at least not under normal circumstances.

The author and his young charges at "the falls" on a peaceful summer afternoon. Due to the steepness of the gorge on which this site exists, mid-day is the only time in which sunlight reaches the stream.

My son had just reached his 12th birthday the previous January, so he was approaching that point that he presumed himself to be quite knowledgeable in many things, and that Dad was beginning to slip a bit. *(And after this experience, I began to think that he wasn't too far wrong, either.)*

We finished loading up the truck with the remainder of Burke's and Jack's camping gear composed of all types of tools, weapons, flashlights and the like. I couldn't help reflecting upon my own previous experiences at this camping site, and the thrills I and my friends had enjoyed in years past. I remembered when my own father had brought my brother, David, and me to this site for outings in our youth.

Every time I looked at the two boys, I had to smile yet again. At 12 and 14 years of age respectively, they both had reached the point in their lives at which camping – especially at a place back in the mountains and as exciting as was this site – represented the ultimate in outdoors adventure.

The two of them had obviously been preparing for this great experience for days, and now they marched boldly around me in their best "*Rambo*" imitations, replete with camouflage clothing and scabbard hunting knives lashed to their legs, flashlights and an array of other paraphernalia dangling from their belts. The knives caused them unconsciously to walk with a noticeable limp as they swaggered around in preparation of entering the "wilderness" to conquer whatever might challenge them.

The recent springtime weather had witnessed an overabundance of rainfall – to say the least – and as the months rolled by, the weather continued to be a bit wetter than normal. The spring months, in fact, had brought forth some of the heaviest rains on record, but a blazing hot and dry July had returned the earth to a powder composition, causing it to easily soak up any brief rains, and the streams had settled back down to normal six-inch levels.

Nevertheless, I was keeping an eye on the weather, because I was well aware that summer thunderstorms can sometimes produce pretty nasty lightning and downpours in northwest Georgia. As Friday, July 21 approached however, the weather seemed to hold the promise of a rainless weekend.

Though I live in the suburbs of Atlanta now, I was raised on a farm only a mile or two (as the crow flies) from our camping spot. I never cease to be amazed at the excitement that spot still conjures up in me. The pungent smells of the moss-encrusted creek rocks and decaying leaves, the crackling drone of the cicadas ("July flies" as we called them), and the water itself falling and splashing over, under and around the unusually large boulders which dominate much of this camping area defy description.

As a child, I explored every cave, every fishing hole, every oddity the mountains there have hidden down through the ages. It therefore wasn't hard for me to understand the excitement the boys were experiencing in their yearning to explore as we proceeded to our campsite.

I drove my Ford Ranger slowly up the historic old dirt road leading back into the mountains to the site, imagining as I often did how it must have been in earlier days, when mules and a wagon (or horses and a buggy) was the only mode of transportation to the old gristmill which had been built well before the U.S. Civil War. The deeply-shaded road, surprisingly, still had some short stretches where the tire ruts were filled with water from the wet months prior to our arrival, and my truck didn't have four-wheel drive, but we made it to the old mill site beside the waterfall just fine.

We were sleeping in an aged pop-up camper which had been semi-permanently parked at the site, compliments of relatives who lived nearby. In those days, they maintained the camper there during the summer months for convenient storage of cooking utensils, minor camping supplies and the like for their children, etc, when they visited the falls – which was becoming rarer and rarer.

The ford (crossing spot) on the stream just below the former site of the old mill – despite its shallowness – was still just a bit too dicey for me to chance crossing in the truck. "Come on," my two little *Rambos*-in-training cajoled me. "Let's drive across."

They, of course, *"had no dog in that hunt,"* since it would be "me" – not "them" – who would have to retrieve my "come-along" winch and laboriously pull the truck, manually, out of the mud if it became mired too deeply to proceed – and that was assuming

The author (standing) with his son and his son's cousin stare in awe at the diminishing run-off from the unusual deluge which had flooded their camping site the previous evening.

I could in fact successfully extract it from the mud myself. If not, I'd have to walk out, and pay someone else to bring a tractor or a four-wheel-drive vehicle back to the old mill site to pull me out. I therefore prudently left the truck parked on the far side of the creek and we carried our equipment across to the old mill site to set up camp.

We waded across ankle-deep water, skirting the section which constantly is a mucky mire, to haul everything over to a shady spot on the lee side of the falls. It took us an hour or so to get everything squared away, and by the time we were finished, the sun was already disappearing behind the mountains, such was the depth of the gorge.

"We're going to inflate the raft," Burke chattered to me from across the creek.

"Not until you get your tent set up," I admonished. I'd slept in the same tent with them on several previous occasions, and was well aware that the preservation of my sanity required separate accommodations for me whenever possible. I therefore had taken up quarters in the camper.

"Where do we set it up?" they inquired in unison, their disappointment obvious. I knew all they wanted to do was to get the tent up as quickly as possible so that they could begin scouting the lower levels of the creek for a place where the water was deep enough to float their raft. They seemed totally oblivious to the fact that we had driven for roughly half a mile along that very creek, and except for the lower section where the creek passes through a pasture, the water was not deeper than a few inches at any spot. Kids are like that though.

"Why don't you set it up here in the clearing below the camper," I offered suggestively, my seeming madness not without a semblance of logic. I wanted them near enough that I might keep an eye on them, but just far enough away so that I could also hope to get some sleep.

The boys, however, knew exactly what I was doing, and countered with a proposal of a site a short distance away on a huge boulder in the middle of the creek bed. The tremendous rock, flat and roughly eight by eight feet on the top side, stands five to six feet above the waters of the creek. It has long been a family favorite as a camping and picnicking spot, so I didn't have a problem with their choice. I had slept on it myself as a *Boy Scout* when I was their age.

After thoughtful consideration of the circumstances, I couldn't see how any danger could possibly be attached to that campsite, so I decided to leave them in peace and let them have their fun. It was a decision which, later that night, would prove to be very nearly disastrous.

The boys finally got their tent set up on the boulder. They then set about the task of inflating their two-man raft. I fired up the Coleman lantern and stove, and threw together some pork & beans and other delicious treats which are oft-times favorites on camping trips. The boys seemed to love it, and, quite honestly, I didn't think the "meal" was too bad myself.

We cleaned up the dishes and I settled into the camper for the evening to do a little reading. The boys scouted out the campsite with flashlights until their batteries were depleted, then settled into their tent themselves.

As is often the case during hot Southern summers, a thunderstorm inevitably began kicking up in the distance with rolling thunder, but it was still quite a distance away, so I didn't give it much thought. Pretty soon, however, I could tell it was headed in our direction, because the booming thunder was gradually becoming louder.

I yelled to the boys that they would have to come inside the camper with me if lightning began invading our little realm, and they definitely didn't like that. Nevertheless, up to this point, the edge of the storm had consisted of nothing but pattering rain and distant thunder.

The storm continued incessantly in the distance until it finally did reach us. The booming cannonades of thunder were now quite loud, and the rain had picked up considerably, and then we began getting lightning. I called out to the boys and told them to come into the camper, and they complied grudgingly.

After approximately an hour, the lightning and thunder ceased, but the rain continued falling steadily. The boys eventually grew bored with the cramped circumstances in the camper, and urged me to allow them to go back to their tent out on the boulder. Since the lightning had ceased, I relented. They tumbled out of the doorway of the camper, scampering to get to their tent before they got too wet from the rain.

Over the years, I had often read descriptions of flash floods and the dangerous circumstances that can prevail under those conditions, but I had never personally been exposed to such circumstances. It certainly wasn't a heavy consideration on my mind on this night, but with the steady rain, I nonetheless was wary.

I actually enjoyed camping during a thunderstorm, and had done it numerous times in the past when on outings into the Blue Ridge Mountains. Call me crazy, but there is something very pleasurable to me about a warm, cozy tent or camper, a lantern, and a good book to read during a thunderstorm.

It was around 9:30 or 10:00 p.m. that I was suddenly aroused from my reveries by my son and his cousin. They burst back into the camper with me. "The water is coming inside our tent and we barely made it over here," they explained, showing me their wet sleeping bags and other equipment. Both of them were drenched, but totally unperturbed by the circumstances. It was all still just one big adventure to them.

Looking back, the words "water is coming inside our tent" should have been a dead giveaway and the alarm bells should have been ringing, but again, it was a remarkably hot, dry summer, and I simply didn't read the danger that was brewing. I just assumed the rainfall was puddling up beneath the floor of their tent, and it was pitch-black dark outside, so I couldn't "see" the prevailing circumstances.

Burke and his cousin piled up into the bunk across from mine, and began playing with bugs in the lantern. I pulled out some treats for them then went back to my reading. I read for perhaps another hour while the boys played a board game they had discovered in storage beneath the bunk. The rain kept

The author's unerringly-adventurous son proudly holds up a stringer of fish he caught in the stream at the foot of the falls circa 1982. (Photo by R. Olin Jackson)

up steadily, never letting up at all. I eventually noticed the hum of an aircraft overhead, thinking to myself that this was an awfully crazy night for small aircraft to be out and about.

The droning of the plane became more pronounced, and it eventually began to sound as if the aircraft was literally coming right down into the gorge to land. The noise from the steady rain almost drowned out the sound of the plane, but it obviously was very near to us. I decided to sneak a peek out to see what was going on.

With all moonlight obscured, the pitch-darkness forbade any surveying of the circumstances. I couldn't even see a few feet away. The droning now had become a whining roar, like the jet aircraft at Hartsfield International Airport outside Atlanta from which I had departed occasionally in the past on business trips.

As I was peering into the darkness, looking skyward to try to determine the source of all the noise, a sudden burst of renewed lightning illuminated the landscape around me, and the vision of what I beheld struck terror into my heart. As explained earlier, under normal circumstances, the creek along which we were camped is little more than a brook on most summer days. There had never been a time in my memory when the average water depth of this stream flowing out of these mountains – at least prior to reaching the lower pastures where it naturally pooled – was more than eight or ten inches deep. I now stood horror-stricken at the malevolence which was mounting before me and shooting over the normally peaceful waterfall above us. The "aircraft" noise I had heard was actually that of a vast and rapidly-increasing volume of water "roaring" down the gorge, shooting fifteen feet or so horizontally off the precipice of the falls and into the creek below.

I stood transfixed at the spot for several moments before returning to my senses. I mean I have personally experienced and witnessed the aftermath of a terrorist attack which caused immense destruction without faltering, but this maelstrom before me now was truly a shocker.

We had been protected in the camper only because we were located on slightly higher ground in a spot behind the protection of a sheer wall of natural stone. It was this secure haven which long-ago had been recognized by the pioneers who had constructed the old gristmill which once existed on this spot.

In the midst of all of the above, I suddenly also noticed that the huge boulder upon which the boys had pitched their tent – normally some five or six feet above the stream, now was almost completely submerged beneath the surging muddy waters roaring down the chasm. There was no sign whatsoever of the boys' tent, life-raft, or anything else they had brought.

I also noticed that a steady stream of cannonades was filling the night with still more noise, adding to the cacophony, but I couldn't figure out what that was either. When I shined my big spot-light up onto the crest of the falls, I was shocked yet again. The water was so ferocious that it was washing large rocks and small boulders down the gorge which were flowing over the waterfall and banging as they crunched and bounced onto the solid stone ledge below the falls.

After witnessing this for a few moments, my sense of self-preservation kicked in, and I dropped into survival mode. My first thought was that I obviously needed to get the boys up on considerably higher ground up the steep hill of the gorge. I knew there was at least one substantial lake upstream with an earthen dam. If it went, nothing but the upper level of the hillside would save us, so we needed to get there, and fast.

As I was quickly ticking off the things which I now needed to achieve, I suddenly happened to think about my truck on the opposite side of the creek. When I had parked it, I had turned it around so that it would be headed "out" when we decided to pack up and leave. As I now shown my spotlight on the truck, my vehicle – which earlier had been parked well up on elevated dry land – now had water flowing almost up to the wheel wells. Once again – shock city.

I dashed back into the camper, slipping and banging my elbow on the door. Cursing to myself, I yelled at the boys "Quick! Get into those rain-suits there," pointing to an emergency item I had chanced to bring along. I knew we were in for a long, wet night, and we were cut off from our access out of the gorge. The last thing I wanted was for hypothermia to further complicate our problems.

Still sitting inside the camper, the two boys were seemingly oblivious to the disaster unfolding around us. When I took them outside to climb up the hillside to safety, they were interested only in the fact that they now miraculously had the "white-water" for which they had so earnestly planned in this outing. Now all they had to do was to find their raft in the maelstrom. Nothing to it.

"Get up the mountainside," I commanded roughly. "Get up there and do not move until I come to get you," I yelled. "Now!" I yelled even louder, my patience fraying. They got the message that time.

"Where's my dad's tent?" Jack shrieked when he realized it had disappeared along with the inflatable raft. For a fleeting moment, I almost laughed.

"Don't worry," I replied quickly. "He'll understand."

"That's right, cause you're gonna explain it to him.....Right?" he pleaded.

"Right," I responded. "Now get up the mountainside."

I next turned my attention to my truck. I started in the direction of what formerly had been our "fording spot" across the "stream." The water there – normally ankle-deep and eight to ten feet across – was now at least four feet deep, and terrifyingly spanned the entire width of the gorge...and it was growing deeper by the moment.

Looking back on it today, I know I should have just let that truck go, but my sense of preservation just wouldn't allow me to do it. I wasn't sure my insurance would cover such a loss, and I absolutely didn't want to have to hike out in miserable rainy weather and attempt to convince a tow truck operator or some benevolent tractor owner (if such even existed) to come take a chance on reaching my truck to pull it out of the mud. No...I had to handle this one myself.

As I started across the surging waters, I noticed to my horror that Jack had plunged into the water behind me, and Burke was running back and forth on the opposite bank behind us yelling at Jack to come back. I had only a moment to send the two of them back up onto the hillside.

I then began wading across the stream. Fortunately, at that fording site, the water current – since it had plunged into the pool beneath the falls – had been interrupted and had not yet picked up unbearable momentum or force. I was able to get across the stream without a great deal of trouble, but my window of opportunity was quickly closing because that water was rising fast.

When I reached the truck, however, I feared I was too late... The water was so high now that I knew it was already up around the engine. It was also up into the rear wheel-wells and lapping inside the door when I opened it. I was almost positive that engine would never crank. It appeared hopeless.

When I jumped inside the cab, I uttered a silent prayer, then put the key in the ignition and turned it. The engine, amazingly, roared to life. I quickly put it into gear and punched it. I mean I didn't spare the horses at all. The tires spun viciously at first, but then caught on some rocks and the truck mercifully shot up to the higher level of the road.

Since I didn't have four-wheel drive, I had purchased very good "mud tires" for the truck, and that little bit of extra protection and preparation had just paid big dividends. Had I had plain street tires, I don't think the truck would have come out of that muck, and the engine and truck interior would have been inundated in just a few more moments with creek water.

With the truck rescued, I then had to re-ford the raging stream and get back up to the hillside with the boys. When I finally reached them, I could see fear in their eyes for the first time, but there was excitement too.

"Let's go look for our raft," Jack yelled. Once again, I just had to smile as I refused them. They simply had no concept of the potential dangers we were facing, and the folly in their immediate desires confounded me.

"Up the hillside," I commanded yet again. This time, however, I left no doubt in the tone of my voice that I meant business. They obeyed and we scurried upward for 50 to 75 yards to a point I felt offered safety.

We huddled up to wait out the storm, and spent the bulk of the night listening to the rain pattering down upon our rain suits as we waited for the deluge to halt and the torrent below us to slacken.

All during the night, the roar of the water and the clattering boom of the boulders being washed down the gorge continued incessantly. I tried to rest, but my pulse pounded into the wee hours of the morning, and every time the sky lit up with distant lightning, the water shooting down the chasm and over the falls shocked me anew. It was "Mother Nature" at one of her most vengeful moments.

By about 5:00 a.m., the rains had finally begun subsiding, and the first signs of daylight had begun peeking over the horizon. I finally had calmed down enough to sleep a little, totally spent from the night's exercises and excitement.

I awoke at about 8:00 a.m. to shrieks of joy. Looking toward the creek, I could see that water was still cascading down the creek through the gorge, but the volume had diminished considerably over the past few hours. The most dangerous period had passed.

"Look Daddy!" my son yelled at me excitedly, demonstrating his prowess at "white-water rafting" in a short stretch of the creek which was in fact still white water and actually deep enough for floatation of the raft. The two mischievous little daredevils had stolen away when I dropped off to sleep. They had somehow located their raft and tent far downstream, both caught on saplings.

The tent was a shambles, ripped to shreds, in fact. The raft, however, amazingly, was still in relatively good shape, and was now captained by two shrieking, laughing little campers, both of whom were totally oblivious to the night of danger which had just passed.

White water rafting indeed.

His Innocent, Darling Daughter

I n pioneer days, to a large degree, children were indeed "seen," and not "heard." Historic records indicate that though most of them enjoyed reasonably normal childhoods, their lives were much more regimented than are the lives of today's children. They had "chores" to keep up with and didn't dare argue or talk back to their parents. They knew that "the belt" or some other handy leather "tool" would be quickly retrieved for use in punishment should those behavioral norms be violated. Those days, however, are soooooooooo long gone.

Today, it seems most children talk back to and argue with authority figures without hesitation. It seems almost to be an accepted norm of daily life. It has been my experience that most children don't even know what the word "chore" means today either. And as the years go by, these "children" seem to grow ever more creative and clever in the ways they seek to deceive their parents.

Take the children of my sister and brother-in-law for instance. Both of those kids enjoyed a cleverness far beyond their years when it came to outwitting not only mom and dad, but each other as well.

Often when their parents were away from home for a short length of time visiting friends, the eldest son – who by then was a teenager and had gained the mantle of responsibility during absences of the parents – was put "in charge of things." This "in charge of" responsibility pertained mainly to his younger sister who he was instructed to carefully monitor, since she was their "dear, sweet, innocent, little darling who was terribly young and vulnerable."

As a reward, my sister and brother-in-law told their eldest son he would receive $10.00 upon their return if he maintained a close watch on everything, and made certain there were no problems. This responsibility included of course the babysitting of his younger sister during these parental absences.

Things went along smoothly in the first few instances in which the parents were away from home. The kids only tied the family cat to the ceiling fan one time, and their parents returned to find everything in order, and their young daughter safe and sound.

At some point in time, however, this adorable little daughter – the apple of her father's eye – suddenly realized her brother was essentially making $10.00 for doing exactly what he always did – lying around and watching television while their parents were gone. The budding little entrepreneur decided she wanted "a piece of the action."

The next time the eldest son was left "in charge" of the domicile, the enterprising daughter demurely watched her parents leave, then turned to her brother and suddenly demanded half of the $10.00 he was being paid to baby-sit her. Her brother, of course, flatly refused. The darling sweet little daughter then "played her ace."

"If you don't give me half, I'm going to tell them you were mean to me," she smiled.

The boy suddenly realized that his sister wasn't playing games. She was serious. That placed him in a tight spot. Even if he agreed to give her half, he had already spent that $10.00 on a baseball glove he was buying from one of his friends. He literally couldn't afford to give half of the money to his little sister – even if he had wanted to.

On the other hand, the young man knew his sister had a valid demand. Their parents WOULD believe *her* instead of *him* if she cried "foul," because he had been previously caught in mischief, and his little sister was so innocent no one could have conceived of misdeeds on her part.

One particularly noteworthy incidence of the son's transgressions was the time their parents had been gone overnight on a Saturday night, and the son had rolled up all the rugs in the house, moved all the furniture in the living room and den into the dining room in order to create an open "party room." He then had proceeded to become a local legend for hosting one of the most talked-about parties ever experienced by his school friends. *(His parents had learned of this escapade later from a neighbor.)*

Little did he realize just how handy that tape recorder was going to be with little sister.

———————————

Clever beyond his years, the young man knew his little sister had him "by the short and tighties" regarding the babysitting money. Suddenly, he had an inspiration. He realized he had a counter-defense right at his fingertips which he had almost overlooked.

Slipping upstairs, the boy retrieved his weapon – totally unbeknownst to his sister – and hid it beneath his bed, then re-engaged his sister in conversation as she continued her extortion efforts with him. Once again, he emphasized that he wasn't about to split the $10.00 with her, and then waited slyly for her reply. He also laid it on pretty thick about how any such "split" would be a deception to their parents, and that he could "never do anything to violate their trust."

This time, to her misfortune and his sly glee, his little sister was even more adamant. "If you don't give me half that ten dollars," she angrily threatened once again, "I'm going to tell Mama and Daddy that you were really bad and that you were ugly and mean to me the whole time they were gone, and YOU KNOW WHO THEY WILL REALLY BELIEVE," she smiled

And down the street she chased little brother after the revelations provided by the tape recorder.

triumphantly. Sighing, her brother just walked away shaking his head, a knowing smile spreading across his own face as he now knew he had "the goods" on her.

When their parents returned home, the two youngsters met them at the door, and the elder son confidently approached his dad to collect his $10.00 for the babysitting. Just as she had threatened, his little sister suddenly wailed to her mother how awful her brother had been, all the while crying abundant crocodile tears. Her performance was truly *Academy Award*-winning material which has now become family lore.

With a scowl on his face, their father took back the $10.00 he had handed to his son, and was about to take further measures to punish him, when suddenly, with a smile on his face, the young man revealed a Christmas gift he had received several years earlier. It was a small tape recorder which had given him many hours of pleasure as he recorded family members and music.

With his family's attention now curiously glued to him – particularly that of his dear sweet innocent little sister whose eyes by now were widening in suspicion – the boy triumphantly pressed the "Play" button on the recorder. There, in startlingly clear stereophonic quality, the voice of his little sister was instantly recognizable to all present, loudly making her extortion demands on her brother, blackmailing him like a seasoned professional.

The last the parents saw of their children that day was their adorable sweet innocent darling daughter – the apple of her father's eye – chasing their loudly cackling son down the driveway with a fireplace poker.

—•⟩⟩ ⟨⟨•—

A Changing of the Guard

Many years ago, shortly after my sweet wife and I moved to our first home in Woodstock, Georgia, we became the owners of a tiny new addition to our family. No... It wasn't a child. It was a kitten which we named "Sammy." Kittens and cats usually "come and go" in a family. They're just naturally aloof and short-lived, particularly in these days of the increased prevalence of coyotes and foxes. To my eventual mild surprise, however, Sammy would become a much noted fixture in our family for many years.

From the outset he was a little bob-tailed Siamese and Maine Coon Cat that had been given to us by a friend to replace a previous family pet which had sadly suffered an early death from feline leukemia. That was back in the early 1980s, before we knew (or could afford) to get a cat vaccinated to protect it against that and other diseases.

The little bundle of energy we called "Sammy" soon matured into quite the personality. His precocious nature was infectious, and he was constantly bouncing around the kitchen and den at our home. One of the first things we did was to take him to a local veterinarian to obtain all of his vaccinations. It paid off too, because for a while, I thought Sammy just might out-live me.

In those days (late 1980s), I had just launched a new business from the spare bedroom of my home – just as countless other entrepreneurial kindred spirits have done over the years. The flagship of my business was called *North Georgia Journal*, a travel & history magazine which eventually grew large enough to be re-named *Georgia Backroads* and which is still in publication even as of this writing in 2025, although under new ownership. It is now one of the longest-published magazines in the state.

Anyway, Sammy and my new business essentially were born at the same time, so it was always easy to keep up with his birthday – 1987 – for veterinarians.

In those early days, Sammy was tiny enough for me to hold him in the palm of my hand. Literally. I didn't know it at the time, but he would eventually grow into the sergeant-of-the-guard of our home, and become almost too large to pick up and carry around, but early-on, he was just another little bundle of joy and mischief.

As a kitten Sammy naturally required a lot of attention, and this trait carried over into his adulthood and, pretty much for the remainder of his life. It seemed all Sammy truly wanted out of life was food, love and attention, – in that order.

Each morning when I would go upstairs to the spare bedroom to begin my day's work on the *Journal*, I'd hear Sammy meowing mournfully downstairs as he tried to locate someone to give him his breakfast. I'd go down to feed him. When he finished, Sammy invariably would bound up the stairs to re-join me. He'd jump up into the chair with me and find a warm spot, and he'd sleep there for much of the day as I wrote and edited articles in my magazine.

I don't really remember from whence came the name "Sammy." I think it was from the lead character portrayed by Ted Danzen on the television sit-com *Cheers*, but I could be wrong about that. The energetic little fur-ball just seemed to strut around a lot and knew instinctively how to "con" his way into pretty-much whatever he wanted, and so I gave him a name reminiscent of a New York bar-fighter. We didn't know it at the time, but the moniker would soon become more than appropriate.

Over the years, my family had "owned" several cats. Of course you never really "own" a cat. You just bring them into your household, and entice them to hang around with good food and shelter. They then decide if they want to "take up quarters" with you temporarily or not. They're almost always aloof and independent, yawning and looking at you like "Why are you bothering me??"

For that and other reasons, the lifespan of many cats is simply short by nature. They fall victim to predators, automobiles, disease, and sometimes sadly simply to neglect. Sammy, however, was never going to fall victim to any of those dangers or maladies. We made certain of that, having failed miserably with several previous pets.

Nevertheless, I initially instinctively felt like Sammy would be short-lived anyway. I knew that realistically, no matter how hard we tried to protect him, the odds simply were not in his favor.

Most cats – especially females that have not been spayed and males that have not been neutered – just aren't happy if you keep them penned up inside your home 24/7, and they will eventually find a way to zip outside into nature, and it's virtually impossible to keep an eye on them throughout the day under those circumstances. I therefore intentionally attempted not to become too attached to the bob-tailed bundle of energy early-on.

My mother used to love to tell the story about how, as a tiny youngster, I witnessed the crushed and mangled remains of a cat which had been run down by an automobile on the road leading to my childhood home. She said for months thereafter, I always referred to anything which was flat as *"Flatter'n a flat cat."*

Much to our surprise, however, Sammy not only survived, he thrived. We fed him nothing but the best foods. We never allowed him to be outside at night when he would be more likely to fall prey to the bobcats, coyotes, and foxes in the abundant wooded areas of rural Cherokee County.

I also maintained regular visits to the vet to keep him up-to-date on all his inoculations. Now when he was a kitten, he didn't know to "hate the vet," but as he aged, those trips became more and more of an exercise in determination. At first, I could deceive him when the time for the annual vet trip rolled around, but he eventually learned that most anything which involved a trip inside my Jeep was not good news for him. The true test of wills, however, didn't begin occurring until Sammy obtained some size and muscle.

I always felt bad about those vet trips too. Despite his obvious displeasure, Sammy would nevertheless trustingly allow me to take him "to" the vet's building, but as soon as we were inside and he smelled those alien "vet smells," he immediately set up a howl that did not cease until we were back at home. I eventually had to start transporting him in a cat-carrier too, just for self-preservation (and one hasn't lived until one has attempted to get a big muscular cat into a cat carrier). It eventually got to the point that he would try to claw his way up to the top of my head in his desperate escape attempts. I hated it too, because it was so very obvious that he truly hated these trips, but I knew if there was to be a decent possibility of a long, healthy life for him, the trips were pretty-much mandatory.

This all continued well enough until Sammy reached full-grown size. At that point, when it became time for him to get his injections, Sammy, who by now was a house-lion, simply revolted. And by that, I mean I literally had to wear the welder's gloves (which the vet always dutifully provided to me) in order to accomplish the deed. *(The vet ultimately reached the point that he wouldn't even attempt injections on Sammy unless I was there, armored with the welder's gloves, to hold Sammy down).* And I hated that even more, because I know he felt I was betraying him, even though I of course was only trying to protect him.

Once back home from the vet, however, Sammy lapsed right back into his old friendly personality. He, in reality, was just a lovable old softie who craved attention.

Sammy's muscular body also wasn't necessarily a draw-back either. He eventually reached the point that we just didn't worry too much at all about his safety outside during the day anymore. In fact, for a good ten or twelve years, he became somewhat of a "patrolman" for us.

Things eventually reached the point that there was no mistaking the "alpha-feline" in our neighborhood. Sammy never left our yard, and after the "loose" neighborhood cats and dogs encountered him, they usually never again ventured into our yard. I watched on several occasions (before I could get to him to intercede) when another male feline foolishly trespassed into his realm. The fur and hide would fly and litter the yard, but it was always from the opposing cat, not Sammy.

As mentioned above, however, Sammy's one weakness seemed to be loneliness. He followed me around like my shadow in order to avoid being left alone. He was strange like that. "Aloofness" was not part of his personality.

As a result, we eventually decided to get Sammy a companion in the form of a tiny female kitten which we named "Prissy." Now most felines are territorial – especially alpha males. A new feline arrival in the household usually isn't immediately welcomed by the established male, so we took it slow.

We kept Prissy penned up in the utility room where Sammy could see and smell her through the plastic cat-door there, but he couldn't get to her. Sammy did hiss and avoid the new arrival for several days early-on, but it wasn't long before it was obvious that his curiosity was getting the best of him. The hissing ceased and he began perching in curiosity right in front of the cat-door window in order to observe her at length.

Soon, when it became obvious that they were no longer at odds with each other, we allowed the kitten out into Sammy's world. Sammy, of

Each day when the author returned home from work in his familiar black Jeep Grand Cherokee, his two-party welcoming committee was always on hand to greet him.

course, was tentative at first, even running from Prissy, but they eventually became inseparable. They ate together, and romped together on a daily basis and slept together every night.

Prissy also became Sammy's "charge," and woe be unto the misguided dog who cockily entered our yard to threaten the new kitten. That, to put it bluntly, was a mistake the opposing cat or dog made only once. Sammy was a terror where Prissy's defense was concerned.

One day, I happened to be sitting in one of our lounging chairs in the yard of our home enjoying the summer peace. Prissy had followed me and was playing nearby. All of a sudden, a big German Shepherd from up the street came trotting aggressively into our yard.

Since I was initially unaware of this dog's invasion of our property, I wasn't able to react immediately to protect the tiny little fur-ball. When I heard her howl, however, I looked up suddenly from my paper just as the dog was set to attack. I jumped up out of my chair to rescue her as Prissy continued to hiss and howl loudly, giving her best imitation of something which might actually be dangerous to the big dog. He, however, clearly was not impressed.

Now I had previously warned the owner of this German Shepherd that if his dog entered my property again, and particularly if he was aggressive toward me or my pets, that I would punish it. I wouldn't end its life, because I'm a natural animal-lover, but I would definitely teach it in no uncertain terms that our yard was off-limits. The owner was one of those high-brow professorial types who just looked at me askance before huffing and walking away.

Prissy, meanwhile, was quickly losing the stand-off with the dog. When I had looked up and seen the circumstances, I was instantly afraid that I was going to be too late to save her – and I probably would have been too. . . . All of a sudden, this blur of gray fury bolted across the yard and flew into the big dog with a vengeance. All I could see was fangs and claws aimed like a bullet-train for a deli-meal of German Shepherd flesh, and I mean Sammy chowed down too.

Most cats under those circumstances – even large cats – will simply threaten a dog and then flee to the safety of a nearby tree or some other elevated post. Sammy, however, didn't waste time with any such nonsense. When his territory was threatened, he became a soldier on a mission, and he took no prisoners. He didn't even pause when he reached the large dog. It was rip and chomp time.

That shepherd howled and leapt back in shock and pain as Sammy ripped at his hide, and the fur flew from that dog's backside. Then the shepherd made an even worse mistake – that of deciding to fight back. That just enraged Sammy even more. Still more rip and chomp, and more fur flying – all of the canine variety.

The neighbor, upon hearing his dog's loud howling, shortly came running across his yard and across the street into my yard to assist his dog, but I was having none of that. "Back across the street professor," I instructed stiffly as I stepped between him and the dog being carved up. "I told you what would happen if you allowed your dog back into my yard."

"Now you - "

"Nope!" I stated firmly, "You had your chance to control your dog, and I've asked you politely on several previous occasions and you just laughed at me. Get back across the street to your property! Now!" I stated, even more aggressively to erase any doubt.

By this point, Sammy had released the dog. He was still standing there with an arched back that bespoke "more blood and guts on the way if you press me." Before he could attack again, however, I swept the big cat up.

At this point, the shepherd shot back across the street to his yard where he immediately set up a very loud and aggressive barking fit. I couldn't help but notice, however, that he wasn't about to leave his yard again. When Sammy attempted to jump from my arms for more Shepherd filet, I turned and walked up to the house, carrying him and Prissy with me.

"Put up a fence. Chain him. I don't care," I admonished the neighbor before walking away. "Don't let that dog back over here on my property again."

Professor just scoffed at me again as he stomped off. Though it still continued to routinely patrol the neighborhood unleashed, the shepherd never again ventured into our yard, and he wore a badge of bare skin thereafter too where Sammy had taken a scalping trophy. From that day forward, Sammy seemed to just dare that big dog to cross the street.

Years went by. . . . Seasons came and went. The ***North Georgia Journal*** continued to grow. I would shortly be converting it into a new publication entitled ***Georgia Backroads*** for wider circulation appeal.

The magazine gradually became profitable to the degree that I was eventually able to purchase office space in nearby Roswell, Georgia, to house the publication's various components. When that occurred, Sammy was left to spend his days alone. . . but he at least had Prissy, and as far as I could determine, he was enjoying his life.

It gradually reached the point of amusement to me. Since the responsibility for feeding the cats – which I did every morning before I left and every afternoon when I returned home – fell to me, both of the animals eventually reached the point that they recognized the sound of my Jeep Grand Cherokee turning into the driveway. They would both converge at the garage, milling about. Prissy's tail would be in the upright "flag" position, as they both greeted me and waited to be petted and fed. I had my own little welcoming committee each day.

I had installed two of those small electronic "cat-doors." One provided access through the garage door so that Sammy and Prissy could come and go safely (via an electronic device on their collars which automatically opened the cat door when they approached it and automatically locked it behind

Old Sammy "on alert status" at the Longfellow Trail home circa 1999. (Photo by the author)

them after they were beyond the door) during daylight hours. Another one was located at the base of the door leading from the garage into the house.

Sammy and Prissy both quickly became acclimated to the devices, and they enjoyed a protected environment in the garage if they so chose. They could also gain access to our home if I chose to unlock the cat-door on the utility room door inside the garage.

At night, I just turned off the switch on the garage exit door to keep Sammy and Prissy secured inside the protection of the garage (and all other wildlife secured outside). In the mornings, I reactivated the switch to allow them access back outdoors.

As Sammy approached ten years of age, I began to notice that he had definitely slowed down a bit. He hadn't actually "lost a step" yet, but he spent much more of his time sleeping in a big cushy lawn chair in a cool area of the patio each day during warm summer weather. In the winters, he spent more and more time inside with us, or in his warm bed in the garage. Each subsequent spring however, when the weather was cool and crisp, he was always up strutting around in his usual manner, seemingly ready for action.

By the mid-1990s, **North Georgia Journal** had a very popular following, and soon began to win editorial awards from the *Magazine Association* *of Georgia*. It was gratifying to see one's work acknowledged by one's peers. Those days were a coming of age as well as for Prissy and Sammy.

By this point in our lives, my sweet wife and I were ready to move yet again – this time to a suburb of Roswell. We had sold our East Cobb home and had contracted to have a new home built to our specifications at Summit Oaks on Mabry Road in Roswell. During construction of this home, we moved temporarily into an apartment.

Sammy was now entering his 15th year – ancient by cat standards – but he seemed to still get around just fine. He wasn't as agile as he once had been, and certainly couldn't jump as high or as far as he had once been able. Converting his cat years to human years, he was somewhere around 100 years of age, though, so I felt like he was doing pretty well, all things considered.

I did notice, however, that he was increasingly cranky. When he was a kitten, he loved to be teased. He'd rip and snort around the house, thoroughly enjoying himself. But by the late winter or early spring of 2001, however, he would no longer allow me to tease him. He just didn't seem to like it anymore, and made that very clear to me... sometimes even flinging a clawed paw at me to emphasize the point.

In looking back, it was almost as if he was trying to tell me something was wrong. Almost as if he was doing his best to communicate to me that he needed something.

Sammy was like that. Sometimes I would swear he was trying to talk to me. If his food bowl was empty, he'd walk over to it, bend down as if to eat, then look up at me with that *"Aren't you going to feed me you big dummy?"* look in his eyes. And just to be sure I got the message, he'd walk away from the bowl, then walk back to it and repeat the procedure all over again until I fed him.

I think Sammy had reached the breaking point when we moved temporarily into the apartment while building our new home – taking of course both Sammy and Prissy with us to the apartment. It was only a day or two before I noticed that Sammy had stopped eating. He'd go to his food bowl as if to eat, nose around in it a bit, then just walk away. He seemed to know he needed to eat, but just couldn't bring himself to do it.

By this point, it was painfully obvious that something was seriously amiss. I took him to the vet and learned the sad news that Sammy was indeed in renal failure. His kidneys were just worn out and shutting down. That was the reason for his inability to eat. He had ceased taking in liquids, and without liquids, his body simply could not process food.

This often happens to aging felines when their environment suddenly is altered (moving into an apartment or into a new home) and they no longer have the home to which they have become accustomed. The stress of the loss of their secure environment – coupled with the wear and tear of advanced age – are just more than they and their psyche can take, and their bodies often respond by shutting down with renal failure.

I tried my best to find ways to entice Sammy back into eating. I bought treats like yogurt – which he had loved when he was healthy – in the hope that the liquid in it would entice him to eat it. Nothing doing. We nursed him along – getting one of those water packs that is injected beneath his skin to provide liquid nourishment in that manner, but that was only a temporary fix.

Looking back, I know I was selfish. It had become abundantly obvious that Sammy had lived a full life and I was now allowing him to suffer just to keep him alive for as long as possible.

When he eventually was so weak that he could hardly walk anymore, it was painfully obvious that no quality of life remained that justified this artificial survival any longer. He clearly just wanted to be left alone to die. His last days were spent beside the toilet and the vet had told us that in their last hours, felines many times will seek out a spot where they know water exists, even though they are unable to ingest it any longer.

At that point, I finally made the hard decision that it was time to take him on that fateful "final journey" to the vet. That was the longest and most difficult trip I have ever made.

In 2001, the *North Georgia Journal* was peaking in both popularity and quality. . . winning awards for excellence. In four more years, I would sell it for a tidy profit and retire to manage my real estate portfolio.

Old Sammy had come almost all the way with me in that career endeavor – right from the first day. I had won awards, but Sammy had never won anything – except my heart.

—•⟩⟩ ⟨⟨•—

Movies and Me:
We Go Back a Long Way

I have been fortunate to attend and enjoy some great movies in my life-time – everything from *Gone With The Wind* and *Butch Cassidy and the Sundance Kid* to *The Bridge Over the River Kwai* and *Jurassic Park*. I am particularly fond of *Westerns*. I believe I've seen every movie ever made by the immortal John Wayne.

My hometown in Rockmart, Georgia was (and continues to be) rela-tively small, compared with many towns in the United States. Despite this fact, it has enjoyed a long tradition of association with the performing arts.

As early as the 1920s, an opera house/theater existed on North Marble Street in Rockmart. It later burned mysteriously, and it reportedly was such a conflagration that it was amazing it didn't burn down the entire town.

Sometime later (I'm not certain exactly when), a more modern movie house was built around the corner on Elm Street near the middle of town. It was once a very popular venue, and thrived in the 1940s and 1950s.

By the time my brothers and sisters and I were old enough to attend the Rockmart Theater in the 1960s, however, it had fallen upon hard times and was in disrepair. Rumors maintained there were rats scurrying down the isles to feed upon the many dropped kernels of popcorn, and dark misdeeds were occurring in the upstairs balcony. As a result, my mother was not an easy "sell" when it came to the attendance of movies there by us children.

Despite this fact, I recall several memorable occasions there. One was a visit made by *Officer Don*, the star of Atlanta television station *WSB-TV*'s weekday evening children's program *The Popeye Club*. This program, pro-duced in the WSB studios from 1956 to 1970, was broadcast weekdays, and was hosted by Atlanta personality Don Kennedy *[who lived a long life, finally passing away in 2024]*.

Because of the show, Kennedy's face became recognizable to millions of baby-boomers of the 1950s and '60s in Georgia. On weekends, the affable host took his show "on the road" in a manner of speaking to theaters all across the state, and the Rockmart Theater was one of the many sites to which Kennedy brought his traveling act.

I also believe it was at the Rockmart Theater that my brother David and I and my sisters enjoyed one of the all-time movie classics – *Walt Disney Productions' "**Old Yeller.**"* I clearly remember my abject despair when Old Yeller had to be shot after contracting rabies.

At the time, we had a dog quite similar to the movie character. His name was "Ginger," but we all just called him "Puppy." He was always like a great big old puppy to us and his devotion was unconditional.

Puppy lived a wonderful dog life, surviving for a remarkable ten to twelve years, never once having received any inoculations for the many diseases that often took down even protected domesticated canines by their 6th or 7th birthdays. He accompanied us everywhere, faithfully following as we rambled over the hills on the outskirts of Rockmart, camping out, fishing, searching for Indian arrowheads, hunting, riding motorcycles, go-carts, and horses. How he survived as long as he did in an environment filled with swiftly-moving automobiles, heartworms, rabies, parvo, and countless other canine killers mystifies me today. We all dearly loved him, and one weekend, after being our faithful companion for a decade or more, he just disappeared, never to return.

When we were small children in the late 1950s, my parents enjoyed going to the drive-in movie theater once located just off the highway between Rockmart and Cedartown. *(The level graded area where all the cars parked and the huge movie screen once stood can still be seen today if one knows where to look.)* As far as I am aware, our parents always took us with them too, which was a huge treat for us. There, many times, were cartoons at intermission, and there were always plenty of "treats" at the concession stand which we sometimes could talk Mother and Dad into buying for us.

We had a 1957 Chevrolet station wagon at that time, and Dad would let down the back seat. Mother, who was an excellent seamstress, had, at some point in time, made a quilted mattress which exactly fit the area and contours of the rear portion of that station wagon. They'd dress us in our pajamas then pile us all back there, along with blankets and pillows, and off we'd go... to the drive-in. If we became too sleepy to finish watching the late movie, we just slept right there in the car. When we returned home, we were all ready to hop right into bed.

One of the most memorable movies (actually the only movie I can remember there) at that drive-in was *The Bridge over the River Kwai*. It was a fascinating story of American and British prisoners-of-war in a Japanese POW camp during World War II. The movie climaxed with an amazing train wreck off the bridge, and it was because of this dramatic conclusion that the movie became indelibly imprinted in my memory. *(Mayhem was high on my list as a child.)*

Most of the old movie drive-in theaters are gone today, victims of time and progress. The one between Rockmart and Cedartown disappeared many years ago. The owners apparently just couldn't compete with the newfangled "televisions" and the indoor theaters in town that could seat hundreds of patrons.

Over the years, I have experienced a number of comical experiences at the movies... A few years after we were married, my sweet wife, Judy, her mother, and I were enroute to a movie at one of the large multiplex theaters near our home in Cobb County.

At that time, we were in Judy's car – a black Mazda 626 – and for those of you unfamiliar with this situation, this model was very similar at that time to several other models by other vehicle manufacturers. To put it in laymen's terminology, my wife's car could very easily be confused with other cars by a buffoon like me. *(I think you can see where I'm going with this...)*

Now let me see if I can let you, ah, "Get the picture, now," as the late famed UGA sportscaster Larry Munson used to say. My wife was driving, and I was in the front passenger seat. We wanted to buy our movie tickets early, so that we could go do a little shopping prior to the movie.

Judy parked in front of the theater, and I got out to get our tickets. I stood in line, trying to be patient as the ticket seller tried to keep up with a line of ticket buyers threatening to encircle the theater. What I didn't know, was that while I waited in line with my back to Judy and our car, she decided to pull ahead a hundred feet or so where she turned the car around and re-parked. At the same time, another car – one of the ones which very closely resembled our black Mazda 626 – pulled into Judy's original parking space.

I finally got our tickets and turned around to walk back to our car. My eyes quickly picked it out, right there in the spot where I had alighted from it only moments earlier. I walked right around to the front door, opened it, and hopped in.

The first thing I noticed was a distinctly different smell – a garlic kind of odor in the car... *"That's funny," I thought to myself... "I've never smelled that in here before."*

I suddenly sensed – rather than saw – people in the darkened rear seat of the car... You know how it is... You *know* you're in your car. You feel certain your wife and mother-in-law are there, so you just assume everything is normal... *(God must truly enjoy moments like this.)*

I noticed we weren't leaving the theater, so I, a little impatiently, said "C'mon sweetie... Let's go."

It was at about this point – as I looked ahead at another car facing us a short distance away – that I truly realized something was amiss. I knew this, because I could see what definitely appeared to be my wife and mother-in-law sitting in that car across the parking lot, and they were clearly enjoying something immensely.

If you've ever been in a situation like this, you know the feeling... You suddenly realize something is terribly wrong about your circumstances, and that it quite likely, now, is not your wife sitting behind the wheel in the car in which you are seated. Your palms get sweaty; you are very uneasy about looking to your left to see who *is* actually sitting there. You feel quite certain by that point that it ain't your wife, but you're simply afraid to look.

"You inna dee wrong carrrrrrrrrrrrr," a sing-song Latino voice suddenly chimed sweetly at me as I turned slowly to gaze stupidly at what clearly was a stranger in the seat beside me. I think it was her mocking smile that got to me the most. I felt like Curly in *The Three Stooges*. I looked quickly into the back seat where I had assumed my mother-in-law was sitting, and a series of beady eyes gleamed back at me from the darkness. They were all munching on tacos, the source of the garlic "aroma" I had smelled.

Words cannot express my mental state at that point. No matter what you want to do, there simply is no way to explain the situation away without looking stupid.

When the author returned from purchasing tickets for his wife, mother-in-law and himself for the movie, he hopped back inside "his black sedan parked exactly where he had left it."

_____

The worst part about it was that this group of Latinos just let me sit there too, like I was actually a member of the family. I'm surprised they didn't offer me a taco. In fairness, they did all have perplexed expressions on their faces. I'm sure they were trying to figure out what this crazy gringo was doing in their front seat.

The next thing I did was to look toward the other car where I had earlier picked out the images of what looked distinctly like my wife and mother-in-law. In retrospect, I should have spared myself that indignity. Judy and her mother were rolling back and forth in their seats exploding in laughter. Their car was literally rocking, such was the extent of their mirth. The situation was turning ugly.

I looked back at the young Latino in the front seat beside me, smiled weakly, held up my hands in that "Oh well" expression, turned and nimbly exited the car. From the back seat, the smell of garlic wafted in my wake.

As I walked back to the car that actually held my wife and her mother, I wasn't sure if I really wanted to get in or not. I seriously considered walking home.

Movies and me. . . .We go back a long way.

Vacation Frustration – and Near Disaster

I n 1987, my sweet wife and I allowed a friend to talk us into leasing a moderately-sized 24-foot recreational vehicle for a vacation getaway. Our goal was to drive from our home in Woodstock, Georgia, to Key West, Florida, and enjoy some time at Hemingway's famous digs – including stop-overs at sites such as "Sloppy Joes." Our inexperience at this endeavor became evident almost from the get-go, and with my 10-year-old son, Burke, in tow, we had a full complement.

The RV we rented had a double-bed, toilet and a small shower in back, as well as a small dinette and fridge mid-way and another "let-down" bed over the driver bay in front, making this house-on-wheels a reasonably comfortable place in which to live "on the road"..... Driving it, however, was quite another matter.

When cruising down the highway (or interstate as it were), the big vehicle swayed frighteningly from side to side if one wasn't overly cautious, and its width seemed to allow it to just barely be "passable" in multi-lane traffic. I constantly feared that the side-mirrors would get whacked off by a passing tractor-trailer.

If one was driving in heavy interstate traffic, we soon discovered this experience was traumatizing. Maybe if I/we had been experienced driving a big-rig such as this down the road, the drive would have been more pleasant and less nerve-wracking, but we were young, totally inexperienced, and yet adventuresome. And off we went.

In order to maintain our time-table of driving all the way to Key West and enjoy a few days there in the limited time we had at our disposal, we knew we weren't going to be able to dilly-dally on this over-850-mile trek.

From our home under normal conditions, it is a 14 or 15-hour drive, and we wanted to pause at some of the sights along the way.

We set out early one June morning and drove all day, stopping for meals along the way. As described, this was in 1987, and there just were not a lot of RV parks in south Georgia and north Florida in those days. On the first leg of this trip – since we had passed no such designated over-nightery for RVs, particularly one which offered "hook-ups" for water, electricity and sewage disposal – we just continued to drive right on into the night, which was obviously a mistake. We should have researched the route a bit better to locate an overnighting spot at the end of each day, but... you know – young and inexperienced. What can I say.

Sometime around 3:00 am, we were on a reasonably main thoroughfare someplace in extreme south Georgia or northern Florida, and if my memory serves me correctly, it was a lonely two-lane highway, not an interstate. I don't know if we had taken what we considered to be "a short cut" or what, but we were all alone on that stretch. No traffic whatsoever, which, strangely, was a bit unnerving.

By this point, we were hungry and tired, and needed a break, and we suddenly happened upon a café/diner which had a prominent sign *"Open 24 Hours."* It was the only sign of humanity we had seen for miles, and the only opportunity for food we had seen for what seemed like hours.

As I turned into the café parking lot, a lone beat-up Ford station wagon was departing from the eatery and pulling out onto the highway. As they passed our RV, I couldn't help noticing that the driver was giving us quite "the once over," and when he immediately turned around and followed us back up to the café, the hair on my neck stood up.

I had not owned nor carried a weapon with me since my Army days some 13 years earlier, but I would have given my right testicle for my .45-caliber side-arm right about then.

As I pulled up and parked in front of the diner, I watched the occupants of the beat-up vehicle – a scruffy unwashed-looking, wild-eyed dude and an equally scruffy female – as they slowly parked and then preceded us into the café. In my duty in the Army, I was permanently assigned to the security detail for the U.S. Army Commander of NATO. I had learned to be constantly alert, observant, and to use as much deductive reasoning as possible in situations of possible trouble. I definitely didn't like what I saw getting out of that station-wagon.

Burke said he just wanted to sleep, so Judy and I locked the two front doors to the RV and went inside to get something to eat.

Inside, I saw that the two scruffys had paused at the counter. When Judy and I took our seats in a booth across the room, scruffy man and woman came over and sat immediately behind me – no matter that there was a whole empty room of other booths. The alarm bells in my head were almost deafening.

We, nevertheless, calmly ordered a meal because we were hungry and exhausted. Judy, meanwhile, was completely oblivious to the entire scenario and danger unfolding around us. I didn't want to say anything to her that would upset her until I could decide what to do.

Our meals arrived in short order, and Judy began eating hers in earnest. Her hunger was obvious. My plate, however, sat untouched.

As explained, the room was completely devoid of humanity with the exceptions of Judy and myself – and the scruffys. Even the waitress behind the cash register had retreated back into the kitchen. Perhaps she had sensed an ominous nature to the return of the scruffys as well.

In those days, my hearing was still pretty good, and as we sat in our booth, I could clearly hear scruffy dude spinning the cylinder on a revolver. I had been around weapons pretty much all my life so the sound of a cylinder spinning in a revolver was instantly recognizable to me. There, quite honestly, is no mistaking that particular sound to anyone who knows weaponry.

I could also hear scruffy woman whispering to him, "Not here. Not yet." That was all it took for me. I instinctively knew that inaction at that point was a fool's errand.

To this day, I really don't know what kept the scruffys at bay. I'm 6'1" in height, but not impressively so. I was in pretty good shape still in those days, having lifted weights every other day in my previous employment at North Georgia College (present-day University of North Georgia), and jogging a mile or two every other day, but I'm certain that scruffy dude wasn't impressed by me.

Judy, meanwhile, as described, had no concept of the dangerous circumstances unfolding around us. I whispered to her, "We need to go," to which she quickly responded simply "Why? No. I'm hungry."

I felt certain that if we started toward the cash register to pay our bill and scruffy dude got up to follow us, I'd have to have a plan of action. Under circumstances such as that in an isolated location, one simply cannot allow one's self to become a victim. Hardened criminals – particularly psychos – in such a setting are not merely going to take a few valuables and then walk away satisfied. They almost always will want more and will be highly unpredictable and extremely dangerous.

It was obvious I was going to have to do something to get Judy's attention. She was weary and had lived a sheltered life and as such, simply did not recognize any of the danger signs. I grabbed her hand and squeezed hard as she prepared to fork more food into her mouth and then I silently "mouthed" the words emphatically "Leave!!!! Now!!!!"

She looked into my eyes and finally her lights flickered on. We both got up silently and walked over to the cash register as I kept an eye cocked to our rear. A waitress quickly reappeared from the back kitchen.

At about this same time, scruffy dude also stood up, and when he did, I was in the process of placing my hand inside my jacket to feign possession of a concealed weapon when a huge cook suddenly appeared from the kitchen and sat down behind the counter with his hands hidden beneath the counter where I am certain he was fingering a firearm of some type. That certainly is what I would have been doing had I been him. To my relief, scruffy sat back down and glared at me.

Judy, meanwhile, had paid our bill and had quickly returned to the RV which she had unlocked. I backed out the door and hopped in the RV and motored quickly away, immediately pushing the big vehicle up to around 90 mph after entering the highway, just hoping we'd attract the attention of a state patrolman or other law enforcement.

After the diner had receded from sight in my side-mirrors – and with no sign of any headlights following us – I relaxed a bit, but I still didn't spare the horses. After 20 or 30 miles, I slowed back toward the speed limit. Thankfully, we never again encountered the beat-up station-wagon or its occupants.

Ever since that vacation, I have had a concealed weapon permit, and if I am traveling anyplace which I deem to have even the slightest potential for being lonely and dangerous, I either go in armed, or I avoid the site entirely – almost always the latter. It's just that simple. It's a sad state of affairs, but that's the world in which we live today. It's a very dangerous place, and one will quickly become a victim if one is not extremely cautious.

We pressed on down the road, and sometime around 6:00 am that morning, with overwhelming fatigue, we came thankfully to a very active RV park with water hook-ups, a sewage dump, and electrical hook-ups for our vehicle. There also was a deli across the way where I loaded up on food for us.

Judy and I both were dirty and "greasy," so we took showers, then chowed down on our food, and then let down the bed for some much-needed rest. That bed above the driver-bay was some of the best rest I have ever had.

Burke, meanwhile, had been sleeping during most of the previous miles (and danger), so he was full of energy and wanted to go play in the play-ground. Normally I wouldn't have allowed that – and I certainly wouldn't allow it today – but it was right in front of a concession stand near where we were parked, and there were a number of people – many quite elderly – who were enjoying a cool breeze and iced drinks, so I let him go. I was really so overwhelmed with fatigue that I just collapsed upon the bed.

After sleeping for several hours, Judy and I were awakened by an exuber-ant Burke. "Look what I found," he said, excitedly, as he handed us a wallet bulging with large denomination bills and a full book of Traveler's Checks. I don't know how much money that wallet contained, but it wasn't the type of money the average traveler would have carried. To me, it "smelled" like drug-dealer money, but I couldn't understand how a book of Traveler's Checks figured into that scenario. Whatever the circumstances, I knew I didn't want to create a reason for yet another confrontation with yet another unpredictable challenger.

"Wow!" was all I could say at first.

"Can I spend it?" Burke said, matter-of-factly.

"Uh, No," Judy quickly replied. "Someone is certain to be searching frantically for that amount money. We'll leave it at the front desk of that little deli. Maybe the owner will stop there when he starts searching for it."

Judy was absolutely right, and that's exactly what we did. To this day, however, the owner of that deli – if he's still alive – probably still gets a good chuckle out of that little incident, because that wallet had a lot of money in it.

After a full night's sleep and breakfast, we set back out onto the road. Later that day we passed Tampa where we found yet another RV park and more sleep during a heavy down-pouring of sleep-inducing rain, before con-tinuing on to Miami the following day to yet another RV park.

It was shortly after this point that Judy and I began to realize we weren't going to be able to achieve our objective of Key West. There simply was not enough time. We had a total of about eight days, of which we were now on the third. By the time we reached Key Largo, we were on our fourth day and knew that we now would have just enough time to get back home before our vacation days expired.

Before we reversed direction and set back out for home, we looked around Key Largo just a bit, finding one or two landmarks from the 1948 *Warner Brothers* thriller of the same name starring Humphrey Bogart, Lauren Bacall, Edward G. Robinson and others. The *Caribbean Club* and wharf where some of the movie's scenes were filmed were still there.

The next day, older and wiser, we headed back in a northerly direction and put Key Largo in our rear-view mirrors. I certainly didn't pause at the 24-hour diner this time, and since that date, I haven't even considered renting another RV.

—◦᠅ ᠅◦—

Impactful Individuals

I n the course of human events – and just life in general – one often looks back to examine that from whence he or she has come. And in so doing, that individual more often than not takes stock of how his or her life was impacted by certain individuals he or she encountered along the way. Some of those individuals still remain, but most of them usually have gone on to the *Great Hereafter*.

I have been blessed to have known a number of individuals who have had a significant impact upon my life. My only regret is that I did not always express my thanks and/or appreciation to those individuals while they were still here among us.

My Grandmother

One of the first on my list of impactful individuals would be my grandmother – **Essie Carroll Hudgins Jordan**. "Miss Essie" as many of Rockmart, Georgia, knew her, was a highly-respected biology and chemistry teacher for at least some 26 years at Rockmart High School, arriving in that realm in 1924 to teach, then resigning several years later after her marriage to Guy Wilfred Jordan in 1927. They raised a family of two girls almost to adulthood prior to my grandfather's tragic death from a terrible industrial accident in 1946, at which time Miss Essie returned to teaching circa 1947.

Just as she was in the community, Miss Essie was an institution in our family. To my brothers and sisters and me, however, "Miss Essie" was known only as *"Namma."* When the "chips were down," Namma was always there for us, no matter the trauma, no matter the problem. She was our "rock" during some very lean and problematic years. Even when my parents were unable to help me, "Namma" was always there, and in my last moments, I am sure I will be thinking of her, among a few others.

By the 1990s, "Miss Essie" had been relegated to a wheelchair due to her bad knees, but she didn't let that slow her down in the least, even occasionally catching a flight to the west coast to see her granddaughter. Her dedication to her profession resulted in the continuation of her high school teaching career at least five or six years beyond the date she was declared "legally blind." She had a huge and lasting impact upon her grandchildren.

Namma came into this world in 1900, during the last days of the Indian wars and travel by horseback in America, and she went out in 1999, during manned space flight into the heavens. As I think I detailed above, she was the most dependable person I have ever known. It was rare to catch her in a situation for which she was unprepared. She always had an answer.

When my mother and father separated in the mid-1960s (and divorced in 1969), Namma was there with help and support for us. When my father suffered the humiliation and indignity of bankruptcy in 1969, Namma again was there with financial support and encouragement for us. When my youngest brother died tragically in his youth, Namma was there to grieve, and wept openly with us, mourning for weeks thereafter.

Namma continued to be our "rock," right up until the last year or two of her life, when she passed away one month shy of her 99th birthday. She never "lost a step," and we had just come to believe that she was going to be around forever.

I can still hear her sweet voice even today, some twenty-five years after her death. That was the greatness of her impact upon my life. She will always have a presence, and even today, when I have an important decision to make, I can hear her sweet calming voice in the background.

Despite our love for her, my brothers and I took great delight in teasing Namma relentlessly – but always in a loving good-natured manner. She had begun losing her eyesight by the time she had reached her late 50s, but that didn't slow her down one whit. She continued a full-time teaching regimen of high school biology and chemistry until she was 70 years of age.

Though we worried constantly about her blindness, it opened up a whole new world of mischief for my brothers. At the grocery store, they would load up her shopping cart with cigarettes, cigars and liquor – to Miss Essie's eventual tee-totaling chagrin – providing a good laugh for the check-out lady. As the check-out lady cackled, we boys stood off to the side whistling a tune and staring up at the ceiling.

Miss Essie engendered so much respect within our community that she was able to shield us children from much of the pain being caused by the woes of our parents. Though my parents and family eventually were denied any type of "financial credit" within the community, Miss Essie's credit was good wherever she went – though she never needed it. She hailed from hardy Scots-Irish stock which simply didn't believe in buying anything for which one did not have the cash on hand to purchase it.

It was Namma's constant impressment of good judgment which served me and my oldest sister and younger brother so well. We learned at her knee to prepare well for life and to respect the good Lord in all things, and her teachings have kept us on "the straight and narrow" now for some 75 years.

My Wife & Son

My sweet wife, *Judy*, and my son, *Burke*, are obviously also among the cadre of special individuals in my life. Burke is a product of my first wife ("Plaintiff," as explained above.).

I have long been impressed by Burke's independence and general acumen for life. He has never – I repeat, "never" – really given me a moment of concern in his life. He matured into one of the most responsible adults I have ever known. Though I am overjoyed at that circumstance, I almost wish he would seek "help" from "old Dad" just occasionally for something.

I am exceedingly proud of his accomplishments in life thusfar, not the least of which are my two wonderful grandchildren and Burke's impressive successes as an award-winning professional homebuilder, estate designer, and property developer. He reached 48 years of age this year (2025), and is retiring, having accumulated far more than he needs to own two homes and other properties and be comfortable and secure for the remainder of his life.

One incident in particular which I will always remember about Burke is the vacation Judy and I took with him back in 1986 to Washington, D.C. We had just checked into our hotel and Burke informed us that he wished to go out into the hallway to "play." Distracted for the moment, I said "Okay, but stay close." Famous last words.

After Judy and I had unpacked our bags and were selecting a restaurant for our evening meal, I suddenly realized that I needed to check on Burke.

The author's sweet wife. (Photo by the author)

In those days, I had nightmares of having to tell "Plaintiff" that something unfortunate had befallen our son. Anyway, when I looked quickly around in the hallway, Burke of course was nowhere to be found.

As I ran back into the room, Judy was watching the television. Nelson Mandela was in town that week and staying in the same hotel in which we had accommodations, and a news conference was being conducted with him downstairs. I grabbed Judy and was just about to go quickly in search of Burke when, to my abject astonishment, there he was "on television," standing with a growing coterie of individuals watching as Mandela was being interviewed. On television??? Were my eyes deceiving me??? This was like a scene right out of the major motion picture, *"Forrest Gump."*

The carpet burned beneath my shoes as I hustled downstairs to where the interview was being conducted. I just hoped "Plaintiff" wasn't watching the same news feed.

Also in the top echelons of impactful individuals in my life is my sweet wife, *Judy*, who has had patience and endurance where my own had quickly been expended, and love eternal where it could easily have been withheld.

I am still dumbfounded that the young woman from the mountains of north Georgia, did not even hesitate to leave her stable environment at **North Georgia College** (forerunner of today's **University of North Georgia**) at which she had been so admirably employed for many years, to blindly follow me in my quest for a profession in journalism. She not only abandoned her stable job, she methodically located yet another stable job in the hustle and bustle of downtown metropolitan Atlanta, Georgia, a place with which she was totally unfamiliar and inexperienced, particularly when it came to "driving" in that mess.

Burke's penchant for impressive achievements began in his childhood, and has not faltered. He began his award-winning career as a builder, property developer and designer shortly after the completion of his college career and he has done nothing but improve his credentials and accomplishments each passing year. (Photo by Olga Jackson)

To my great fortune, *Judy* married me a few months later, and has been with me through "thick and thin" ever since, and I'm here to tell you, there have definitely been some "thins" along the way. Life was exceedingly difficult in the early 1980s, after the trauma from the policies of the 1976-1980 Jimmy Carter presidential disaster began to be felt by the populace. No jobs. Sky-high interest rates. Burgeoning crime. Just as with my grandmother, Judy has been a rock as well... always resourceful, prudent, unhesitatingly kind, deliberate, and loving. I would not have made it to whatever I am today without her.

The United States Army

Back in 1971, some ten years before I met *Judy*, I had volunteered for service in the *United States Army* after – in the shadow of my father's bankruptcy and other familial ills – tiring of a starvation diet and the constant struggle of a pauper in pursuit of an education at the *University of Georgia* in Athens.

"Uncle Sam" saw fit to train me as a military policeman, and, following additional instruction at *Advanced Individual Training (AIT)* school, I was shipped to *Heidelberg, Germany*, where I shortly found myself serving in the *529th Military Police Company*, the protection unit for the *U.S. Army*

Commander of NATO, Gen. Michael S. Davison. I was a security specialist in the *Top Secret* realm of the *U.S. Army European Command Complex* at the headquarters of the *United States Army in Europe (USAREUR)*.

My duties – along with a company of other MPs – revolved around the security of one of the foremost generals in the entire Army. Though I saw him on an almost daily basis, I can honestly say that I can count on one hand the number of times we conversed – and those invariably were two-word conversations. "Yes sir," and "No sir." Am I glad to have known him? Yes. I have to say I am.

The *529th Military Police Company* – for obvious reasons – was composed of top-notch military policemen and other security specialists. To my good fortune, the *529th* was named as the top military police company in the entire United States Army *(Brigadier General Jeremiah P. Holland Award)* in 1974, the final year of my tour of duty.

Am I glad I joined the United States Army in 1971? Yes. Resoundingly so. Without exception, the United States Army is one of the best things that ever happened to me, and, quite frankly, I would be a much-lesser person today were it not for that three-year expenditure of time and training. It has served me well.

University of North Georgia Years

After returning stateside and finishing college at *Georgia State University* in Atlanta as planned, I endured the "Plaintiff" years, then eventually secured employment as director of media services and sports information at the *University of North Georgia*. Sometime around 1983, I was able to interest the producers of the local *FOX* affiliate *WAGA-Television* in Atlanta in a feature on the college. At that time, *WAGA* produced regional programming called *"PM Magazine."*

Those of you who weren't around in the early 1980s probably won't have a clue as to who the late *Virginia Gunn* was, but if you don't, she was quite the little "fire-cracker" in her day. Lovely Virginia started out as a "weather-caster" at *WAGA*, but was so talented that she was quickly promoted to the co-hosting helm of *PM Magazine*.

Not only was *Virginia* drop-dead gorgeous, she was an absolute spit-fire daredevil as well. She came up to the mountains of north Georgia to pursue not only a *PM Magazine* feature on the college, but also on the U.S. Army's *Frank C. Merrill Ranger Camp* in the mountains near us.

I later was told the *Army Rangers* eagerly awaited *Virginia's* appearance at Camp Merrill. The men of this elite unit no doubt were hoping to take this "weathercaster" on a somewhat terrifying UH-1 ("Huey") chopper ride through the mountains, and a mountain rappelling adventure on those same mountains, and in general, just frighten the do-do out of her. Much to their surprise, however, *Virginia* not only was "game" for all of these adventures, she reveled in them, thrilled with every moment she spent in the chopper and elsewhere as the always-impressive *Army Rangers* showed off their skills. That was *Virginia Gunn* in a nutshell – always a trooper clamoring for adventure.

Interestingly, *Virginia* and her even-more-famous husband – author *Bill Diehl* – once owned and lived at an estate in Cherokee County which today is only five or six miles from my home. They, however, departed years ago, *Bill* sadly succumbing in November of 2006 to an aortic aneurism while living in Cherokee, and *Virginia* tragically dying several years later at St. Simons Island, Georgia, to which she had returned (she and Bill having also lived there for a number of years early in their marriage) to finish out her life.

Bill was the author of several best-selling books, not the least of which was *Sharkey's Machine* (1978), famously-converted to the silver screen in 1981 in a major motion picture starring and directed by *Burt Reynolds*, and co-starring *Brian Keith*, *Bernie Casey*, and others. In 1992, Bill struck gold again with *Primal Fear*, adapted into the 1996 film of the same name starring *Richard Gere* and *Edward Norton*.

I am thankful I was at least introduced to the beautiful Virginia Gunn back in 1983. The feature which eventually aired on *PM Magazine* helped spread the message about the beauty and value of an education at what then was the small institution of North Georgia College. It also didn't do my career any harm either.

In 1980 when I arrived at what was known as "the military college of Georgia," the student enrollment was just cresting at 2,000. Today, that enrollment is well over 18,000, and quickly climbing, and the *"University of North Georgia"* is a major educational center of the Southeast, if not the entire United States. I can honestly say the world is a lesser place today in the absence of *Virginia Gunn* and her ever-so-talented husband, *Bill*.

Also while at the *University of North Georgia*, I was fortunate to make the acquaintance of a popular sports writer at the *Atlanta Constitution*

Best-selling author and rising star humorist Lewis Grizzard (seated) signs the author's book. "Never let the facts get in the way of a good story," he said.

who also was a best-selling author. **Lewis Grizzard** came to the college campus as a featured speaker in either 1983 or '84 (I can't recall exactly), and I was able to casually get to know him during his visit. Needless to say, Lewis, as always, quickly won over the student-body.

Later, during my employment with a public relations firm in Atlanta, one of the agency's clients was, coincidentally, Mr. **Grizzard**. Our firm represented him during the years when he was so preeminent upon the speaking circuit and as a rising stand-up comedian who made two appearances on *The Tonight Show* in Hollywood, starring the immortal *Johnny Carson*.

The last time I spoke with **Lewis**, he looked at me and quipped *"Don't ever let the facts get in the way of a good story,"* quoting a line from one of his *New York Times* best-selling books. I asked him if he would write that little admonishment and sign his autograph with it in his book (which I had just dutifully purchased). He said *"Sure."* I still have that book and will always cherish it.

Lewis, sadly, also left us far too soon in 1994 at the somewhat youthful age of 47, from complications involving heart surgery at Emory University

Hospital in Atlanta. Millions mourned his passing. I was one of them.

Was I glad to have met *Virginia Gunn* and *Lewis Grizzard*? You bet.

A Business of My Own

After a four-year stint with the public relations firm, it, to my shock, just went out of business one day. Never saw that one coming at all. I decided at that point to strike out on my own, and founded *Legacy Communications, Inc.*, publishing a quarterly travel and history magazine called *North Georgia Journal* which I later converted into *Georgia Backroads* magazine. It eventually became quite popular regionally, and earned a number of editorial awards.

During my days with *Legacy*, I took a phone call one day from the lieutenant-governor of Georgia, *Zell Miller*. *Zell* said he had an article in which he thought I might be interested. I of course was flattered. I chatted with him a few moments and then urged him to send his manuscript on to me so that I could look it over. He said "It's already in the mail."

I wound up publishing *Zell's* article. After that, I kept in regular touch with him, and a few months later, he won the 1991 Georgia gubernatorial contest. One of the things which I eventually requested of *Zell* was a telephone number at which I could reach him with editorial questions during the day, and he said "Here. Here's my direct line at the governor's office."

Was I proud to have known *Zell Miller* personally? Yes. Resoundingly so. Even though it was a political gamble, just having his name associated with my magazine definitely raised its credibility, and though he could sometimes be abrasive, Zell, nevertheless was extremely popular, and always exceptionally kind to me. In my mind, he was one of the foremost Georgia politicians of the past 100 years.

Interestingly, years later, I learned that an individual with whom I had grown up in my youth - Keith Sorrells - had coincidentally been assigned to Zell's security detail after a successful career in the Georgia State Patrol. Small world.

It was also during my days as the owner and publisher of *North Georgia Journal / Georgia Backroads* that I chanced to be introduced to a fellow by the name of *Hugh Jarrett*. Now Hugh's name isn't one that inspires immediate recognition from those unfamiliar with the gospel and rock & roll music worlds, but fans of those realms recognize him immediately.

Hugh in fact, was one of the founding members of the *Jordanaires* who were the backing vocals group for *Elvis Presley* during his glory years as a recording artist and movie star. *Hugh*, with the *Jordanaires,* appeared in most of *Elvis's* early movies and in his break-out appearances on programs such as the *Ed Sullivan Show* broadcast from New York.

When his days with *Elvis* and the *Jordanaires* came to a close, *Hugh* came to Atlanta where he owned a nightclub and became a popular radio disc jockey. In his later years, he also reentered the acting world, appearing in a number of television prime-time

The late Hugh Jarrett at his home in Cherokee County, Georgia. (Photo courtesy of Doc Lawrence)

features, including fairly regularly in *"In the Heat of the Night"* with *Carroll O'Connor.*

The day *Hugh* strolled into my office, I have to confess I didn't really know who he was either, because his days with *Elvis* (the 1950s) were just a little bit before my days of enjoying rock & roll music. Nevertheless, I got to know *Hugh* and thoroughly enjoyed having him around. He was immensely entertaining. The stories he could tell were priceless and seemed never-ending. *(One of his funniest involved Pat Boone and his toupee. It's even funnier because Hugh wore a hairpiece too.)*

Hugh eventually reached the point that he was just a bit "down on his luck," and I began casting about for ways to raise his spirits. I emailed *Zell Miller* one day asking if he would help nominate *Hugh (Jarrett)* to the *Georgia Music Hall of Fame. Zell,* a big fan of gospel and country music, said he would do his best. When he learned of his eventual election, *Hugh* was overjoyed to say the least. Though it was late in the cycle, I like to think it helped resurrect his waning career just a little bit prior to his untimely passing.

A few years later, I learned that *Hugh* had passed away from complications involved in a tragic automobile accident. I consider it an honor to have known *Hugh Jarrett.* Today, he sleeps the eternal sleep in the cemetery of his former church in Cherokee County.

—◦⟩⟩ ⟨⟨◦—

What Is It About a Southern Accent? Really?

How well I remember as a child, watching old black and white Westerns on television on Saturday evenings with my father. *[This was back in the late 1950s and early 1960s, when there were a total of three whole television channels available for viewers in northwest Georgia, and only two of them actually functioned, since Atlanta's WXIA-TV (Channel 11) had such a weak signal at that time that it was only viewable from inside the Atlanta metro area.]* Invariably, my father would complain about how the villains in these Westerns (but never the heroes) almost *always* had a Southern accent.

At the time, I just didn't think that much about it because I was viewing these television productions from a child's innocent unassuming perspective. Today, however, when I chance upon one of those old Westerns, I see exactly what Dad meant.

The villains in those serials and features very definitely have distinctly Southern-affected accents, and it very obviously isn't happenstance either. The reason I know it's not accidental is because none of the villains were actually actors who hailed from the South. They very clearly were actors from the Mid-West, Western, or Northern states who were intentionally "imitating" Southern accents.

I'd like to think that this was all just some little anomaly which was innocent in origin, but in all honesty, I really don't think that is the case. There are just too many instances of this nefariousness. Dare I say it? Was there a darker intention afoot here?

There simply is no way to escape the fact that the objective very definitely was to portray *"the good guy"* as having either a "non-regional" or

Mid-Western or "New York" or even Hispanic accent, while portraying *"the bad guy"* as having a distinctly "Southern" accent. Now why was that done? What was the actual intent of the producers and directors who very obviously created this scenario?

And before any of you start with that *"Oh you're just being overly sensitive"* nonsense, it doesn't take a phonetic genius to understand a particular accent being portrayed in a particularly unflattering role time and time again on television. I think you know what was going on just as well as I do. Is that really being overly sensitive?

When one thinks about it, this situation could not only be classified as unflattering, but *intentionally* defamatory too. Why else would one so obviously portray a specific culture in this negative capacity over and over again?

Now *"Hollywood"* with its plethora of outspoken "celebrities" would never admit this circumstance, nor would many who don't actually hail from the South. Just ask them. It is for this and other reasons that *Hollywood* has lost so much of its sparkle and allure in recent years – particularly to Southerners. It has become such a disingenuous and divisive arena – in more ways than one.

One might ask *"Why is this allowed in a Hollywood which supposedly has been so rigorously indignant and quickly outspoken any time any other culture or ethnic group is marginalized or insulted?"* Well, that's a good question, and one that bears exploration. As stated above, this unsavory proclivity has continued right up to the present day, and no one says a word about it. Why is that?

One of the most ironic aspects of this whole Southern accent defamation in *Hollywood* is that the actors negatively-portraying Southerners invariably are not natives of the South. No. Back in the 1950s and early '60s in particular, *Hollywood* consistently used (and continues to use) "fake" Southern accents in major motion pictures and television Westerns in order to portray its "pseudo-reality," because *"Hollywood"* and television producers, directors and other executives more often than not have refused (until very recently) to hire anyone with a natural Southern accent. Now why was/is that? Why, in particular, do Southerners sit around and just accept this circumstance with no complaints whatsoever? Why do Southerners readily patronize major motion pictures and television serials which portray their culture as ignorant, evil and revolting?

Even in the 1960s when *Hollywood* actually did begin hiring a precious few actual Southerners with *real* Southern accents such as Claude Akins, Dub Taylor, and Jim Nabors into their acting "brotherhood" in motion pictures and television programming, they cast them almost exclusively in the roles of outlaws, degenerates, and general idiots. Right up until the movie **Deliverance** (1972) with Burt Reynolds, Jon Voight and Ned Beatty it was extremely difficult to identify a major motion picture role (excepting of course with the obvious **Gone With The Wind** cast) which portrayed a Southerner in a distinctly positive manner.

So why is this not perceived and recognized for the moral dilemma that it actually is? *Hollywood's* more recent indignation at bigotry and racism would be admirable were it not being exposed more and more as little more than a charade of self-righteous hypocrisy. One can only presume that the Akins, Taylors and Nabors of the acting world were simply desperate enough to allow themselves to become the pawns of rich producers and directors.

Both Claude and Dub were Georgians, and Jim is an Alabamian. Dub was actually born in Richmond, Virginia, but grew up in Augusta, Georgia, where his father was a cotton broker. He, interestingly, got his start in *Hollywood* after playing for the *Alabama "Crimson Tide"* in the 1937 *Rose Bowl* gridiron classic. Those were still *Depression*-era years, and after the '37 football season had expired, Dub just decided that rather than return to the poverty in Georgia, he'd remain in California to search for employment. He eventually was successful too, finding steady work as an actor portraying idiotic white Southerners.

Claude was born May 25, 1926, in Nelson, Georgia, and was a perennial "bad-guy" in Westerns of the 1950s and '60s. Prior to that, he had somehow miraculously made it to *Broadway* in the late 1940s where he actually won a part in the hit play, **The Rose Tattoo**. His surprise success on the New York stage led him to *Hollywood* in 1953 and a role in the *Academy Award*-winning film, **From Here to Eternity** where he portrayed – you guessed it – the evil individual with his Southern accent. He was *"Sgt. 'Baldy' Dhom."* Even though the name almost certainly was purposefully created to sound unappealing and sinister, it could hardly have been more insultingly-so *("Dhom?" Really?)*, and adding insult to injury, Claude wasn't even listed in the movie credits for his work, either. Perhaps, however, that was a blessing in disguise?

By the 1960s, when *Hollywood* discovered Claude was from the South and could provide a "believable" Southern accent, they began casting him as the "heavy" in a number of productions – mainly Westerns. If you watch **Rio**

Bravo (1959) – a very popular old John Wayne movie – you'll see Claude cast yet again in the role of a low-life criminal – with his semi-obvious Southern accent. Interestingly, Akins – apparently ashamed of his accent – actually does his best to disguise his Southern drawl in this and other performances, but it bleeds through nonetheless. I can't count the television Westerns and other motion pictures in which he appeared as "the heavy." They're just too numerous to list.

After years and years of ridicule and grinding away to lose his accent, Claude finally semi-"made it" in a lead role after being cast as *"Sheriff Lobo"* on the brief run of the television series **B. J. and the Bear** (1978-1981) and later in a similarly-brief *The Misadventures of Sheriff Lobo*, a spin-off series. After a life-time of mainly "bad-guy" roles in *Hollywood*, however, Claude passed away in 1994 at the relatively-young (at least by today's standards) age of 67. His net worth at death was listed as barely $2 million. Was that the result of poor money management on Claude's part, or of a lifetime of employment as a desperate actor at minimum wage?

As I said, at the time that I was watching Claude, Dub, and others in television Westerns, I was but a youngster, and a "Western" was a "Western" to me, regardless of who was speaking with what accents. I was totally unconcerned with that aspect of the production, being focused instead upon the hero of whatever particular episode was being featured. As long as **Roy Rogers, Hopalong Cassidy, The Lone Ranger, The Cisco Kid** and **The Rifleman** carried the day, that was my only concern. In my childhood imagination, I rode off into a thousand sunsets with them – accent or no accent – heroic guns a'blazin.'

My dad, however, wasn't fooled for a second, and he definitely wasn't pleased. The obviously deliberate nature of this defamatory practice by Hollywood was just too much for him to stomach.

So just what is it about a Southern accent that so naturally attracts a negative connotation? What causes it to be so routinely and naturally associated with denigration, ridicule, and shame? Why are Southerners intentionally painted with this negative brush-stroke?

I'll never forget how surprised I was when, in the early 1970s in one of my college journalism classes, one of the smug self-assured professors sniffed that "professional broadcasting companies would not stoop to hiring an individual with a Southern accent." Was it really possible that such discrimination – based solely upon an accent and one's heritage – was actually flying along so tolerantly and unopposed beneath the radar? Didn't Southerners speak proper English just like any other American? What exactly is the problem here?

I'll grant you there are indeed ample numbers of Southerners with heavy Southern accents who are downright obnoxious and totally intolerable. You and I both have encountered them on the highways and interstates of the South, or on Saturdays and Sundays at baseball and football games, and at neighborhood gathering spots *(Read "Memories of the 1960s and a Place Called Gus's" in this book.)*. But so what? News flash! Southerners didn't invent obnoxiousness and intolerable behavior.

Equally obnoxious and intolerable behavior can be routinely experienced at a *New York Yankees* baseball game *(I've experienced that personally)*, or in a Boston bar *(I've experienced that too)*, or right on a downtown Chicago street – assuming one survived. Southerners didn't patent the practice of being a jackass, so why are they the ones who most often are insulted and ostracized? Why are they constantly singled out for abuse, mockery, and insults?

The worst part about this discrimination (and whether one is willing to admit it or not, discrimination is the name of the game here) is that it isn't a veiled or hidden ostracization. It is an openly accepted policy – both by academia and the professional world. You speak with a Southern accent, you can pretty much forget about a career in broadcasting, no matter that a rather large portion of the nation is composed of Southerners.

So, again, what fosters this anomaly? I can't be the only Southerner to have noticed it. I know there are others of you out there who are well aware of this bias, but who apparently have just decided to accept it (or else you just have no moral backbone) and remain silent.

Are Southerners just afraid to speak out on issues such as this? Do they just not care? Have Southerners been cast in the lot of racists and inferiors for so long that they've just come to accept that role as a natural consequence of their heritage? Have we been brow-beaten into stupidity identification so long that we have come to accept it as normal? What's the deal here? Really.

By the time that my journalism professor was making his condescending statements about a Southern accent, I had already served in the United States Army for three years in a high-level security position, and had seen a bit of the world, so I pressed that professor further, to which he responded, "Americans simply don't want to hear a Southern accent. They want to hear an 'American from the heartland' who has no accent."

Really? You're going to shovel that load of warm steaming do-do over to me and expect me to sniff it? What about the millions of "Americans" in Southern states? Do you really think they're put off by a Southern accent?

And while we're at it, what about the multitudes of broadcasters and actors with the thick Boston accents, or the Californians with "Valley Girl" accents that one constantly encounters in television commercials? Or the actresses and actors with a thick Bronx accent *(Read Fran Drescher on **The Nanny**)*? I love Fran Drescher. She's probably one of the sweetest individuals in television, but I gotta tell you... She isn't even close to speaking like "an American from the heartland." Okay?? And how about the many Latino broadcasters, actors, and comedians now in "show business?" You're telling me all of those are "heartland with no accent?" Ironically, Blacks with Southern accents are totally acceptable, but not Whites. What's the story there?

Even worse, those occasional White Southerners with Southern accents who hit the lottery and gain celebrity status are nevertheless routinely harangued and constantly humiliated into submission by their colleagues. In more recent times with more Southern talent breaking through, the late Burt Reynolds, the late Kenny Rogers, Julia Roberts, Holly Hunter and Billy Bob Thornton – to name just a few – have collectively appeared on a national stage and in hundreds of movies, acting alongside a plethora of other superstars, but the first thing most all of these actual Southern actors do upon gaining "star" status is to initiate a desperate campaign at *losing* any remaining vestige of their Southern accentual identity, because they're made to feel ashamed of it. Why is that? What is fair or proper about that?

Billy Bob Thornton – a hugely-popular actor – has speech patterns now that often just sound ridiculous to me. He is so obviously ashamed of his Southern heritage that every "i" and "e" and "u" are painfully elongated in pronunciation in a desperate bid to erase even a hint of a Southern twang.

Thornton was born on August 4, 1955, in Hot Springs, Arkansas, the son of Virginia Roberta Faulkner, a self-proclaimed psychic, and William Raymond "Billy Ray" Thornton, a high school history teacher and basketball coach. Billy Bob's journey to success is a story of talent and determination, but it ironically was his Southern accent in his mesmerizing portrayal of a mentally-disabled Southerner which ultimately helped to make him a star.

Thornton's breakthrough came with the major motion picture ***Sling Blade*** (1996) which he wrote, directed, and in which he starred as "Karl Childers" who had been released from a mental hospital where he had spent the bulk of his life after murdering his mother and her lover. The film not only won Billy-Bob an *Academy Award* for *Best Adapted Screenplay* but also established him as a multi-faceted talent in Hollywood – but as what? That's right. A brain-damaged Southern murderer. And since the day he gained fame, he's been running from his Southern heritage, doing everything in his power to bury it.

As far as I'm concerned, Billy Bob Thornton is one of the greatest actors to come along in a great while. His performances are riveting, and don't get me started on one of his most recent productions – *"Land Man"* – to which I am addicted. I began watching it one night, and simply could not stop. It was five or six hours later that I realized there were other things I very badly needed to do. But please, Billy, be proud of that from whence you have come. Okay?

This shame of Southern identity is so pervasive that the school children of the South today rarely ever have Southern accents anymore. They – and quite often their parents as well – have very determinedly eliminated the accent if they have even a hint of such a "burden," because they don't want to "stand-out" among their peers and set themselves up for abuse or ridicule. To unabashedly display their heritage is simply too painful, and those students who are so-identified – particularly with a Southern accent – instantly become a target for abuse.

This abusive "shaming" which is so routinely directed at those with a Southern accent apparently is achieving its intended goal too. It now appears that in the future, a Southern accent may indeed be a thing of the past. It is literally a disappearing aspect of Southern culture. I'm told quite frequently *"Wow. You have a Southern accent. I never hear that anymore."* My grandchildren have no Southern accent whatsoever, and my son barely has one. I, nevertheless, am certain that one day, their children's children's children will mourn the loss of that cultural identity.

A few celebrities, however, have very stubbornly held on to their Southern heritage. Harry Connick, Jr., Ben Johnson, Tommy Lee Jones (to some extent), and Holly Hunter represent a few rare examples of Southerners who have risen to star status and – to their credit – nevertheless retained at least a measure of their Southern persona. But almost certainly as a result of that determination, they also are often relegated by Hollywood producers, directors and filmmakers to status as "co-stars" with other big-name co-stars, rather than as solo marquee attractions.

Even worse, as mentioned above, when Hollywood producers and directors have desired to actually portray a character with a Southern accent, do you think they routinely use an actual Southerner in that role??? Of course not... Don't be ridiculous. More often than not, they still prefer to take an actor from New England, the Mid-West – or someplace other than the American South – and ask him or her to *fake* a Southern accent that sounds so ridiculous that it often becomes the death knell for that particular motion picture.

Take for instance Val Kilmer in the hit movie *Tombstone* (1994). Val is one of my favorite actors too. For his role in this extremely-popular movie, he studied all aspects of the family and history of John Henry "Doc" Holliday. And he did a great job too... but he isn't a Southerner, and non-Southerners who are portraying a Southerner, always over-emphasize and erroneously characterize a Southern accent.

Take, for instance, Ben Kingsley's recent role in *War Inc.* (2008) starring John Cusack and Marissa Tomei. The only "criminal" in that entire motion picture is Kingsley, and how does he speak? That's right.... with a very pronounced – though nevertheless pathetic-sounding – Southern accent.

Another such production – *Two Guns* (2013) – stars Denzel Washington (another of my favorite actors) and Mark Wahlberg. It is an excellent drama, but in the villainous role it also stars Bill Paxton with what?... That's right... yet another pathetic and very obviously fake Southern accent.

Or take *The Glimmer Man* (1996) with Steven Seagal, Keenan Ivory Wayans and Brian Cox. Seagal portrays an ex-CIA operative who teams up with Wayans to bring down a corrupt CIA "handler" (Cox). Who's the only individual with a Southern accent? Why it's the corrupt CIA handler, of course, with Cox providing yet another ridiculous rendition of the accent.

Or take *Most Wanted* (1997) with Keenan Ivory Wayans, Jon Voight, Eric Roberts, Paul Sorvino and Robert Culp. Once again, one evil individual (Voight) with the poorly produced fake Southern accent.

And then there's *The Sheepman* (1958) starring Glenn Ford, Shirley MacLaine, Leslie Nielsen and Pernell Roberts which I recently caught on one of the cable channels. The outlaw "heavy" was portrayed by Pernell Roberts who of course had an obviously-affected Southern accent, and, once again, it was ridiculously faked too. Amusingly, it seemed that midway through this production, Roberts apparently realized just how ridiculous he actually sounded, because he gradually began "losing" his "fake" accent, so that by the end of the movie, he barely had a fake Southern accent at all anymore.

Watch the movie *M*A*S*H* (1970). Who's the individual portraying the "idiot" in that production? Why it's Tom Skerritt in the role of *"Duke Forrest."* And what does Tom Skerritt solely have?? Altogether now.... "yet another ridiculously-fake Southern accent."

Interestingly, in the original 1968 best-selling book by H. Richard Hornberger *(who wrote under the pen name of Richard Hooker)*, *"Duke Forrest"* was portrayed as the primary side-kick of *"Hawkeye Pierce,"* but in Director Robert Altman's movie version, Elliot Gould's *"Trapper John McIntyre"* is elevated in stature to the starring "side-kick" role, and Skerritt's *"Duke Forrest"* is reduced to a supporting role. Why was that? And what does Elliot Gould have? Altogether again now.... that's right... a very noticeable "New York" accent.

Unsurprisingly, Skerritt refused to reprise the *"Duke Forrest"* role in the television version of *M*A*S*H.* Wonder why?? Was it that by that point, he simply had grown weary and frustrated with the reduction in character from "second" to "fourth fiddle?"

Indeed, DeNiro, Nick Nolte, Clark Gable, Vivian Leigh, Robert Mitchum, and many others have faked a Southern accent at some point in their careers, and have looked and sounded ludicrous in the effort. Did *Hollywood* actually think Southerners spoke like the characters in the immortal *Gone With the Wind* (1939)? Really?? The only reason real Southerners swallowed that tripe at all was because in 1939, they were finally getting a little worldwide "semi-positive" exposure after being mired in the Civil War ashes of poverty and relegation to obscurity for 75 years.

And then you might say, "Well what about the country music stars?" Well? What about them? The fact of the matter is, they are a direct reflection of the huge acceptance of Southern mores and traditions by a huge segment of America at which *Hollywood* had turned up its collective nose for over 40 years. By the 1970s, country music stars carried so much clout that *Hollywood* producers and mass media in general simply could no longer *afford* to ignore the financial windfalls they represented. This, however, has not stopped *Hollywood* from continuing to portray many country music stars and Southerners in general as buffoons and in-bred idiots any chance it gets, nor has it stopped many country music stars from attempting to grind away their Southern accents after falling prey to the standard abusive treatment *(RE: Jim Nabors).*

This of course isn't to say that admirable roles portraying Southern characters are never cast with actual Southerners now-a-days. No. Far from it.

I'll be the first to admit that. *Steel Magnolias* (1989) is a good example. Nevertheless, I also know the score with admiration and respect when it comes to a Southern accent and Southern culture in general on the national stage. . . . and I think deep down, most other people do too.

It's so easy to simply overlook the fact that at least 11 states in our nation are considered distinctly-"Southern" states, and that's not even considering border states such as Virginia, West Virginia, Kentucky, Missouri and Florida. There are millions of "Americans" in the South who rarely see or hear a truly-positive and life-affirming reflection of their own "Southern" culture or identity on the silver screen or in broadcast media. Why have Southerners so willingly bought into this negativity toward their culture?

All the above being considered, it is truly ironic that the few examples of television programming featuring the culture of the South which have miraculously made it into a *"Prime Time"* broadcasting slot have many times been monstrous hits. *The Dukes of Hazzard* (1979-1985) was one of the most popular television sit-coms of all time, as were *Hee-Haw* (1969-1993) and *Designing Women* (1986-1993). Despite this fact, both *The Dukes* and *Hee-Haw* productions again went out of their way to portray Southerners as toothless in-bred idiots at every opportunity.

Though he was born in New York, the star of *Dukes* – John Schneider – grew up in Atlanta, Georgia, where he acquired just a tiny bit of a Southern accent, but it was barely noticeable, because he worked strenuously at controlling it.

The highly-successful *Designing Women* starred Delta Burke, born in Orlando, Florida; Jean Smart, born in Seattle, Washington; Dixie Carter, born in McLemoresville, Tennessee; Annie Potts, born in Nashville, Tennessee; and Meshach Taylor, born in Boston, Massachusetts. Both *Designing Women* and the later *Evening Shade* (1990-1994) were written and produced by Linda Bloodworth-Thomason, a native of Poplar Bluff, Missouri, who let her Southern roots shine in both productions and who, thankfully, was adamantly averse to a negative portrayal of the South and/or its culture. Linda, sadly, is/was a rarity. Burke, Dixie Carter and Annie Potts all three unabashedly freely conversed in their unrestrained natural Southern accents in the portrayal of their characters, much to the delight of their "Southern" viewing audience, and they all three portrayed (and were) very astute, attractive Southern ladies too.

Evening Shade, set in Arkansas, starred Burt Reynolds, Marilu Henner,

Hal Holbrook, Michael Jeter, Charles Durning, Ossie Davis, and Elizabeth Ashley. It also presented a positive portrayal of the South and Southern culture, but it nevertheless again required the determined Southern-born Bloodworth-Thomason to achieve such an admirable presentation.

I remember years ago, watching Robert Klein as he was being interviewed by the always self-infatuated Bob Costas as the two of them viciously mocked the late South Carolina Senator Strom Thurmond. Now I was never a Strom Thurmond fan by any stretch of the imagination. God knows he was an anachronistic dinosaur that desperately needed to slip quietly into extinction via the LaBrea tar pits long before his time, but Costas and Klein were brutal in mocking Thurmond's *Southern accent* as much as him personally. I couldn't help marveling that what they were doing was the purest form of bigotry that one could imagine, and they didn't even seem to realize it – or if they did, they just simply didn't care. It, sadly, has become solidly mainstream and acceptable to taunt, ridicule and demean Southern culture.

Compounding the problem today are native Southerners like Jeff Foxworthy who whole-heartedly gladly self-flagellate. I like Jeff. He hails from a town – Marietta, Georgia – that I have often called "home," and he was even a member of a church to which I once belonged. I think he's probably one of the most talented comedians to come along in many years. He's a native of Georgia who reached the big-time and, to his credit, never felt compelled to lose his Southern accent. In the process, however, he nevertheless *has* felt compelled to earn millions by making Southerners look like simple backwoods idiots.

Foxworthy is so talented that he ultimately attracted a huge following, ringing up the "cha-ching" dollar signs in *Hollywood's* eyes until they simply could no longer ignore him either – thick Southern accent or not. They gave him a rare opportunity for a network television situation comedy [*The Jeff Foxworthy Show* (1995-1997)] which once again made Hollywood producers gazillions and him even more famous and wealthy.

Maybe you feel it's funnier to make Southerners look stupid, Jeff, but pleeeeeeeaaaasssee . . . . find a way to add a little intelligence and dignity to the mix, or at least poke equal fun at all regions of the United States. Okay? Millions of people will thank you.

One of the few celebrities who was a bright shining light of inspiration to Southerners everywhere unfortunately disappeared from the scene far too quickly, succumbing as a young man to heart failure in 1994. The late Lewis

Grizzard knew exactly how to poke fun AT ALL CULTURES – Southerners included – while reserving a full measure of dignity for the South in the
process. He also took his very pronounced Southern accent with him everywhere he went – even into the studios of *Hollywood* – making no apology
for it anywhere. He was proud of it, stating often that "*God* speaks with a
Southern accent."

Lewis was an exceptionally-talented, award-winning, nationally-syn-
dicated newspaper columnist with the **Atlanta Constitution**, a **New York
Times** "Best-Selling" author with a string of popular books, and a Southern
humorist who appeared throughout the United States, including in *Hollywood* several times on **The Tonight Show** starring the immortal *Johnny
Carson*.

I spoke with Lewis a few years prior to his death. He mimicked the
words from one of his books as he wrote in mine: *"Don't ever let the facts get
in the way of a good story."* I still have that book, and I treasure it. It occupies
a permanent position of respect and prominence on a vanity bookshelf in my
home today.

I can't help but believe that Lewis often looks down from his heavenly
typewriter desk today, smiling broadly in that "knowing" sort of way that he
made so famous, and wishing he had just one more chance to give "the finger"
to some earth-bound sassy journalism professor critical of a Southern accent.
Sic 'em Lewis.

—•⁊⁊ ⁊⁊•—

After All That We've
Been Through

L ooking back over the years, there has been a plethora of good times, bad times, laughter, tears, agony and ecstasy in my family. It just seems like the day-to-day life in my family has leaned a little bit more to the "tears" and "agony" side, than to the "laughter" and "ecstasy" side.

I don't know why this is. Some families just experience more than their share of this type of thing. Some families bring it upon themselves; some others are just fated in that direction.

I can honestly say that I have only scratched the surface on the ill sides of and bad experiences in my family too. There are many, many things which I have chosen not to relate in detail.

- My grandfather Jordan, the chief chemist at Southern States Portland Cement Company in Rockmart, was tragically killed in 1946, when he was accidentally dragged into heavy machinery where his life was instantly snuffed out.
- Several cousins, nephews, an aunt, and a sister all committed suicide. Both my aunt and my cousin hung themselves – my aunt from the limb of a tree in her front yard in Cartersville, Georgia and my first cousin from the rafters of a barn.
- Both my father and mother were alcoholics during the formative years of my brothers and sisters. My father eventually obtained professional treatment and recovered to go on to a reasonably auspicious career late in life – but not before almost burning down our home and engaging in a number of other very traumatic incidents.

For reasons unknown today, the year 1980 was a particularly devastating year for our family:

- My first wife abandoned me in January of that year, leaving me with a mountain of debt and relocating to Louisiana with my three-year-old son, removing any chance for me to see him without a 9-hour, 600+ mile drive. I therefore was only able to see him for a couple of weeks each summer. I loved him dearly (and still do) but, due to Plaintiff's very distant residences, I was not able to raise or protect him during his formative years.
- My brother Guy, after being charged and convicted of what amounted to nothing more than a simple prank in 1975 had his life ruined forever by a vindictive individual. In 1980, Guy subsequently died after being poisoned by a presumed tainted recreational drug. He was only 23.
- My sister, Mary, after being viciously beaten and robbed in 1972, was later beaten and abandoned by her husband while on vacation in Rome, Italy in 1980. That same year, she was divorced from that individual who shortly committed suicide via a gunshot wound to the head. In 2014, after being diagnosed with the deadly disease MSA, Mary opted to commit suicide rather than face the ravages of this disease.
- Other than my brother, Guy, two of my nephews in my immediate family sadly and tragically died from drug poisoning/overdoses at a very youthful age.

As stated, the incidents above represent only a portion of the tragic events faced by my family over the years, but lest you be misled, a lot of good things also occurred. Following years of heart-break and disappointment, we eventually began to see a light at the end of the tunnel. Even better, this time, it wasn't an onrushing train.

My surviving brother, after returning from service as a military policeman in the *United States Army*, took advantage of the *GI Bill* and earned a *Bachelor of Science* degree in biology from *West Georgia College*. He subsequently gained employment with the *Georgia Department of Natural Resources (DNR)*. Capitalizing upon his training in the *Army*, David earned a position within the law enforcement branch of *DNR*, rising to the top non-politically-appointed rank of Wildlife Technician IV and enjoying a distinguished career. His sometimes dangerous work required that he receive the same training as the top law enforcement units in the state. He later was featured in several major articles in the statewide *Atlanta Constitution* regarding *DNR* and the progress it was making with the state's wildlife resources. Today, after raising a son and a daughter, he is retired and lives in a fine home with his wife on an estate of well over 100 acres.

My surviving sister, following graduation from *Emory University* in Atlanta, entered the world of real estate sales. She ultimately became so successful that she was named to the *"Million Dollar Club."* She also had the good fortune and taste to marry well, her husband being an honor graduate of the *University of Georgia* where he earned a degree in *Journalism*, and *Georgia State University* in Atlanta where he earned a graduate degree in *Public Administration*. He subsequently rose to the top echelons of Georgia state government, being appointed a Division Director in the *Georgia State Merit System*, where he worked closely with the *Georgia State Legislature*. He also has been a bulwark of unfailing support within our family during all the hard times.

Even my father eventually was graced with good fortune by the good Lord. He somehow attained not just an average law degree, but a *Juris Doctorate* degree surprisingly enough. After retiring from a position with the *U.S. Department of Agriculture* in Atlanta, he moved to northeast Georgia's Forsyth County where he subsequently was appointed to a judgeship in that municipality, being re-elected twice to the bench, and gaining the respect in the legal world he had so coveted in his youth before retiring from this second profession after a distinguished twelve-year career.

And as for me, I've done okay too. In my second nuptials (which I finally got right), I married an angel.

Living a Whole Life

Connecting Body, Mind, and Spirit

Dr. Peter Patterson

Cheval Press

COPYRIGHT © 2025 PETER PATTERSON
All rights reserved.
Sun City West, Arizona

LIVING A WHOLE LIFE
Connecting Body, Mind, and Spirit
First Edition

ISBN   979-8-9904276-4-8   *Hardcover*
       979-8-9904276-5-5   *Paperback*
       979-8-9904276-6-2   *eBook*
       979-8-9904276-7-9   *Audiobook*

LCCN   2025900876

This book is dedicated to the late Evan Oswald, who taught me so much about living a joyful, intentional, and wholly interconnected life.

It's also dedicated to every single person on their journey to becoming a community elder. We can all learn so much from you about what it means to age well and to accept loss with grace.

Contents

Foreword

Reading Dr. Pete Patterson's book filled my heart with joy and put a smile on my face. In this work, he shares his inspirations and insights with you, the reader, drawing from his rich experience as a medical doctor. His intention is to enrich your life, making it more fulfilling, inspiring, and joyful. It is truly a gift of wisdom and encouragement.

Many in the medical field excel in treating the body but often overlook the critical aspects of mind and spirit. However, these elements are just as vital for our overall health and life satisfaction.

This book offers a straightforward approach to integrating the three essential components of holistic living: body, mind, and spirit. Life can sometimes feel overwhelming, but the fundamental truths are timeless and simple. It's easy to be misled by "quick fixes" and "expert advice" that promise wholeness. Instead, the enduring principles that Dr. Pete presents have stood the test of time and, while they require effort, they genuinely work!

Read the book, choose a starting point that resonates with you, and begin practicing. Like any skill, practice fosters strength and empowerment.

It has been a pleasure to collaborate with Dr. Patterson over the years. His sincerity and dedication to the wisdom he shares are genuine. I hope you find great value in his insights.

—**DR. GAIL CANTOR**
Director of Belonging and Spiritual Life, Endicott College

Introduction

I've been a doctor for more than fifty years. In that time, I've seen hundreds of patients and served as a consultant for a diverse array of businesses within the health care space. And yet, despite all the advances we've made in medication and medical technology (and there have been many), almost every single day—even now, decades later—I am reminded of a simple yet profound statement my father used to make: "When you get the human spirit lined up behind healing and recovery, good things happen."

Unfortunately, the opposite is also true. When a physician (or anyone in a position of influence, for that matter) says something discouraging or negative during someone's recovery, it can halt progress in its tracks.

Even though I first heard my father make this statement nearly seventy years ago, it's only within the last decade or so that science has started to understand and accept this simple truth. Luckily, though, it *has* gotten on board: many experts are beginning to understand that healing is about more than just attending to the physical. There are numerous studies exploring and supporting the idea that mindset is crucial for healing too.

Those studies are accurate, but they miss out on something even more important: the role that spirit plays in health. The power of the human spirit is immense, and yet people often underestimate it. The power of spirit, not just the human spirit but something bigger, is what connects us all. Unfortunately, the awareness and understanding of this connection is missing in the world today, especially in Western cultures where we have become so captivated by the power of science. Many people are enamored with evidence-based medicine, as if that's the whole story and the final or best version of the truth. But it's not the whole story. The realm of spirit encompasses everything. It's how we connect with each other and with the world around us.

The threefold model of understanding ourselves—the model of body, mind, and spirit, in other words—isn't something new. It's part of the design of the human experience that has been with us from the beginning. However, it's often presented as though these are three separate entities, when in fact, they are deeply interconnected. We'll explore each of these aspects of ourselves in depth in this book, but I want to emphasize, first and foremost, that *the spirit is the gateway to understanding the whole human and, as such, it is the key to true well-being.* Once you see and understand this, things that once seemed mysterious or beyond comprehension will begin to open up.

The problem is, people often try to approach spirit through the intellect. Indeed, we live in a world where intellect and rational thinking are highly valued, and so people think they can reach the spirit through their mind, by analyzing and understanding it logically. But that's where they get stuck.

In reality, we can't *think* our way to spirit. It's not something that can be explained or described purely through intellectual means. To truly connect with the spirit and achieve the kind of well-being that we are all capable of, we need to move beyond just the mind, or just the body, and embrace body/mind/spirit in their entirety. That's what I want to help you do. In this book, I want to provide you with a framework for seeing and connecting with the spirit, and therefore your own well-being, in ways you may have never considered before.

Before we go any further, I want to be crystal clear: When I talk about spirit, I am not talking about religion, and certainly not organized religion. I am talking about spirituality in its purest form, separate from any specific religious system.

That said, spirit can absolutely include religion. Christians can access the flow of spirit. So can agnostics and atheists. Buddhists can too—and so can Muslims, Jews, Hindus, pagans, and followers of every other type of religion, organized or not. That's the beauty of this: Spirit and the flow of spirit is accessible to *everyone*, no matter what you believe or where you come from.

Whatever traditions you follow, I'll tell you right now—spirit can't be forced or controlled. You can only open yourself to it and let it move through you. You can only allow yourself to experience it. But when you learn how to do that, you will have the key to unlock true and complete well-being.

Spirituality and the Whole Person

So how did I come to the understanding that spirit is just as important to well-being as body and mind? After all, my view is quite different from most people in the health care field, especially doctors. Well, to answer that question, we have to go back to 2016. That's when I got the opportunity to design the curriculum for a program at the Glencroft Center for Modern Aging (also known as Glencroft Senior Living, or just Glencroft).[1] They were starting a program focused on the total health of their residents, and they brought me on board to provide an outside expert perspective on the subject.

What I discovered while creating that curriculum laid the groundwork for much of what I'll be writing about in this book. I worked alongside a dear friend of mine, Reverend Doctor Gail Cantor, who played a significant role in helping me come to my understanding of the significance of spirit *and* the interconnectedness of body, mind, and spirit. Gail started out doing communications work for corporations years ago, but her own spiritual awakening led her to become an ordained interfaith minister. She's now the Director of Belonging and Spiritual Life at Endicott College in Massachusetts—a role I find incredibly inspiring.

Gail helped me design the curriculum I delivered at Glencroft. She's now focused on other endeavors, so I'm

---

1   https://www.glencroft.com.

carrying this message forward. But we still keep in touch, and she's been an ongoing source of wisdom and support throughout this journey.

This book, in many ways, is the continuation of that work—a guide for understanding spirituality in a way that is accessible, meaningful, and relevant to everyone, regardless of religious background. My goal is to help people connect with the spirit, the true essence that ties us all together, and to do so without the boundaries or limitations often imposed by traditional religion. That's what makes this work so important today.

But returning to that original question: What made me open to these concepts in the first place? After all, many doctors wouldn't even consider this type of thinking. The importance of "spirit" just never enters into the picture for them.

Honestly, I think it's in my blood. My father was a physician, as was my grandfather. Medicine has always been in my genes, but what truly shaped me was how my father interacted with people. Listening to him, observing his approach, and seeing how he connected with patients on a deeper level—that's where this openness to something more than traditional medicine started for me.

I could see that, for my father, it was about more than just treating the body. He wanted to understand the person as a whole, connect with their spirit, and guide them through their own healing journey. That's the foundation for everything I've learned and continue to share.

Don't get me wrong...when it comes to health, the body and mind are vitally important too. In fact, to be truly healthy, every part of us must be in harmony and supported. Focus solely on the body, and your health will suffer. Focus solely on the mind or the spirit, and your health will suffer too. As I learned from my father, you need to attend to *all* of it.

I remember being thirteen or fourteen years old, sitting just around the corner while my father spoke by phone with his patients. Even though I could only hear his side of the conversation, the way he interacted with them was powerful and unmistakable. It was clear that he wasn't just a doctor treating symptoms—he was truly connecting with people. By taking the time to focus on the whole person, he made a profound difference in a lot of people's lives, even though it wasn't always immediately apparent how big that impact was. That didn't bother him, though. He used to say to me, "You never know how much good you're doing," and as I've grown and practiced medicine myself, I've found that to be incredibly true.

My father influenced me in other ways too. Career-wise, I took one of the few pieces of direct advice my father gave me, which was to start with general practice before diving into any specialization. Through that experience, I came to understand my father in a more profound way. There's something intangible that happens between a doctor and a patient, something you can't always point to or explain. It's not always about the medicine or the treatment plan—often, it's about the connection. That is something my father understood instinctively and intrinsically.

That is why I've always been open to the idea that there's something more at play—something beyond the physical realm. My father never explicitly said so, but I sensed it. Now, to be fair, my father was a devout Roman Catholic, and like many people, he had a view of the spirit that was intertwined with his religious beliefs. As a result, I'm not sure he was fully open to the broader idea of spirit that I've come to understand over time—the one that sees spirit as encompassing but not constrained by religion. But he certainly laid the seeds of understanding in me. I just took the lessons I learned from him and further developed them.

Throughout the book, I hope to help you open up to that deeper spirit, and to share some practices you can use to keep your spirit, mind, and body whole and healthy. Yes, doing so takes effort and discipline, but trust me—it is well worth it.

Let's begin the journey.

ONE

The Whole Person

"
Health is a state of complete harmony of the body, mind, and spirit.
"

—B.K.S. IYENGAR

OVER THE COURSE OF MY LIFE, OUR UNDERSTANDING of how to achieve health and well-being[2] has drastically improved. Back in the 1960s, for example, physical fitness wasn't as emphasized as it is today. There were essentially two groups who were committed to fitness: joggers and bodybuilders. They represented two extremes on the fitness spectrum. But over time, society came to realize that moving your body and staying physically active is essential to living a healthy life. Today, it is common knowledge that staying active is foundational for well-being. Everyone needs to practice some kind of regular exercise in whatever way they are able to do so. In other words, physical fitness isn't just for the joggers and bodybuilders, or for a certain age group or gender. It's for every human.

Of course, as I mentioned in the introduction, I believe that well-being is about more than just physical fitness; it's about the mind and spirit too. In the same way that we've collectively embraced physical fitness, we need to recognize the importance of training our minds and spirits.

---

2   I deliberately use the term "well-being" rather than "wellness" throughout the book. That's because I want you to remember that we are talking about an entire state of being for your body, mind, and spirit. It's much bigger than simple wellness.

If you ask most people today how to achieve well-being, they will point to two things: 1) moving the body to stay fit and 2) fueling the body with proper nutrition. Those are both good starts, but they overlook a critical component: *learning to change your mental and emotional state.* So many people are missing that third piece—the ability to manage and adjust both their mental condition and their spirit.

Being able to consciously shift your mental and emotional state from negative to positive is just as important as keeping your body in shape. That means consciously moving yourself from the dark side to the light, from stress and overwhelm to clarity and well-being. Just like physical exercise, this requires practice and attention.

All of this is to say that the real journey to well-being involves integrating all three domains—body, mind, and spirit—because they are all interconnected. It might seem surprising to hear a doctor say this, but it's true. We've come a long way in understanding the importance of the body, and now it's time to fully embrace the role that the mind and spirit play in our overall well-being.

Sadly, most people don't even realize that they can change their mental and emotional state, let alone understand how to do it. They believe they are at the mercy of their thoughts and feelings. But they aren't—and if they want to experience true well-being, they must learn to accept this truth. As the Roman poet Horace put it, "Rule your mind or it will rule you." Or as Reverend Gail once said to me, "The mind is a great servant, but it's a heartless taskmaster."

There are some people, especially high performers, who have figured this out instinctively. I saw some great examples of this during the 2024 Paris Olympics. Before her final balance beam routine, US gymnast Suni Lee said she felt exhausted from the relentless days of competition. However, she was seen on camera just before her routine giving herself a pep talk as a way to self-motivate to push through the fatigue and put on a gorgeous performance. Gymnast Jordan Chiles did something similar during her floor routine. Both of these high-performing athletes—and dozens more like them—have learned how to change their own state rather than allowing their thoughts and feelings to dominate them.

This kind of mental and emotional agility doesn't come naturally. Again, it requires training. And while most of us won't master it right away, learning to move from a place of negativity to a place of calm and clarity is a skill worth cultivating.

In my own life, I've had moments where I felt trapped in what I call "the alarm ringing"—that internal, frantic state where everything feels dark and overwhelming. In the past, I would often sit in that discomfort for days before it hit me that something needed to shift. Now, I can move through that phase and shift my state much more quickly. But that's how it begins for many people, with an awareness that something in their life needs to change—even if they don't yet know how to change it.

Out of the Blue

On the other hand, many people miss the ringing of the alarms. They don't even realize something needs to change! They live in the chaos, headed for a crash that they don't even know is coming.

Medical providers see this all the time. Case in point: I managed an ICU for a number of years during my medical practice. When a patient would come in after a heart attack, they would often say things like, "Doc, I don't have time for this heart attack! It came out of nowhere! I was just living my life, and then, out of the clear blue sky, *bam!* Heart attack! And now here I am."

I would respond, "Hmm...so, do you smoke?"

The answer was often something like, "Yeah, about a pack and a half a day."

Then I'd ask, "Do you exercise?"

They'd typically reply, "No, not really."

Every question I asked, whether it was about what they ate or whether they drank, would reveal that the warning signs were there. Those alarms were blaring, but they were too disconnected from their body, mind, and spirit to hear them.

This became almost a running joke. Whenever I would ask these questions, especially the one about exercise, I'd get the same response. And not only that: When the question of exercise in particular came up, they would suddenly become timid and passive, as if even talking about working out was exhausting. But here's the thing—heart attacks (along with so many other diseases and health crises) don't just happen out of nowhere. They're usually the result of years of poor habits: smoking, drinking, a bad diet, and a sedentary lifestyle. Yet so many people live that way and then are surprised when their body gives out. They'll say, "I don't understand. I was just going about my business when this heart attack struck me down," without recognizing the years of neglect that led them to that moment.

The same holds true for the mind and spirit. The truth is, calamity almost never comes out of the blue. Whether it's our physical health, our mental state, or our emotional

well-being, everything is connected. And by paying attention to how we move, fuel, and manage our bodies, minds,
and spirits, we can shift the trajectory of our lives. The tools
are available to us, but we have to be willing to use them.

Pause and Reflect

People often live their lives on autopilot without pausing
to examine whether they're headed in the right direction.
This lack of self-reflection is one of the great tragedies of
human existence—the unexamined life. Too many of us go
through the motions, never stopping to ask the important
questions: *Am I moving in the right direction? What am I not
hearing or paying attention to? What do I need to change, and
who can help me do it?*

For those who are tuned in to the idea of self-examina-
tion, these are powerful questions. Personally, I've developed a practice that helps me reflect and reset at the end
of each year. It's something I've been doing for about a
decade now. At the close of each year, I sit down with my
good friend Reverend Gail, and we debrief. With her guidance, I reflect on what I accomplished and what I didn't,
what projects I started but didn't finish, and even what I
abandoned because it just wasn't going to work out.

If you want to include this practice in your own life, I suggest starting with the following questions. Give yourself time and space to journal on these questions, and see what comes up.

- How was [current year]?
  - What improved from the prior year, or over the course of the current year?
  - What became more apparent as an issue that needs to be addressed?
  - What thrilled you about [current year]?
  - What disappointed you about [current year]?

- What is your intention or hope for [upcoming year]?
  - What do you want to improve?
  - What issue(s) do you want to address?
  - What goals and intentions do you have?

- Energy imbalances in life show up as confusion, recurring issues, settling for going along with something, a chattering mind, fear, and/or hesitation. What do you think may be out of balance? In what way?

- What else is on your mind as the current year ends and the new year approaches?

Even though it's helpful to go through this practice at the end of each year, this process isn't about making traditional New Year's resolutions. It's much deeper than that. It's about creating the new year with intention, focusing on meaningful goals and themes that resonate beyond just temporary fixes or superficial resolutions. For me, this has been an invaluable practice that has helped me to consistently examine my life and make adjustments where needed.

I'm a note-taker by nature, so I keep detailed records of these debriefs every year. I jot down everything that Gail and I discuss, and I also record our calls to ensure that I capture the important insights that come from these conversations. Usually, a clear theme or goal for the upcoming year emerges from our discussions. It's never very specific or highly detailed—just the core ideas, the meat of what needs to be focused on. And each year, I use those notes to keep myself accountable and aligned with my intentions.

For example, one year I realized that my life had improved in terms of my work. However, I knew that I needed to spend more time focusing on developing my spiritual strength. I also realized that I wanted to become "more of myself"—more authentically me—in all domains of life. Yes, I had some specific goals within those overarching points, but by doing this exercise, I had a larger purpose for the next year—one that would let me develop into someone whose well-being was holistic. Or, as I like to say because it captures the essence of what I'm talking about far more effectively: "*wholistic.*"

While you might not adopt this same exact approach, I want to invite you to regularly pause, take a step back, and reflect on what's working, what isn't, and what you want to improve. This is a great way to continuously and regularly examine your life, identify areas that need attention, and seek out the right people to help guide you through those changes.

I am fully convinced that regularly examining the mind, body, and spirit as a whole is essential to living a fulfilled life. Yes, you need to move your body and eat well in order to stay healthy (we'll talk more about both of these things later), but just as importantly, you need to embrace the practice of intentional self-reflection in order to support the mind and spirit and create a *wholistic* approach to living a healthier, more purposeful life.

Let the words you're reading right now be the catalyst for you to begin this process and start making the deep changes you need to make for your whole self!

Your First Step

At this point, you know that when I talk about *true* well-being, I believe it's essential to consider *the whole person*: body, mind, and spirit. Well-being isn't just about physical health; it encompasses all aspects of who you are. That means you need to give plenty of attention to your mental and emotional state as well as your spiritual growth.

I often think of well-being like a diamond. You have to examine it from different facets because each facet offers a unique perspective that ultimately reveals the brilliance at its core. In the same way, you need to look at your health and happiness—or, more accurately, your joyfulness—from multiple angles to truly understand and nurture yourself.

There's so much more to life than the physical realm we see. We are developing the technology to go to the stars—and might even one day move beyond our galaxy—but I believe that before we confront the infinite, we must first learn to connect with ourselves and the spirit that flows through everything.

Awakening to the power of the human spirit is the first step toward healing the whole self, and from there, you can connect to something greater than yourself. Many cultures native to North America referred to this "something" as the Great Spirit. But whatever you call it, it ultimately comes down to a profound realization that spirit drives everything we do—how we live, how we connect with others, and how we navigate life.

That's where joy comes in—and it is not just a feeling, but a manifestation of that connection to spirit. It's where compassion comes in too, as well as intentionality. As you'll see in later chapters, all of these things link the body, mind, and spirit in a way that is at once simple and profound. That said, I do want to make it clear that although body, mind, and spirit are all interconnected, we're going to deal with them individually in order to help you understand how each plays a role in your experience of well-being.

The beautiful thing about this journey is that it's never too early or too late to start. Whether you're young and just beginning to explore what well-being means to you, or you're further along in life and looking for renewal, there's always an opportunity to grow and evolve into the best version of yourself. Ease yourself into a better, healthier life, find balance, and do it in a way that works for you.

Start viewing yourself from different facets, like that diamond, to fully appreciate the whole in order to achieve your full potential as a human being. Then you can begin to live a full, active, and purposeful life that is rooted in whole-person health—body, mind, and spirit. Fully integrated.

Bear in mind, I'm not giving you an explicit roadmap that you have to follow. There are no requirements or demands here. Everyone's journey is unique. Rather, I'm here to guide your thinking, show you facets of the diamond, and invite you to look deeper. Ultimately, whole-person health is about recognizing that we all face challenges to body, mind, and spirit, but we don't have to let them overrun our best thoughts and intentions.

My hope is that I can help awaken you to your connection to something greater, something beyond yourself, and in doing so, you will discover your innermost essence. Can you imagine if we could all come together in a meaningful way and honor what an extraordinary creation the human being is at every stage of life? Once you've embraced body–mind–spirit in the way I describe in this book, you'll be well on your way to doing just that.

Connecting Eternal Truths

In this threefold model of the human being, I often talk about the body, mind, and spirit working together as one integrated whole, but it's important to remember that this is just a model. It's not a dogma or an absolute truth. Instead, it is a framework I use because it can help people see how these elements interact. Your body, mind, and spirit are not separate parts. I merely distinguish them so we can better understand how they work together.

I also want to remind you before we go any further that this whole-person perspective isn't new. It is actually ancient wisdom, found in cultures all over the world. My goal is to bring it to a deeper level of awareness in today's Western context.

Let me share a personal story that grounds where I'm coming from. As I said, my father was a physician, and as is often the case, I also became a physician because of his influence. He used to say something that stuck with me: "A good surgeon who knows what to say and how to say it on the first post-op day can take ten days off a patient's recovery."

Is what he said scientifically true? Maybe. Maybe not. Honestly, that doesn't really matter. What does matter is the meaning behind what he was saying, and that is absolutely valid: Words—both which ones are chosen and how they're delivered—can significantly improve healing. Conversely, saying something careless or offhanded during a patient's recovery can halt progress and even cause complications. My father knew this from years of experience.

He saw it over and over again in his own patients. And I've experienced the same thing in my own practice.

This story reflects not just my father's philosophy but also the depth of responsibility I feel in the work I do. My goal is always to utilize my years of experience and dedication in connecting eternal truths with the realities we face every day.

Please know, as we continue through the book, that I recognize it's sometimes a struggle to make ancient wisdom relevant to our modern lives, especially when our minds are constantly buzzing with chatter. However, sometimes all you really need to do is pause, take a deep breath, and try to be discerning about your thoughts. That is often the most powerful way of balancing body, mind, and spirit.

So, with that in mind, let's talk about each of these facets of ourselves, and then examine their connection to joy, compassion, and intentionality.

Practices for the Whole (Wholistic) Self

On a regular basis, sit down and debrief on
how you're doing. Ask yourself these important
questions: "What's working? What isn't working?
What do I need to pay attention to? What do I
want to improve? Who will help me do it?"

Remember that while the body, mind, and spirit are
interconnected, breaking them down into separate parts
is often a good way to start to develop true well-being.

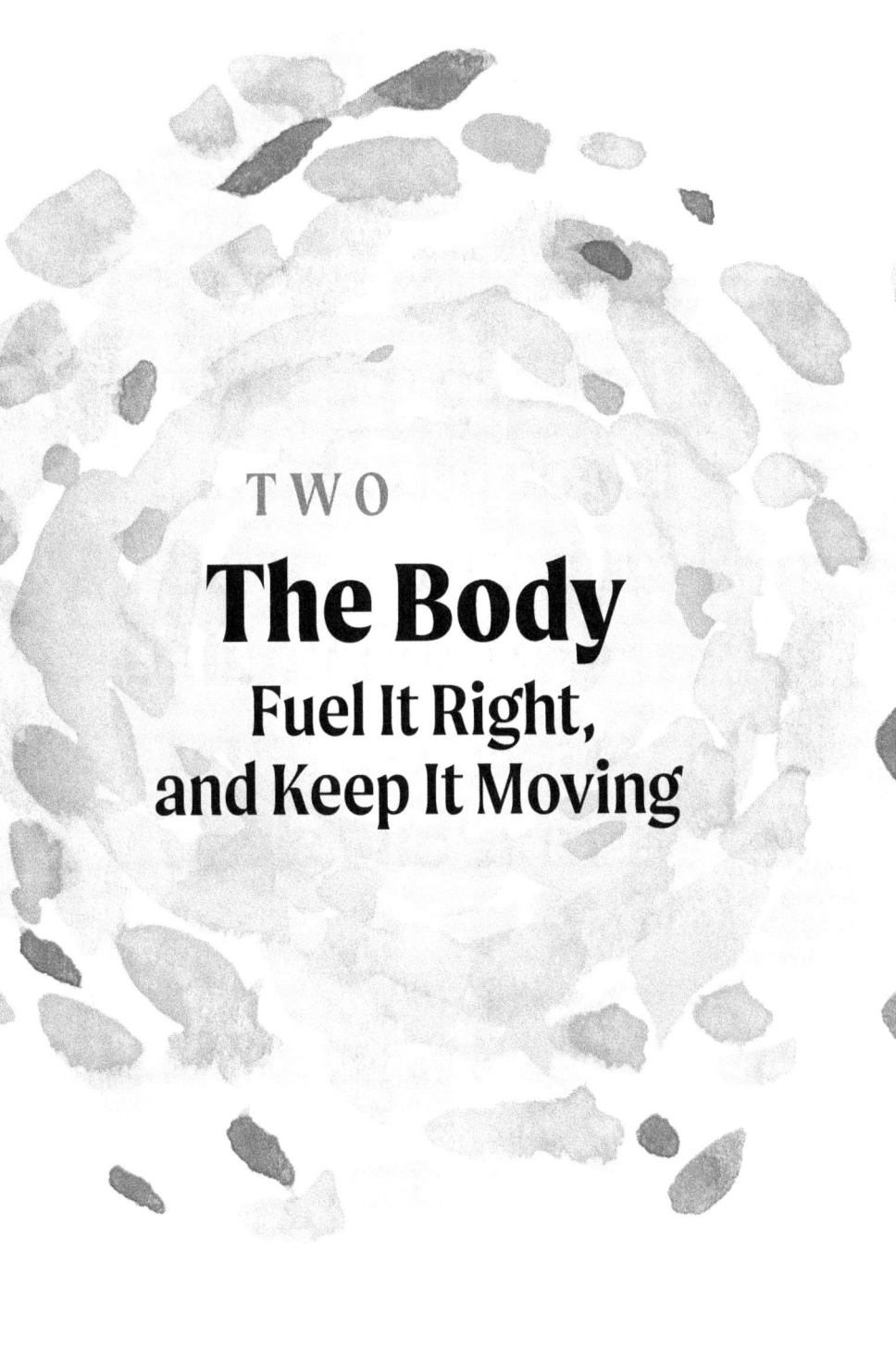

TWO

The Body
Fuel It Right, and Keep It Moving

"

To keep the body in good health is a duty...otherwise we shall not be able to keep our mind strong and clear.

"

—BUDDHA

L ET'S BEGIN OUR JOURNEY INTO *WHOLISTIC* WELL-
being in an unlikely place—the physical. Because
most people are already at least passingly familiar
with the importance of keeping the body healthy (at least
in theory!), I find it's often a good jumping-off point to talk
about well-being.

The first thing to keep in mind is that exercise is crucial to maintaining a healthy body. There's no need to over-
complicate this—when it comes to exercise and healthy
living, particularly for older adults, I always start with one
essential point: *Any exercise is good exercise.* Whether you're
taking regular short walks or following a structured workout plan, *movement* is key.

Sometimes, staying motivated can be tricky. I know
some people who go on walks with friends because they
find that the social aspect makes sticking to the exercise
part easier. If that works for you, great! If not, you'll have
to get creative with your motivation. One lady I know
pays herself for each hour of exercise she completes in a
day. She puts that money in a special high-yield savings
account and uses it to treat herself to a nice meal or a nice
outfit once she's accumulated enough to do so. I think
that's a pretty clever way to prioritize exercising, but
you can also keep it as simple as finding an activity you

inherently enjoy so that you stay committed, or scheduling exercise times in your calendar and treating it like any other appointment.

If your goal is only to get your body moving regularly, any of these techniques can work. However, if you want to take things a step further, an organized program that engages all of your muscles is ideal.

One lady I know pays herself for each hour of exercise she completes in a day. She puts that money in a special high-yield savings account and uses it to treat herself to a nice meal or a nice outfit once she's accumulated enough to do so.

For example, my fitness routine each week involves alternating between two different upper body workouts, which are split into two different sessions (upper one and upper two). I also regularly engage in a lower body workout, and I do cardio on the non-strength training days. Why do I have two upper body days every week? Well, as my coach Jim explained to me, we have twice as many muscles in the upper body compared to the lower body, so it makes sense to divide the upper body exercises into two different days. That way, every muscle group gets attention without overloading the body.

As an added bonus, working out under the watchful eye of my trainer keeps me accountable. Coach Jim and I have a standing appointment; knowing that I'm paying for his time and that he's waiting for me means I show up, even on days when I really don't feel like it.

Now, I don't prescribe specific routines for everyone, so I'm not saying you should adopt my workout schedule. However, I encourage you to find an exercise approach that works for you—whether that means going to the gym, following a home workout plan, or going for a walk. This morning, for example, wasn't a gym day for me, so I took a walk around the block. I time my walks to see how far I can go in six minutes. Why six minutes? Because it's the gold standard to determine aerobic capacity and endurance. Plus, even though it might not sound like it, six minutes is a long time to walk, especially if you're moving as quickly as possible. It gets your heart rate up, your blood pumping, and your circulation moving, all of which are good for whole-body health.

This morning, for example, wasn't a gym day for me, so I took a walk around the block. I time my walks to see how far I can go in six minutes. Why six minutes? Because it's the gold standard to determine aerobic capacity and endurance. Plus, even though it might not sound like it, six minutes is a long time to walk, especially if you're moving as quickly as possible.

You can easily incorporate six-minute walks into whatever exercise routine you decide to follow too. If you need to slow down or even stop completely to rest, feel free to do so. Incorporate these walks a couple of times per week, and over time, see if you can increase the distance you're able to go. It sounds simple, but exercises like this can make a big difference, especially for people with heart conditions or mobility challenges.

Speaking of heart conditions, I've had my own experience managing heart failure. Back in 2006, I was diagnosed with left ventricle dysfunction. My ejection fraction (EF), which measures the heart's ability to pump blood, dropped to 35 percent, but with the help of medication, it's now back up to 55 percent. At one point, it was even as high as 60 percent, which is considered excellent for someone with my history. In general, medication and the exercise routine I've described to you have allowed me to manage my condition well.

However, about a year ago, I was at the gym for one of my regular workouts. A few minutes into my warmup, I started feeling short of breath. I already had an appointment scheduled with my cardiologist for the next day, so I decided to wait to talk to him about it. At my appointment, the cardiologist measured my BNP, which is the biochemical test for left ventricle function. My results came back in the hundreds, which indicated acute systolic failure. However, it was only one episode; while we've continued to monitor my heart health closely, with the help of exercise, medication, and changing my state (more about how to do that later), I continue to remain active and enjoy good health.

In case you're curious, here's how heart failure affects the body: Normally, your heart is shaped somewhat like a football with one end cut off, but as heart failure progresses, it can start to resemble a basketball—rounder and less efficient at pumping blood. When combined with regular exercise, the medications I take have been nothing short of miraculous, helping to "remodel" my heart, bringing it back from that basketball shape to something closer to a football again. I'm lucky; this type of medication has only been available for about twenty-five years, which is relatively recent in the world of heart failure treatment.

I owe a lot of my recovery to a great cardiologist in Kansas City, who first discovered my condition during a routine insurance medical check. The EKG showed a right bundle branch block, which is a disruption in the electrical pathways of the heart. Initially, I didn't think it was a big deal, but after a scan, we discovered my low EF. It was a shock, but it's worth mentioning again that with the right medical treatment and exercise, I've been able to manage my condition and recover my well-being—and this can be the case with many other chronic health conditions as well.

I share this story because I want you to understand that I am living the reality I stated at the beginning of this chapter. Regular exercise, no matter how simple, is vital for maintaining health, especially as we age. And for those dealing with medical conditions like heart failure, staying active and following the right treatment plan can make all the difference. Ultimately, by incorporating movement, proper diet, and monitoring your health, you can improve your quality of life, even in the face of significant challenges.

So whether you're starting with a walk around the block or thinking about a more structured program, remember that it's never too late to begin. Small steps lead to big improvements, and your body will thank you for taking care of yourself.

Practicing Moderation

My diagnosis is why I've committed to walking on the days I'm not in the gym, and why I take my medication religiously. I am serious about staying in shape, especially as I age. But, I'm also realistic about what I can do. I'm a bit like Detective Provenza from the show *The Closer*, who famously said, "I don't run."

Well, that's me. I don't run, but I do walk as fast as I can—for those six minutes at a time. Timing myself keeps me motivated and lets me measure my progress. (I can walk almost a quarter of a mile—1,150 feet—in six minutes. Compare that to many heart failure patients, who may struggle to walk across the room without pausing for breath, and you'll see why regular exercise is so important to *wholistic* well-being.)

Exercise isn't the only part of the equation, however. Nutrition also plays a critical role in physical well-being. I've always been on the heavier side, but I manage to keep my weight around 210 pounds. To control my weight, I prioritize eating fruits and vegetables, and I am mindful of how much protein I consume. And of course, I practice portion control—though admittedly, I struggle with that at times.

When it comes to nutrition, my best advice for you is this: Remember that the key to eating well isn't about avoiding certain foods altogether; it's about moderation. I like to tell people there are no bad foods, only bad amounts. It's the same principle I learned in therapeutic drug monitoring during my medical career. With medication, you measure the drug levels to ensure the dose is right. With food, you can enjoy whatever you want, as long as you don't overdose. There's no need to deprive yourself of delicious meals. Just enjoy them in the right quantities.

Of course, I know that some of you want a bit more guidance than that. If you aren't sure where to start, I can offer a few suggestions. First, try to enjoy a variety of foods from all the different food groups (including fruits, vegetables, grains, proteins, dairy, and oils/solid fats). That will help ensure your body's nutritional needs are met, and it can also help reduce the risk that you'll develop diseases like diabetes, high blood pressure, and heart disease. If you struggle to get enough protein throughout the day to maintain muscle, try adding seafood, dairy, or legumes like beans, peas, and lentils. You can also incorporate more fruits and veggies into your day by eating them as snacks (bonus: Lots of grocery stores sell pre-cut varieties, which are often more convenient than slicing and chopping them yourself, if more expensive).

Staying active and maintaining a balanced diet are both about finding a sustainable rhythm that works for you. Again, there is no one-size-fits-all solution, but by paying attention to what your body needs and practicing moderation, you can enjoy life's pleasures while still taking care of your health.

If you want more guidance on healthy eating, there are a lot of resources available to help. One of my favorites is USDA MyPlate (www.myplate.gov), which replaced the Food Guide Pyramid. You can customize it to fit your needs and preferences, and it has a lot of free tools and resources to help you make healthy food decisions.[3] You can also work with a registered dietician or nutritionist—a Google search may yield nutritionists and dieticians in your area. Your doctor may also be able to recommend someone, or your local gym may have a nutritionist on staff.

I know what you might be thinking: "Moderation is easier said than done!" Trust me, I'm right there with you! I've had my fair share of overeating episodes. One of my biggest challenges is that I eat so fast that by the time I realize I'm full, I've already consumed a shocking amount of food. I used to try the conventional advice to help myself slow down: not eating in front of the TV, chewing each bite twenty times, and so on. Nothing really seemed to work, though, until I tried my newest approach.

---

3   Note that I am not affiliated with MyPlate, nor do I receive any compensation from it. I simply present it here as a good option if you're looking for information about healthy eating.

Now, I play a (rather frustrating) game at each meal: I try to make sure I don't finish what's on my plate before my wife, Margaret, finishes hers. She's a *slow* eater, so to make sure I don't finish before her, I use all sorts of tactics. I cut my food into smaller and smaller pieces, chew more, and put my fork and knife down between bites. I think it works because, unlike the things I tried before, I can make it into a game. Sure, it's a little annoying to eat so dang slowly, but it's a good way to stay mindful and engaged with the process rather than rushing through it—and to reduce how much I eat at any single sitting. As a bonus, it adds to my overall enjoyment of my food, as I have more time to notice the flavors of the dishes!

Making this switch has changed my whole approach to food. Before I started trying to match Margaret, I—like so many other people—absolutely inhaled my food. Slowing down is teaching me to pay attention and, more importantly, to *listen* to my body.

Ease Your Way into Health

Easing into health, then, is about doing three things: 1) get moving, 2) ensure proper nutrition, and 3) find a balance with how you fuel your body. To achieve these things, listen to your body and figure out what works best for you. Then consistently apply it in your daily life.

If you're in a skilled nursing facility, you may think your opportunities for exercise are limited. Many facilities have small gyms or spaces for exercise, but they often lack the kinds of structured programs that make a real difference. In that case, I recommend online programs like ZoeLife.[4]

ZoeLife (from the Greek word zoe, which means "vitality") is a highly organized program designed to bring movement and activity to skilled nursing care residents or homebound individuals, even those who use a wheelchair or have limited mobility. The program offers a range of activities that engage both the body and mind, promoting a sense of vitality in elderly individuals who may otherwise feel disconnected from physical activity.

Programs like ZoeLife are important because they don't just focus on physical fitness. They create opportunities for people to engage mentally and spiritually as well. That's what makes it such a well-rounded approach to well-being, especially for older adults who might not have the same mobility or independence they once did. The purpose is to foster vitality in all aspects of life, even as we age.

4   https://www.zoelifeonline.com

Here's a tip for you as you start to explore how you can ease into health and well-being: Look for online classes that you can sign up for. In today's highly technological world, you don't have to be present and in-person in order to get moving and make progress. For example, I've delivered virtual exercise sessions to people who couldn't otherwise attend a gym class. I ask them to keep their cameras on, so I know they are participating. It has been eye-opening to see how much you can accomplish, even in that format.

During virtual sessions, I take people through some exercises (they vary based on what my attendees can do, but I always aim to include both upper- and lower-body exercises, along with stretching), introduce some breathing techniques, and even toss a little meditation in there. That simple engagement gets people into the right mindset and spirit, and it introduces them in a practical way to the idea that they can *change their state.*

Move the body to be well, fuel the body to be well, and be able to change your state. Those are the keys to physical well-being, and you don't need a rigorous program to achieve them. Spend thirty minutes a day moving (yes, you can break it up if you need to). Get your heart rate up a few times per day. Introduce more balance into your diet, practice portion control, and focus on healthier foods. That's it. That's how you start to ease into a healthier life and begin the process of changing your state.

Intentionally Pursuing Vitality

As we age, the body experiences an inevitable decline in physical capabilities, so we have to be intentional about compensating for it. Take Gordie Howe, the legendary NHL player. He played hockey for decades. In the latter years of his career, late into his life, he could no longer skate as fast as the younger guys. However, he was smart enough to compensate for this by trying to anticipate where the puck was going to be. He didn't chase it around like the young guys. His strategy shifted to accommodate the decline in physical capabilities, and as a result, he was able to continue playing—and winning—for many more years.

As my father used to say, "The human body doesn't wear out—it rusts out from disuse."

Of course, that's not a license to give up on maintaining your physical abilities as you grow older! As my father used to say, "The human body doesn't wear out—it rusts out from disuse." In other words, it's not age alone that limits us, but how we treat our bodies.

People who neglect their health through overeating, drinking excessively, smoking, and avoiding exercise are the ones who pay the price.

As my father joked, "When the feeling of exercise comes over them, some people lie down *immediately* until the feeling passes." He was absolutely right—and I can tell you beyond a shadow of a doubt that doing so is what leads to the rusting out he warned about.

Physical fitness, at its core, is about three main components: strength, flexibility, and endurance. These are the pillars of movement, and as we age, we must continue to work on all three in whatever ways we can. As much as possible, I encourage people to try to avoid becoming dependent on things like walkers and wheelchairs.

Keep moving, stay engaged with your body, and focus on maintaining the essential qualities of strength, flexibility, and endurance. Aging may slow you down, but it doesn't mean you have to let your body rust out. By paying attention to these three aspects of your bodily health, you can live with greater vitality, no matter your age.

And remember, if you need programs like ZoeLife because you're in a skilled nursing facility or other long-term care, they are available to you (currently, ZoeLife is only available at Glencroft, although that may change in the future). As a reminder, the ZoeLife program was designed with a specific theme in mind: pursuing vitality through a full, active, and purposeful life. It's a different way of looking at things, especially for people in retirement communities like Glencroft. Too often, there's a misconception that places like that are where people go to live out their final days. And the truth is, without a meaningful program that treats people as lifelong learners and encourages them to keep building and growing, it can easily turn into the sad stereotype of a facility where people go to die. However, we should be pursuing vitality at every stage of life. We can never start too early, and we should keep pursuing it into our later years.

Seeking a full and purposeful life should be a universal goal for everyone, at every age.

Practices for the Body

Start moving! Find an exercise routine that works for you, whether that means going to the gym, following a home workout plan, or taking regular walks.

If you struggle to commit to a regular exercise routine, find creative ways to stay motivated. Pairing up with a friend or family member, paying yourself for each hour of exercise you complete, or signing up with a trainer who will keep you accountable are a few tactics you can try.

Take steps toward better nutrition. Prioritize fruits and vegetables, be mindful of how much protein you consume, and practice portion control. You don't have to avoid the foods you enjoy altogether. Just practice moderation.

As you age, focus on maintaining the essential qualities of strength, flexibility, and endurance so your body doesn't "rust out."

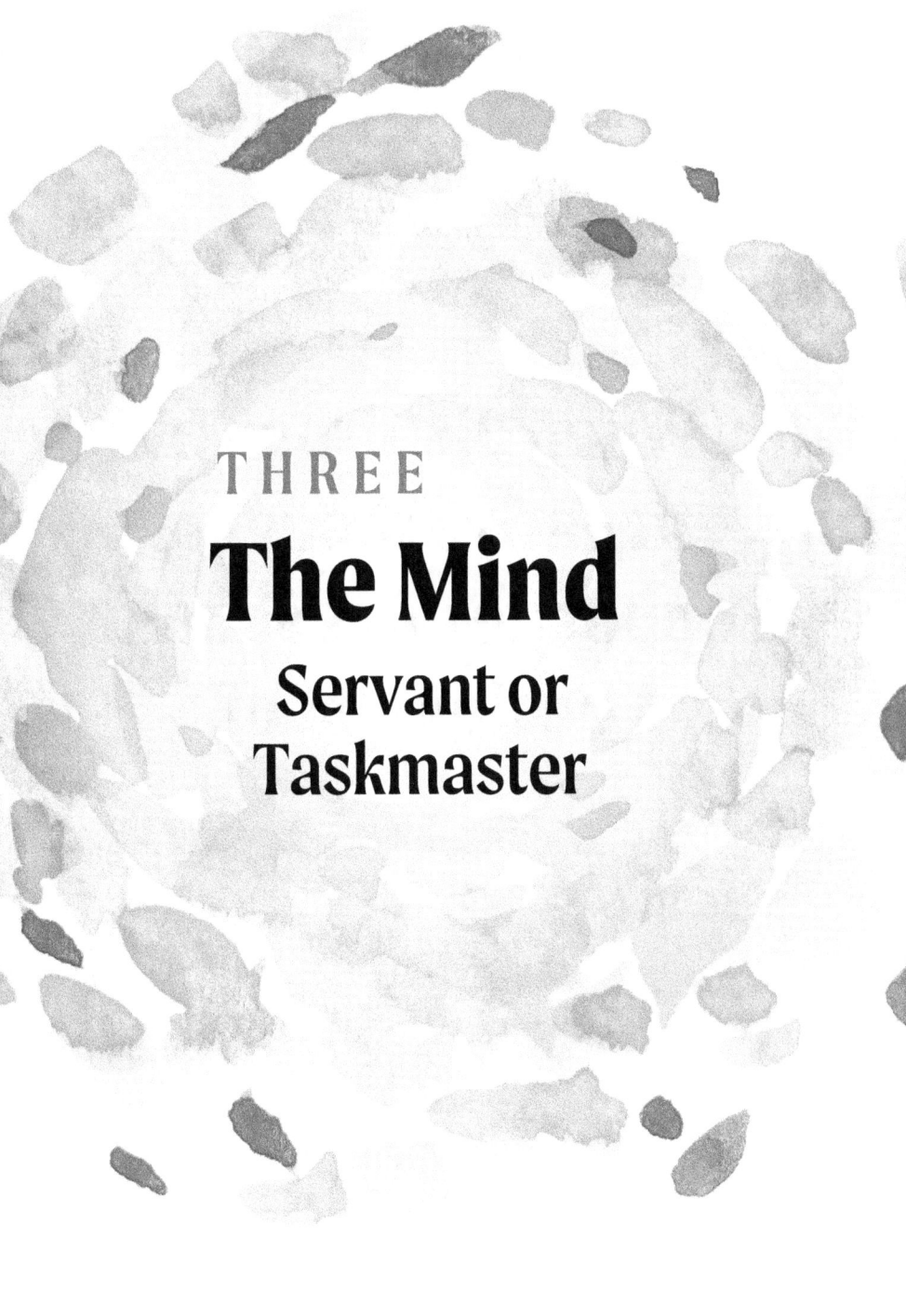

THREE

The Mind

Servant or Taskmaster

When disturbed by negative thoughts, opposite ones should be thought of.

—PATANJALI

I LIKE TO TELL MY PATIENTS, "THE MIND CAN BE A GOOD and faithful servant, or it can be a terrible taskmaster." What do I mean by that? Simple: Many (if not most) people let their minds run the show, flooding them with a steady stream of negative thoughts that can lead to anxiety, depression, and even suicidal ideation. In the medical field, we talk a lot about mental illness, but I'm convinced that many of our mental struggles come from an untrained mind and an underdeveloped spirit.

I know this is a bit of an edgy (or even controversial) statement to make, but I firmly believe that if people trained their minds and spirits, many of the cases of depression, anxiety, and despair we see would cease to exist, or at least lessen in intensity. That's because mental illness doesn't just appear out of nowhere, and it's not merely the product of a chemical imbalance. It is, in large part, the result of unchecked thoughts and emotions running rampant because we haven't learned how to manage our internal world.

Now, having said that, I want to be crystal clear about something. In no way, shape, or form am I saying this to make people feel guilty about their own struggles. And, I am most definitely *not* saying, "If you have depression or anxiety, it's your fault!" Quite the opposite, actually. I see an opportunity here for people who are suffering. More than that, I see hope. If you're tired of living with depression, post-traumatic stress disorder, or other mental health challenges, there *is* another way. And no, you don't necessarily have to turn to medication for help. You can learn to change your state.

Now, I am not dismissing the use of medication entirely. I'm a doctor, for goodness' sake! I'm well aware that many medications can be helpful tools in the treatment of mental health issues (and other diseases too, for that matter). But medication can only go so far. For true well-being, the fundamental shift needs to come from within, from learning how to manage and control your response to the external events that induce negative emotions and mental states. The emphasis has to move away from relying solely on drugs to a focus on developing inner resilience.

Let me share something with you that illustrates this point beautifully. Viktor Frankl, famed psychiatrist and Holocaust survivor, served as a doctor in Auschwitz. According to Dr. Frankl, his experience there taught him that while we can't always control what happens to us, we can always control how we respond. As he is often credited with saying, "Between stimulus and response there is a space. In that space is our power to choose our response.

In our response lies our growth and our freedom." That's the inner resilience I'm talking about—and it's a message I think the world needs to hear now more than ever.

Getting Your Mind off Autopilot

A big part of building inner resilience is turning your mind into something that serves you, not the other way around. That means *you* decide how to manage the thoughts that come into your head—or at least decide which ones you give your attention to.

Most people don't realize that their minds are on autopilot, constantly running like a radio that never turns off. They don't control what thoughts pop into their heads. Thoughts just arrive, uninvited, and many of them are negative. Their minds serve up a steady stream of judgments, assessments, and criticisms. But guess what? *It's all just noise.*

Why are our minds like this? The answer lies in our biology. We are wired for survival, for fight or flight, and this instinct goes deep into our neurobiological makeup. As a result, our minds constantly react instinctively to everything, looking for trouble, seeking escape, worrying about predators around the corner, and so on. It's not something we invented or have complete control over; it's simply part of being human. The bad news is that we can't necessarily stop it. We can't turn the radio off or unplug it.

So, if we can't stop the mind from babbling all the time, what can we do? The key is not in silencing the mind, but in *directing our attention*. That's the real secret—and the good news.

This is why practices like breathing exercises are so powerful. When you focus on your breath, it disrupts the mental chatter. You take your attention away from the judge, jury, and executioner in your mind, and direct your mind toward something as simple as breathing instead. *And in the process, you realize you don't have to accept or believe every thought that passes through your head.*

If more people truly understood this, many could find relief from suffering. Our inability to separate from our thoughts is what causes so much inner anguish. (Interestingly, a lot of corporate exercises, like those that focus on the "five dysfunctions of a team," are counterproductive for this very reason. As soon as you start focusing on dysfunction, you reinforce the belief that you have a messed-up team.)

Most of us are never taught to do anything about the negative thoughts that come into our heads. Instead, we just believe them. So really, is it any wonder that so many people suffer from anxiety, depression, and so on? Or that, as a society, we don't have a good approach to addressing those problems? But once you understand how to achieve true well-being and change your state, the solution appears. Indeed, it's stunning to me how often we work on "fixing" what's broken instead of shifting our attention to what's already working.

This is something people need to understand, and the earlier in life, the better: The constant mental chatter each of us experiences is not who we inherently are. That clamor is an automatic mechanism, a noise that runs in the background. Learning to separate yourself from the mental din is a critical lesson that applies to people of all ages.

Picture the human mind as an airport TV that's blaring nonsense in the background while you're trying to read a book. You can't turn it off, but you can choose where to place your attention. You can ignore the television and focus on the pages in front of you. It might take a few minutes, but eventually, the sound from the TV recedes into the background, and you don't even notice it. Right? It's still making noise; you just don't pay attention to it. The same holds true for the negative thoughts in your mind.

Just like you can ignore the TV while you're sitting in a packed terminal waiting to board a plane, once you understand this concept, you can start to free yourself from the endless cycle of reactive thinking.

Breaking the Loop

Remember, our minds have this habit of getting stuck in repetitive loops, triggered by old patterns and habits. That means we live much of our lives reacting rather than responding. The key to breaking these loops and freeing ourselves comes from learning how to catch those automatic thoughts and shift away from them. To do that, you have to train yourself to recognize when your mind is stuck in the endless, inane loop of the radio broadcast.

Again, you can't necessarily stop the mind's automatic thoughts, nor can you wrestle them to the ground. But you can direct your attention elsewhere. That's where practices like breathing exercises come in.

Breathing is a tool to redirect your focus away from those automatic patterns and bring you back into the present moment. It's about marking the territory of your mind and choosing where to place your attention.

When I conduct breathing exercises with a group, I like to begin every session with an invocation, a kind of grounding intention that sets the tone for the work we're about to do. I often say something like:

I am intending that our work here today supports everyone in their insights into whole person health and well-being—body, mind, and spirit, integrated as one full expression of life. May we not let the challenges of life take us over and overrun our best thoughts and intentions. May we have compassion for ourselves, for others, and for life itself. I dedicate all of our work today to that purpose, and I hope you do as well.

Reciting an invocation like this helps anchor the session and reminds everyone (myself included!) of our shared goal: to honor what an amazing creation a human being is, at every stage of life. When you engage in breathing exercises, you might consider reciting your own invocation, or repeating the one I just shared. While you don't have to say it out loud, taking a moment to silently offer up your own personal invocation or prayer can help mark the moment as sacred and make it easier for your mind to change into a different state.

Breathe and Be Present

My favorite breathing exercise is a form of meditation called "The Eye of the Hurricane." Here's how it works: First, find a quiet place where you won't be disturbed, either indoors or outdoors, depending on your preference. Sit comfortably, but keep your spine straight, and rest your hands on your knees or in your lap. Begin taking deep, intentional breaths. Inhale deeply through the nose, hold it for a moment, then exhale slowly through your mouth.

Visualize yourself in the eye of a hurricane, the calm center amidst life's chaos, surrounded by wind and rain. Become the stillness, even as the storm swirls around you. As negative thoughts and feelings arise, acknowledge them without judgment, but gently bring your focus back to your breathing.

At first, you might find yourself getting attached to every thought that comes into your mind. That's totally fine; in fact, it's normal! Be gentle with yourself. Each time you notice that your attention has wandered away from your breathing, bring your attention back to your breath, envisioning yourself at the center of the storm all the while. Over time, you'll catch those moments of inattention more quickly. Eventually, your thoughts will quietly drift in and out without distracting you.

If you're new to breathing exercises, I suggest starting with a five-minute session once or twice per day. Over time, as you become more accustomed to the practice, you can gradually increase how long you spend in each session. However, remember that even short sessions are powerful ways to cultivate peace and presence, especially in turbulent times.

There are other breathing exercises you can do, of course. Another popular and highly effective one is known as "Box Breathing." Breathe in slowly, deeply, and calmly for a count of four (or three, or five—whatever is comfortable for you). Hold your breath for the same amount of time you breathed in. Then, breathe out (again, for the same length of time). Finally, hold your breath for the same count before taking another inhalation. Repeat this pattern ten times, once or twice per day.

"Box Breathing" is especially powerful because it quiets the sympathetic nervous system, which is responsible for the "fight or flight" response, and activates your parasympathetic nervous system, which controls the "rest and digest" response. We take rapid, shallow breaths when we're stressed, so box breathing is a way to trick your nervous system into settling down and relaxing. Plus, like "The Eye of the Hurricane," this type of breathing is meditative. While you're busy counting the length of each part of your breath, your mind can't grab onto other thoughts. Put all of this together, and suddenly you're in the process of changing your state from stressed to relaxed.

Whether you choose to use "The Eye of the Hurricane," "Box Breathing," or some other kind of breathing exercise, one tip is to practice it *before* you get stressed. It can be hard to focus on your breathing when you're in the middle of something stressful, especially if you aren't familiar with the technique. But, if you make it a point to incorporate your chosen breathing technique into your everyday life—say, when you first wake up in the morning and again when you lay down at night—you'll be better equipped to utilize it when things get tough.

Breathing exercises allow us to integrate body, mind, and spirit so that we can engage with life in a more powerful and meaningful way. Remember, the concept of body, mind, and spirit well-being is about embracing a wholistic approach to life, in which these elements don't exist as separate parts competing with one another but come together as a unified force.

Eliminate Unnecessary Suffering

At times, one of these aspects might present itself more strongly. For example, you may face a physical problem, or your mind might be preoccupied with worries or thoughts about a person or a group—politics, for instance, is a good example of how people get caught up in mental struggles. We're often torn between perspectives, unable to see the legitimacy in both sides, and this leads to unnecessary tension.

When we view body, mind, and spirit as separate, we create a lot of suffering for ourselves. I often tell people that there are two kinds of suffering: necessary and unnecessary. Necessary suffering is what we can't avoid, like the pain after a car accident. It's part of life, something we must endure as we heal. But unnecessary suffering is the kind we create in our minds—the self-torture that comes from dwelling on things, overthinking, and letting our thoughts run wild. This kind of suffering is avoidable.

What we're doing here is learning how to eliminate the *unnecessary* suffering. It's not something that can be overcome completely—no book or teaching will make it disappear forever. But you can learn how to deal with it in a way that stops you from torturing yourself. The trick is to direct your attention to the present moment, to whatever is right in front of you, and to let the feeling pass. Just as importantly, this must become a lifelong practice.

In reality, this concept is simple and incredibly powerful. The three deadly R's—regret, remorse, and resentment—are all manifestations of the babbling mind and the unnecessary suffering we carry within us. Quieting the mind is a key part of overcoming all of it.

When we quiet our minds, we can tune into something greater than ourselves—something bigger than our small, personal concerns. And when *that* happens, we can usually find a sense of peace and perspective. This is why I use breathing exercises as part of my teaching. Wherever you are, whatever you're feeling, you can always direct your attention to your breath. Breathe in, breathe out, and be conscious of where the breath is coming from. This is a simple yet powerful way to ground yourself, to quiet the mind, and to reconnect with your body and spirit.

The bottom line here is that breathing exercises are about learning to direct your attention, silence the clamor, and embrace the whole of who you are—body, mind, and spirit. This is something anyone can do at any time. Breathe in, breathe out, and be present. If you can do that, you will be well on your way to changing your state.

Practices for Quieting the Mind

Recognize that the constant mental discord you experience is not who you inherently are. Start training yourself to redirect your attention away from the steady stream of negative thoughts.

When the negative thoughts are loud, try breathing exercises to disconnect from them. Practice "The Eye of the Hurricane." Breathe in, breathe out, and be conscious of where the breath is coming from. Visualize yourself as the calm center amidst life's chaos.

Try "Box Breathing" to shift from "fight or flight" to "rest and digest." Breathe in for a count of four, hold your breath for a count of four, breathe out for a count of four, and hold for a count of four. Repeat this pattern ten times.

The time to get good at breathing exercises is not in the midst of a traumatic or stressful event. Incorporate them into your daily routine so that when the going gets tough, you'll be able to utilize them more effectively.

FOUR

Spirit
A Force
of Healing

"

Spiritual healing occurs as we begin to consciously reconnect with our essential being—the wise, loving, powerful, creative entity that we are at our core.

"

—SHAKTI GAWAIN

A T THIS POINT, WE'VE TALKED ABOUT SOME WAYS TO get the body healthier. We've also discussed ways to quiet the mind and change your state. So now, it's time to turn our attention to the third pillar of *wholistic* well-being: the spirit.

The human spirit is something we all come equipped with from the factory. Yet it doesn't get the attention it deserves. That's due in large part to the fact that people often associate spirit solely with religion, which, frankly, is a mistake. Spirit and spirituality are not the same as religion. Don't get me wrong—there's nothing wrong with many of the spiritual practices within religion, but we must recognize that while the spirit includes religious structures, *spirituality* is all-encompassing.

In essence, the human spirit is a force of resilience, healing, and vitality. It's part of what makes us whole, and learning to engage our spirit is just as important as taking care of the other aspects of ourselves.

The lack of attention that most people give to spirit (whether they recognize it or not) leads to a whole host of problems. Even though many people are unaware of its influence, the spirit inspires, uplifts, and guides us through all aspects of life. We now have a much broader understanding of fitness and know that maintaining our bodies requires intentional effort and regular practice. The same is true of the spirit. It's always there, part of our natural wiring, but it must be developed through practice to fully realize its potential. We'll discuss some ways to do that here, but the main thing that I want you to take away is that attending to spirit is just as crucial as exercising, eating right, or quieting your mind. To paraphrase G.I. Joe: "Now you know...and knowing is half the battle."

Finding Connection to Spirit

Spirituality, like physical fitness, is different for everyone. Some people connect with their spirit through service to others, through a deep sense of purpose or mission. Others find their spiritual grounding in nature.

I think of my daughter, who lives on the coast of British Columbia and often takes photos of herself in the forest. I tease her about "forest bathing," which is a term used to describe how some people connect with their spirit by surrounding themselves with nature. But in reality, she's onto something. By spending time in nature, she's taking care of her spirit. The funny thing is that people who engage in these activities might not even realize they're accessing their spirituality because what they're doing feels so natural. It is their way of "going to church," and that deeper connection to spirit is something worth cultivating—being fully awake to the experience.

> *If spending time in nature fuels your spirit, then forest bathing might be something to try. It's simple to do. Just get outside into nature and notice how the light plays through the leaves of the trees. Listen to the sounds around you. Breathe in the scents all around you. Much like the breathing exercises I described in the last chapter, forest bathing helps stop your mind from getting swept up in every single thought that comes along. It's a way to drop into mindfulness and support your body, mind, and spirit in achieving wholistic well-being.*

Some people might disagree with me saying this, but you don't literally have to go to a forest to practice forest bathing, either. If you don't have a forest near you (and many people don't), going for a walk in the park offers some of the same benefits you would experience if you were forest bathing in the traditional sense. If walking in a park isn't possible, bring the outside in. If you can, open the windows in your house or room, place some potted plants (and maybe some rocks, pinecones, and/or shells) around, and listen to recordings of forest sounds while you do one of the breathing exercises I described in the last chapter.

Engaging in acts of service or going into nature aren't the only ways to connect to spirit. Some people find their connection through meditation, and others through study. But study alone, in my opinion, doesn't provide direct access to the spirit. Deep spiritual access requires more than merely gaining knowledge; it requires making a core connection between body, mind, and spirit. Indeed, *everything* stems from that core connection. And yet, in Western culture, we miss this point. That's a natural result of our belief that science is the ultimate truth, or that science alone provides the whole story. Even though I'm a doctor of Western medicine, I can tell you unequivocally that this viewpoint leads to problems. Science can explain a lot, but it doesn't account for—or even provide space for—things like intuition and spirituality.

For example, where does creativity come from? It doesn't arise from evidence or data; it comes from a deeper, more intuitive place. This is why I often remind people that evidence-based practices, while important, are not everything. If we rely solely on science and evidence-based knowledge, we miss out on the richness of our inner world and the spirit that drives us toward something greater. The key is to find balance and remain open to that spiritual depth, even when we can't explain it through logic or data.

By developing an awareness of your spirit and practicing ways to connect with it—whether through meditation, nature, service, or something else—you open yourself to the most important aspects of living a full and meaningful life. And while not everyone may reach this understanding immediately, it's worth preparing yourself to dive deep into the spiritual side of life. That's where the true magic lies.

The Elements of Spiritual Strength

It's one thing to talk about the integration of body, mind, and spirit; it's another to actively engage in it. However, when you make that core connection, you strengthen the spirit, and because everything is connected—wholistic, remember?—that, in turn, strengthens the mind and body.

To guide you in this process, it may be helpful to look at the elements of spiritual strength. If you can master these things, you will be well on your way to integrating your body, mind, and spirit into a unified whole.

1. **Recognize the Riled-Up Mind:** The first step is to recognize when your mind is racing—whether it's

filled with anger, fear, or reactive thoughts—and understand that this isn't you. Detach from that state and let it go by focusing your attention elsewhere. Breathing exercises like the ones I described in chapter 3 can help.

2. **Practice Compassion:** Compassion is about feeling deeply for another's pain, and it starts with being compassionate toward yourself. The word compassion literally means "to suffer with," and true compassion means being present with others in their suffering, not pitying them. We'll look more at compassion in chapter 7.

3. **Trust in How the Universe is Unfolding:** The next element is to trust that the universe is unfolding exactly as it should. This is about embracing the belief that, no matter how chaotic or difficult things seem, nothing is fundamentally wrong.

4. **Answer the Call:** Spiritual strength involves recognizing and answering the call to action in your life. There are moments when you know it's your time to step up, whether it's a calling

from within or an external responsibility. It's like hearing a phone ringing—it will keep going until you pick it up...so answer it!

Spiritual strength isn't something that just happens. It's something we train and develop. And the foundation of this training starts with self-care, so include yourself in the care and compassion you offer others.

Practices for the Spirit

Find the most impactful way for you to connect
with the spirit, whether that's meditation, being
in nature, acts of service, or something else. Then,
incorporate that into your everyday life.

Practice the elements of spiritual strength: 1) recognize
when your mind is "riled up" and redirect your attention,
2) develop compassion for yourself and others, 3)
trust in how the universe is unfolding, and 4) answer
whatever call to action is coming from within.

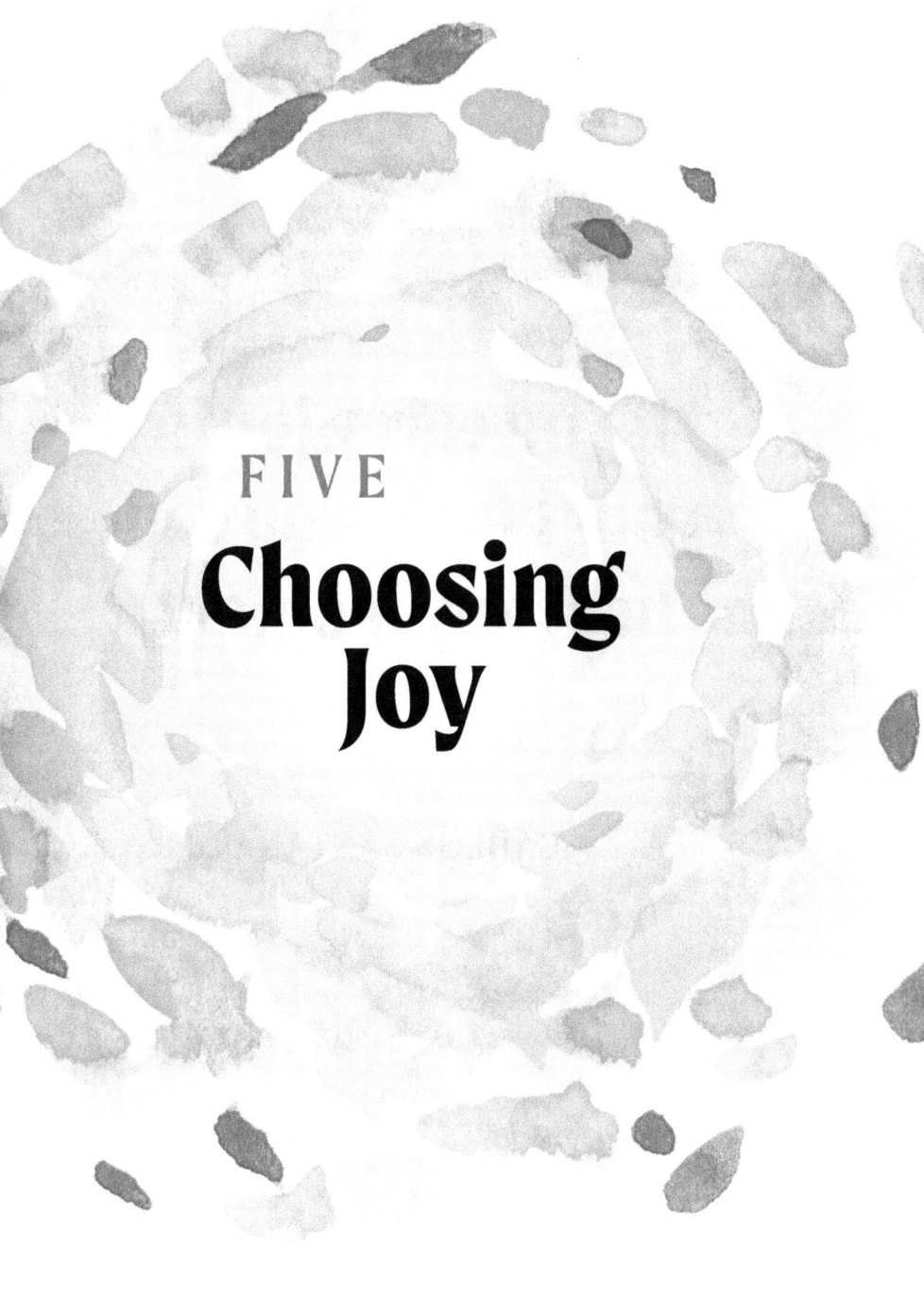

FIVE

Choosing Joy

"

If you carry joy in your heart, you can heal any moment.

"

— CARLOS SANTANA

WHEN IT COMES TO BODY AND MIND WELL-BEING, I've found that most people "get it," at least on a superficial level. But when it comes to well-being of spirit, things aren't quite so straightforward. Many people equate spiritual well-being with how happy they are. However, when they start talking about happiness, I remind them of one very important fact—and it's one I want to remind you of, as well: Joy is not happiness, and happiness is not joy. They are not the same thing.

So, what's the difference? Happiness is circumstantial. When things are going well, we're happy; when things go wrong, we're sad. It's tied to the ups and downs of life. But joy? Joy is deeper. It's something that stays with you through the highs and lows. Joy isn't about riding the waves of emotion, it's about finding something profound even in the midst of difficulty. And here's the important part: If you want to achieve true well-being of spirit, you need to be able to tap into joy.

Joy exists in both the good times and the bad. That may sound surprising, but it's true. When you're joyful, you can find something to appreciate even in life's challenges. Often (though not always), that appreciation comes down to the fact that the low moments usually lead to growth and transformation. So, as we explore joy more deeply throughout this chapter, keep in mind that happiness comes and goes, but joy remains constant and available.

Joy Is Constant

Given all this, you might be asking yourself one very important question: "I'm not experiencing joy—so what am I doing wrong?" Well, the first thing you need to realize and accept is the previous key point that joy is always available. Because it's already present, you don't have to create it by changing your circumstances; you just have to tap into it.

You see, joy is not merely an emotion or a reaction to outside stimuli, but a practice; and it's a practice we can all embrace. No matter what you're feeling right now, whether you're happy or sad or something in between, joy is available to you. It's available no matter what, but only if you choose it.

The problem is that most of us are stuck in habits that counteract joy. We default to negativity, gossip, or complaining. It's like an unwritten rule that when we sit down with other people, the conversation will naturally drift toward the struggles or frustrations we've faced. Even if you consider yourself a "champion of joy," like I do, you can easily find yourself slipping into this negative flow, nodding along, and agreeing, "Yes, that's so terrible. Everything is awful!"

What happens then? You start feeling like your joy has been stolen by others, and your resentment builds. It's easy to blame others for ruining your good mood, but here's the reality: You don't have to participate in the negativity. Instead of joining in on the complaints and grumbling, why not connect with joy? Share something positive, something you're grateful for, and celebrate the simple privilege of being alive.

An African proverb says, "Community is where people come to contribute their gifts."[5] That's such a powerful idea. Community should be about giving, not just commiserating. It should be about contributing something meaningful to those around you, not dragging each other down. Imagine how much more joyful our connections *and* our lives would be if we focused on what we can give rather than what's going wrong (or did go wrong, or might go wrong).

I've seen examples of this in my own life, just as I'm sure you've seen examples in yours. Think about Hurricane

---

5   The quote is sometimes attributed to Parker J. Palmer, an author, educator, and activist who was committed to spirituality and social change.

Helene, which devastated portions of Florida, Georgia, South Carolina, and North Carolina in September 2024. Helene was an undeniable tragedy, and its ramifications will continue to be felt for years to come. And yet, if you talk to the people who lived through it, many of them will say that the outpouring of support from other people in their communities and the country at large were bright spots through the horror. People came together to collect food, water, and other necessities for each other. They came together to get those supplies distributed too. And throughout it all, the people who were being helped and the ones doing the helping found solace in the sharing of those much-needed gifts. The impact didn't end there, either. The stories about linemen and search/rescue teams coming from sixteen different states—and even Canada— to help restore power and locate missing people demonstrated the power and pull that true community has on a larger scale.

The bottom line is that we are here to contribute, not just to take, and it's in this exchange that we find deeper meaning. And once someone understands this, they can start tapping into joy. Gratitude plays a huge role in this. In fact, joy and gratitude go hand in hand, and they can be both passive and active. First, you can passively experience joy, just going along with whatever life throws at you, like a leaf floating down a stream. But you can also actively choose joy when you bring intention to it. When you make a decision to find joy in your work, in your day, in the people around you, or even in the challenges, life takes on a different energy.

While this message is appropriate for older people who have lived long enough to experience life's ups and downs, I think it is even more important for younger people to hear. I had a close friend who spent years teaching at a university, and during her last three years as a professor, not a single term passed without one of her students either attempting or committing suicide. These incidents were not isolated; they were part of a recurring pattern. Whenever my friend talked to me about what her students were going through, I couldn't help but think about the importance of what I'm sharing with you in this book. The younger generation is in desperate need of tools to navigate life's challenges, and the sooner they can develop this perspective, the better.

The earlier you can awaken to joy, to stewardship, to your role in this world—and help those around you do the same—the more resilient everyone will be when life inevitably gets tough. People, both young and old, must learn to not just survive but thrive by awakening to the joy that's always available to them, no matter what life throws their way.

No matter your age, learning to cultivate joy is crucial to your well-being. According to the Centers for Disease Control and Prevention (CDC), the suicide rate in the United States reached an all-time high in 2022.[6] Nearly 49,000 people died by suicide that year, which is equivalent to one death every eleven minutes.[7] Seniors—particularly men over the age of 75—were (and are) particularly at risk. This may be due in large part to the feelings of loneliness and isolation that many senior citizens experience. Add in serious issues like chronic illness and pain, grief over losing loved ones, financial troubles, cognitive impairment, and/ or a loss of self-sufficiency, and it's clear why older people may be more likely to attempt to take their own lives. However, I truly believe that it doesn't have to be this way. By tapping into joy—and focusing on body, mind, and spirit wholistic well-being—many of these issues can be dealt with more effectively.

6   Centers for Disease Control and Prevention, *Vital Statistics Rapid Release,* November 2023, https://www.cdc.gov/nchs/data/vsrr/vsrr034.pdf.
7   Centers for Disease Control and Prevention, "Suicide Data and Statistics," October 29, 2024, https://www.cdc.gov/suicide/facts/data.html.

Joy in the Tough Transitions

When I say that joy is *always* available to us, I mean it. That includes finding joy where you might not expect to— whether that's in your job or in the tough transitions that are a part of life.

The book *The Joy of Work* by Bruce Daisley talks about finding joy and deep satisfaction in what we do. As Daisley writes, "Joy at work isn't just about feeling happy all the time; it's about finding purpose and connection in what we do."[8]

I've personally found joy in the work I'm currently doing in Las Vegas, where I am running a large clinical laboratory and promoting antibiotic stewardship. That's true despite the fact that there have been many challenges. Case in point: It's brutally hot in Vegas, but many of the tests we do require keeping the sample cold from the moment it gets taken all the way through analysis. We had to establish a dedicated team to figure out how to do that, consistently and without errors. It wasn't easy, but when you get right down to it, challenges like this don't have to take away from our joy. The fact that they exist is fine. In

---

8 Bruce Daisley, *The Joy of Work: 30 Ways to Fall in Love with Your Job Again* (New York: Random House, 2020).

fact, every challenge we've faced, and all the ones we'll face in the future, are fine. Maybe they're more than fine. We are working hard and pushing through the tough stuff, and that gives me a sense of purpose and joy.

Sometimes, challenges are more personal than solving a cold-chain problem. Recently, our lab manager, Mark, resigned due to a diagnosis of stage IV prostate cancer. Understandably, he wanted to focus on getting better. Fortunately, he gave us plenty of notice, which allowed us to recruit a replacement. As it turned out, we hired a woman who had held the position before him. She'd had to step down for her own health reasons, which have since cleared up. Her interview was outstanding, and it reminded me of how joy can be found even in tough transitions. And she has been spectacular in her new role.

Before he left, Mark told me he wanted to stay on as a contractor for a period of time to help us with a special project. That project was a business plan to establish a microbiology lab in Las Vegas, something we lacked at the time but desperately needed if we wanted to keep our clients.

When he said that, I was amazed. So many people in his position would have stopped working immediately, and nobody would blame them. But perhaps I shouldn't have been surprised that Mark chose to stay onboard while we tackled the challenge of establishing a microbiology lab. That's because Mark has a unique perspective on his illness—one that really struck me.

One day, he said, "I want this microbiology project plan to be my legacy, before the cancer gets me." He knows he's dying of prostate cancer and understands the gravity of his situation. However, he hasn't allowed his circumstances to steal his joy in the work he's doing. Instead, he's continuing to live his life with purpose and do what he can to help others. That certainly contributes to his joy. Plus, he doesn't see his cancer as a fight, and I admire that.

Too often, people approach illness with a combative mindset. They want to fight the enemy—and win. But I always caution them against taking that perspective. I tell them, "Don't put that energy in your body." Sometimes, it's wiser to let go and relax enough to truly live in a state of joy.

In both the process-related challenge of keeping samples cold and the more personal challenge of witnessing a friend and colleague dealing with cancer, I could have spent my time worrying about how things would turn out. I could have stressed about how to handle the obstacles and let the uncertainties we faced interrupt my peace. But instead, I consciously chose to take a different approach. I adopted the mindset that no matter what comes our way, there is still joy to be found. I focused on what I could give to others and found things to be grateful for, and you know what? Joy naturally followed. If you can train yourself to seek joy whatever comes your way, I can all but guarantee joy will find you too.

Stop Trying to Control Everything

Bringing joy into your life doesn't come from overthinking or following a rigid set of steps. It's not about finding the perfect formula or constructing just the right set of circumstances. Joy comes when you relax, when you stop trying to control everything, and when you let go of the need for everything to be perfect.

I remember a great quote from Pema Chödrön, an American Buddhist monk. She said:

> Awakening is essential. Times are difficult globally. Awakening is no longer a luxury or an ideal; it's becoming critical. We do not need to add more depression, more discouragement, or more anger to what's already out there. It's become essential that we learn how to relate sanely with difficult times. The Earth seems to be beseeching us to connect with joy and

discover our innermost essence. This is the best way we can benefit others.

That quote captures so much of what we're trying to explore here—how to connect with joy even when the world feels heavy. The problem is that not everyone wakes up, even though they may physically grow older. So many people chase happiness rather than doing as the Earth "beseeches us" to do—connect with joy and discover our innermost essences.

David Brooks, a columnist for the *New York Times*, has explored this very idea in his writing. He talks about how our culture is obsessed with happiness, but not joy. Like me, he draws a distinction between the two: Happiness is fleeting, but joy is something deeper.

As he writes, "Happiness usually involves a victory for the self. Joy tends to involve the transcendence of self [...] Joy is the present that life gives you as you give away your gifts."[9]

"Joy is the present that life gives you as you give away your gifts." How beautiful is that?

9   David Brooks, "The Difference Between Happiness and Joy," *New York Times*, Opinion, https://www.nytimes.com/2019/05/07/opinion/happiness-joy-emotion.html.

When we think about the founding principles of our nation, even in the Declaration of Independence, the founding fathers talk about "the pursuit of happiness." But happiness, by nature, is temporary. It comes and goes. Joy, on the other hand, is something we can cultivate and enjoy, no matter what's happening around us or to us. Better, perhaps, for them to have talked about "life, liberty, and finding the connection to joy."

Appreciate the Ups *and* the Downs

In life, there are always going to be ups and downs. The real secret to joy is learning to appreciate both. It's not about getting through the tough times as quickly as possible, but rather embracing them. And you know what? When you understand that challenging times are just as valuable and meaningful as the good times, you're getting somewhere.

I know this probably sounds like a very advanced concept. Finding joy in challenging situations doesn't come easily, but I believe that once you can learn to appreciate the downs just as much as the ups, you will unlock something profound. Life is full of contrasts, and that's what makes it rich and meaningful. The Buddhists have a deep understanding of this. They recognize that all of life is suffering in some way. But remember that there's necessary suffering, like healing from surgery or trauma, and then there's unnecessary suffering, the kind we inflict on ourselves through worry and fear.

In the end, joy is about accepting the full spectrum of life and understanding that both the highs and the lows are essential. When we stop trying to control every outcome and instead focus on appreciating what is, we can find true joy.

Connecting to Joy

Joy is not happiness, and happiness is not joy. The
difference is that happiness is circumstantial—
when things are going well, we're happy; when
things go wrong, we're sad. It's tied to the ups and
downs of life. Joy, on the other hand, is constant. It
stays with us through the highs and the lows.

True spiritual well-being only comes
once you learn to tap into joy.

One way to start to access this ever-present joy is
to notice when you're gossiping or complaining.
Break the pattern by sharing something positive or
something you're grateful for instead. Do what you
can to celebrate the simple privilege of being alive.

Try adopting the mindset that no matter what comes your way, you can choose to focus on what you can give to others. You can choose to find things for which you are grateful. If you do that, joy will naturally follow.

Most of all, remember that joy comes when you relax, when you stop trying to control everything, and when you let go of the need for everything to be perfect—or, as I like to think of it, when you stop resisting the flow of the stream and start rowing in the same direction it's going.

SIX

When a Door Closes

"

Joy does not simply happen to us. We have to choose joy and keep choosing it every day.

"

—HENRI NOUWEN

A T THIS POINT, YOU MAY BE ON BOARD WITH HOW important joy is to your well-being of spirit, but you may also be struggling with the idea that joy takes practice—that it's a skill you must develop. You might also be finding it difficult to wrap your head around the idea that you can find joy in difficult moments. This is probably especially true if you're going through tough times in your life right now. If that's the case, you're probably thinking, "There is nothing good about this horrible situation. How can I possibly find joy in it?"

I understand completely. Some years ago, I was suddenly fired from a job I loved. At the time, it felt like the worst thing that had ever happened to me. I was devastated, and the blow to my confidence was immense. As I was reeling from the shock of it all, a member of my staff—a woman I respected very much—said to me, "Someday, you'll see this as the best thing that's ever happened to you." I bit back the first response that popped into my head and smiled at her, but inside, I was rolling my eyes. I had just been let go, and she wanted to tell me it was a good thing? *Yeah, right.*

As the days passed, though, and I gained some perspective, the pain of my situation lessened. I found a new job. I was still able to provide for my family. I realized I was still capable, still me, and there were people out there who valued my talents. And you know what? Even though I couldn't comprehend it at the time, it turned out that my colleague was right. If I hadn't been fired from that job, I never would have started down the path that has led me to where I am today. I might not have gotten as deeply into antibiotic stewardship as I have, and I doubt I would be writing a book about *wholistic* well-being, either.

Losing out on either of those parts of my life—not to mention everything else that happened, either directly or indirectly, as a result of that situation—would have been a tragedy. So yes, as it turns out, losing that job *was* one of the best things that ever happened to me. It was an eye-opening realization, and one that has helped me hold onto joy during other tough times in my life.

The truth is, when a door closes, it can feel like the end of the world. And in some ways, it *is* the end of the world, at least the world as we knew it. But that's how life works. It breaks *down* before it breaks *open*. The key is learning to trust that a breakthrough is on the horizon.

Think of it this way: You're standing at the open door of an airplane, parachute on, and your heels are dug in, resisting. You don't want to jump. But eventually, you're either going to jump of your own volition, or you're going to get pushed out of the plane. With time, you learn to embrace the situation, despite the fear and the uncertainty you might feel. You've witnessed others who trust the process jump without hesitation—and you use that to bolster you until you can draw on your own experiences of success. That's the kind of growth that develops resilience of spirit. It's the kind of growth that develops spiritual well-being.

Life moves in phases, and sometimes a change or challenge feels like a loss, like something's ending. But once you understand that every ending brings an opening into a new beginning, a new trajectory, you can approach these moments with more grace. Instead of viewing hardship as something to fear or avoid, you begin to see it as an opportunity for something new. That's where joy comes in—not just in the easy moments, but in learning to appreciate the hard ones too.

Opening Up to Joy

Years ago, I attended a seminar where I was introduced to bodywork, which is a therapeutic technique that involves manipulating muscles, fascia, and energy systems in order to release tension or stored emotions. For many of us, it was the first time we'd experienced something like that. I remember a young woman next to me who had experienced recurring pain in her leg as a result of an accident she'd had years earlier. During her session with the therapist, she suddenly cried out. Afterward, she told us that when the therapist touched her leg in one particular spot, the memory of what had happened to her came flooding back in an instant, as though it had been locked away in her body. After that moment, though, the pain released, and she was able to move in a much freer way.

This is a powerful example of how the body holds on to experiences. According to the book, *The Body Keeps the Score* by Bessel van der Kolk M.D., the body stores memories, emotions, and trauma, often in ways we aren't even consciously aware of. As the author writes, "Trauma is not just an event that took place sometime in the past; it is also the imprint left by that experience on mind, brain, and body."[10] And just like that young woman, when we unlock those memories, we experience profound (and sometimes unexpected) release.

This is a perfect example of the connection that exists between body, mind, and spirit, and it's something I've personally felt during yoga classes. In poses designed to

---

10 Bessel van der Kolk, *The Body Keeps the Score: Brain, Mind, and Body in the Healing of Trauma* (New York: Penguin, 2014).

open the hips—where emotions are said to be stored—I've found myself crying without any clear reason. It's like a dam breaks, and emotions I didn't even know were there come rushing out. Afterward, I feel lighter, as if some pain deep within me has been released.

I'm far from alone in this. Many yoga teachers refer to the hips as the body's "emotional junk drawer." Our hips revolve around the iliopsoas muscle, which connects the upper and lower body. When that muscle gets tight, it causes pain and interferes with our posture. That can lead to headaches, fatigue, stress, and even depression. But that's not all. Our kidneys and adrenals are located in the psoas; when that muscle is constricted, it can have an effect on the sympathetic nervous system. Stress can get "trapped" when the psoas gets tight (which can happen for a variety of reasons, including sitting for too long—which, let's face it, is common in our modern society). But as you start to stretch and release that muscle, the stress that's been trapped gets released, and it may exit the body through reactions like crying.

To release emotions in your hips and the rest of your body, try stretching, massage, yoga, or even somatic exercises (body-awareness practices in which you focus on what you're experiencing internally while you perform various exercises). One of my favorite stretches for emotional release and psoas health is the "Seated Butterfly" pose. To do this stretch, sit on the ground with a straight spine and relaxed shoulders. Bring the soles of your feet as close together as possible, and let gravity gently pull your knees down. If you need to, support your knees with blocks, pillows, or blankets. Don't force anything, and only go as far into the stretch as is comfortable. You shouldn't feel any pain when you do this! At first, only hold the pose for twenty seconds or so; you can gradually build up to longer periods as you get looser. This is far from the only stretch that will release the hip flexors, of course, but it's a good one. However, if you're new to stretching, it's a good idea to work with a yoga instructor to find stretches that are ideal for you (and to make sure you're doing them correctly).

You can also strengthen your psoas with an exercise known as the "Psoas Hold." While standing, bend your right knee and lift your upper leg. Stay balanced on your left foot (you can hold on to a chair or use a wall for support if needed) while keeping your right knee and thigh at hip level, or as high as you can comfortably lift your leg, even if it's just a few inches off the ground at first. Hold this pose for about 30 seconds, then slowly lower your right leg. Next, repeat with your left leg. As you do this exercise, remember that it's important to maintain proper form. If your head bobs forward or you notice that your back is rounding, don't lift your leg up as high. Regularly perform this exercise, along with the "Seated Butterfly" pose, to both keep your hips in good shape and increase your joy.

When we release the stored energy from past experiences, whether through bodywork, movement, or becoming more aware of our emotions, it frees us. It opens us up to joy, healing, and a deeper connection to ourselves and the world around us. That's exactly what we're aiming for. Remember, the joy is already there; we just have to open ourselves to it.

As the Hindu monk Paramahansa Yogananda put it, "From joy I came, for joy I live, and in thy sacred joy, I shall melt again."[11] In other words, joy is something eternal and sacred, something we are meant to experience, and something we can choose.

Martin Buber, the famous author, political activist, and philosopher, put it this way: "The beating heart of the universe is holy joy." That imagery is so powerful, connecting joy to the very rhythm of life itself.

---

11 Paramahansa Yogananda, *Whispers From Eternity* (Dakshineswar, West Bengal, India: Self-Realization Fellowship, 1960).

Tools for Finding Peace

So yes, we're made for joy. And yes, cultivating a joyful spirit takes practice. It's a skill that must be developed. One of my favorite tools for doing that is reciting a personal mantra. I keep quotes that resonate with me posted on my wall; some of my favorites are:

"I release things that no longer serve me."
"I am at peace with what is happening."
"I release the need to replay situations in my mind."
"I am gentle with myself and others."

These are just a few examples of mantras—there are many more that are just as powerful. You can go online to find examples, or make up some that resonate with you.

Mantras are especially useful because they help you redirect your attention when you get hooked by circumstances. Of course, to be effective, you have to catch yourself when you start to spiral. When you find yourself feeling down and blaming the world around you, it's easy to slip into a negative mindset and think something like, "Those people are really jerks," or, "Everything is terrible!" But remember, that's just your automatic mind taking over.

To escape this negative cycle, start repeating a mantra to yourself in order to redirect your thoughts ("I transform negative energy into love and light" is a good one). As you repeat the mantra, allow your body to relax. Keep repeating your chosen phrase until your mind lets the negative thoughts go.

As I've mentioned several times, and as you'll discover when you start this practice, you can't necessarily shut your mind off, but you can always turn your attention elsewhere. That's the real power you have. And remember, because of the interconnectedness of body, mind, and spirit, breathing exercises can also help.

Breathing is such a fundamental tool. When you're stressed or upset, your breath becomes shallow. It's a physiological response, but you can interrupt it by pausing and reminding yourself to breathe deeply. Focusing on your breath—breathing in deeply, breathing out deeply—helps bring your attention back to the present moment. For me, I focus on a point where the breath flows through my body, right where the trachea splits. It's a grounding exercise that reminds me to be present and brings me back to a place of calm and joy.

Breathing isn't just about filling your lungs; it's about creating space for joy to flow back into your life. It's one of the simplest yet most powerful ways to regain control when life's circumstances pull you away from your center, and it's a great way to find the beauty and grace in whatever you're going through (doubly so when you couple it with a mantra!).

Now, you might be wondering, "How does a breathing exercise make any difference when I'm having a bad day?" The answer is simple: Breathing interrupts whatever negative state you're in. It disrupts the inner voice that says, "Everything's messed up," and makes room for something new. It might not take you directly to joy, but it certainly opens the door for intentionality, compassion, or whatever else you might need in that moment.

Then again, when life feels like a complete shit show, as it often does, I remind myself that maybe joy isn't the immediate goal. Sometimes it's about being mindful, not mindless. To get to that place, sometimes *equanimity*, a state of mental calmness, is more attainable—just being able to accept that "it's all part of life." For me, equanimity means staying calm and balanced, knowing that everything is exactly as it should be, because I am exactly where I need to be. Equanimity is not about holding hands and singing "Kumbaya" in the midst of chaos, and it's not about pretending that everything is okay. Rather, it's about finding peace within myself, no matter what's happening internally or externally.

At the end of the day, your ability to breathe, center yourself, and find some sense of equanimity during difficult times is a powerful tool. It's how you can navigate the ups and downs of life, knowing that while happiness may come and go, peace and balance are always within your reach.

So, if you find that joy feels too far away on a given day, maybe you can aim for equanimity instead. That's very much a worthwhile practice too. Equanimity is an incredibly powerful state to cultivate—in fact, it's not just a stop along the way to joy, but a key part of the journey. After all, joy isn't a station on the train track of life that you simply pass through. Although it's ever-present, it's more fluid; it's not a fixed destination. Equanimity, though, can be a steadying force, giving you a sense of peace even when things are uncertain. It's a place of balance that can hold you until you find your way back to joy.

Practices for Finding Joy

The next time you find yourself in a conversation
where people are complaining or grumbling, rather
than joining in, try to connect with joy. Share
something positive or something you're grateful for,
and celebrate the simple privilege of being alive.

Consider participating in therapeutic bodywork
or yoga in order to release pent-up emotion from
past trauma and open yourself more fully to joy.

Begin collecting meaningful and inspiring phrases
that you can use as personal mantras the next time
you're feeling down. When you find yourself slipping
into a negative mindset, repeat one of your mantras
to yourself in order to redirect your thoughts.

Use breathing exercises to bring yourself back to the present
moment and create space for joy to flow back into your life.

Be gentle with yourself. If you can't get immediately
to joy, you can always aim for equanimity.

SEVEN

Growing in Compassion

"

If you want others to be happy, practice compassion. If you want to be happy, practice compassion.

"

—HIS HOLINESS
THE XIV DALAI LAMA

A T THIS POINT, YOU UNDERSTAND THAT JOY IS A BIG part of maintaining the well-being of spirit. But it's not the only component. When our minds are on autopilot, it's easy to fall into pity, whether for ourselves or others. These pity parties are instinctive, something we tend to do without even thinking about it. But they don't serve our bodies, our minds, *or* our spirits. Know what does? Compassion.

Sometimes when I say this to someone, they look at me blankly. "What's the difference between compassion and pity?" they ask. "Aren't they essentially the same thing?"

My answer to that is an unequivocal no. They are *not* the same thing. Pity is about feeling sorry for someone (or ourselves), but compassion is something deeper and more empathetic. It's about truly understanding someone else's experience or our own experience without judgment or condescension.

The word compassion comes from two parts: "*com*," meaning "with," and "*passion*," meaning "to suffer." So compassion literally means "to suffer with"—to feel what another person is feeling, to truly be present with their experience. Pity, on the other hand, is more detached. There's no shared feeling, no real empathy. You might feel badly for someone else, but when you pity them, you hold them at arm's length. You don't really connect with their situation or their pain. Pity just doesn't go that deep.

As important as the distinction between compassion and pity is, it's only part of what you need to understand to cultivate compassion. Another piece of the puzzle is recognizing that life, by its very nature, is filled with challenges, and compassion helps us navigate those challenges together. But here's the catch: Our culture often sends the message that life *shouldn't* be a challenge. Everywhere we look, the message is clear—if something is hard, it's a problem that needs fixing. But that's simply not true. Life is supposed to have ups and downs; it's all part of the experience. Even the joyful moments can present challenges.

For instance, when my grandchildren come to visit, it's always a wonderful time, but it's still a challenge. I joke that I need to make sure the cupboards are locked, or they'll get into things they shouldn't! Having them around fills my heart, but let's be honest—their boundless energy and never-ending questions can be tiring. Similarly, having a new puppy is a joyful experience, but it comes with its own set of challenges. House training, puppy-proofing, and dealing with the chewing, the barking, and the constant demands for attention can be overwhelming at times. Does that mean that children and puppies are bad?

No, of course not! But they are what I like to refer to as "up challenges"—good things in life that still require effort, patience, and sometimes a lot of energy.

The key to dealing with challenges of any kind is to embrace both the ups and downs with compassion. That goes both for what we experience and what others go through. In other words, we can choose "to suffer with" and find the joy in the hardships. When we approach life this way, we begin to see that every challenge, whether it's a high or a low, is an opportunity for growth *and* an opportunity to connect with joy. Compassion allows us to face life's difficulties without judgment and with an open heart, knowing that so-called problems are just part of the journey.

We Can All Cultivate Compassion

Like joy, compassion is something you absolutely can develop and cultivate, whether it comes naturally to you or not. However, it must start with yourself. You can't offer real compassion to others unless you first learn to be compassionate toward yourself. You must treat yourself with the same kindness and understanding that you would extend to a friend in need. Once you learn to do that, you'll find it much easier to open your heart to others.

The doorway into compassion is gratitude. Gratitude softens us and makes us more receptive to the world around us. It's also what makes us more able to care about people. And, just like joy, compassion is something that can help get you through the hardest times. There's a story about a Russian Orthodox priest named Father Arseny who was imprisoned in a Soviet gulag during Stalin's reign. Each night, Father Arseny would gather the men of the camp around him and ask them to list the things they were grateful for that day. Can you imagine how hard it must've been for those men to feel grateful amid so much deprivation and suffering?

One man in particular, though, became Father Arseny's champion in the camp, and he would enthusiastically participate in the gratitude exercise. On one occasion, he managed to come up with thirteen things he was grateful for in the prison camp.[12] Thirteen things! If that doesn't show how gratitude can be cultivated by anyone, anywhere, and in any situation, I don't know what does.

Why did Father Arseny put such a focus on gratitude? I believe it's because he knew how important it was for

---

12 Vera Bouteneff, *Father Arseny, 1893-1973: Priest, Prisoner, Spiritual Father* (Yonkers, NY: St Vladimir's Seminary Press, 1998).

maintaining spiritual well-being. He understood that even in the darkest times, gratitude opens the door to compassion and even joy, and he was committed to helping the men around him get through what was happening to them with their spiritual well-being intact.

As impressive as Father Arseny was, he's far from the only one who has recognized the power of gratitude and compassion. There's another story I've heard about a Buddhist monk who was imprisoned by the Chinese after they invaded the country. He spent eighteen years as their prisoner, and in that time, they forced him to denounce his religion and tortured him repeatedly. When he was finally freed, he went to India to meet the Dalai Lama. The Dalai Lama asked him whether he had ever been afraid during the eighteen years he spent in the Chinese prison. His answer? He had been afraid of one thing and one thing only: losing compassion for the Chinese.[13] Pretty incredible, right? But what's even more incredible is that he *didn't* lose his compassion and, as a result, he was able to maintain his mental, emotional, and spiritual well-being, despite the horrendous circumstances he found himself in.

13 His Holiness the Dalai Lama and Victor Chan, *The Wisdom of Forgiveness: Intimate Conversations and Journeys* (New York: Riverhead Books, 2005).

Just like joy, compassion is a choice. Remember, joy is not about your circumstances. Joy is an internal declaration. You can choose to be joyful, just as you can choose to be compassionate. It's a privilege to be alive, with all the challenges and opportunities we face. Life is not a problem to be solved. It's a gift to be embraced, and compassion helps us do that.

Shift Your Outlook

Compassion and joy are closely linked, and when you start to practice them, you'll notice a shift in your entire outlook. The automatic pity parties and complaints will begin to fall away, replaced by a deeper sense of empathy and gratitude. And that's where true compassion—not to mention true well-being of spirit—lives.

Compassion has been a big area of growth for me personally. It's easy to have compassion for people close to you—your spouse, your family—but expanding that circle to include people who are frustrating or challenging? That's been my real growing edge. Take, for example, people who believe in certain political ideas that I fundamentally disagree with. Extending compassion to them? It's not easy. But that's the new frontier for me. I have been learning to include even those people in my circle of compassion, without necessarily accepting or tolerating the beliefs and behaviors that go against my values.

Remember, compassion is not about blind acceptance. It's about holding space for empathy while still recognizing the things that don't feel right.

Speaking of politics, in today's world, wouldn't it be refreshing to hear a message that says, "We are more alike than we are different"? We're so caught up in the divisions—whether it's politics or social issues—that we forget our shared humanity. Whatever side you're on, the current public conversation is often driven by a belief that the people who disagree with us are jerks (or worse), and that it's our job to "save" the country from them. But there's no cheese at the end of that tunnel. That mindset only deepens the divide—unless someone steps in to interrupt the narrative. And the only sustainable way I can see to do that is through compassion.

One way I've started building my compassion for people I find difficult is by regularly practicing a "**Loving-Kindness Meditation**." The steps are relatively simple, and you can practice this meditation yourself in the privacy of your own home or room. First, sit or lie down in a place where you won't be disturbed. Close your eyes, and take a couple of deep breaths. Next, imagine that you are experiencing total well-being of body, mind, and spirit. Imagine feeling unconditional love for yourself, exactly as you are. As you focus on this feeling, say (either out loud or in your head; it really doesn't matter):

"May I be happy."
"May I be safe."
"May I be healthy, peaceful, and strong."
"May I give and receive gratitude and compassion today."

Take a few moments to bask in the feelings of loving-kindness these phrases bring up. Then shift your focus to someone in your life you're very close to. It could be your child, your spouse, your parent, your best friend... even your pet. As you think of that being, let your gratitude and love for them wash over you while you repeat the same four phrases you said earlier. Next, think about an acquaintance you know—someone you're more neutral about. Extend the same feelings of loving-kindness to them, while repeating the phrases you used before. Finally, repeat the process with someone you find difficult. (Keep in mind that you can switch who you think about for each category each time you do the meditation to give yourself more practice.)

Do this meditation a few times per week, and over time, you will find it easier to bring up loving-kindness and compassion toward everyone, including the people you struggle with.

Accessing Gratitude

All of that said, I have personally found that the most sure-fire and effective way to access compassion and joy is through gratitude. We've all been guilty of throwing ourselves a little mental pity party now and again for our troubles. I'm no different. It's part of the automatic mechanism of the mind. The chatter of the mind is always going to be there, and so are the pity parties that come out of it. You can't get rid of them entirely, nor can anyone talk you out of them or "cure" them.

But you know what? That's fine. The goal is not to eliminate these things, but to get better at interrupting them. Over time, you can develop the ability to shift your state, going from a feeling of "everything is messed up" to realizing, "Hey, the world's actually a pretty bright place, and thank God I'm still breathing." That's what it looks like to shift from pity and negativity to compassion and gratitude.

A simple exercise to access gratitude is to make a daily list of things you're grateful for, no matter how small. You might start with two or three things a day, but with practice, you'll notice the list growing. That's because you're training yourself to see the good in even the most challenging situations, and as you do this, you are also developing greater compassion and accessing joy more frequently.

On the days when I struggle to come up with even one thing to be thankful for, I remember the story of Father Arseny. I'm not in a prison camp, and yet there are days when gratitude feels out of reach. But it's a reminder that gratitude—and by extension, compassion—is a practice. We often get so disconnected from that sense of appreciation for the life we have that it becomes easy to overlook the little blessings in the midst of chaos. There are always blessings, all the time and in every situation, but you must be willing to recognize and acknowledge them.

When I speak about compassion, especially with groups of people who are lifelong learners, I always start by reminding them that compassion grows and develops over time. It's not something that's "fully baked," as though you reach an endpoint and you're done. It's a constant process of breakthroughs, big and small. As we broaden our horizons, we expand our circles to include those who challenge us. Like joy and gratitude, compassion grows with practice—and it's never too late to start.

Bring Compassion into the Process

Our culture tells us constantly, like a refrain, "If you have a problem, solve it as fast as possible." The issue is, when we try to apply this problem-solving mentality to many of life's challenges, we end up being incredibly hard on ourselves, on others, and even on life itself. This approach divides us—it splits the body, mind, and spirit—because it leads us to try and reduce the problem to its smallest part and then go after it, neglecting to consider the whole.

I can tell you that in much of Western medicine, we tend to take the same approach: "Just take a pill or opt for surgery, and make it go away." We focus on the quickest fix rather than addressing the full picture, and our patients sometimes suffer for it.

I've experienced this firsthand on more than one occasion, both as a doctor and as a patient. For example, I have an appointment coming up with an orthopedic surgeon to drain a cystic mass in my leg. When we first became aware of the mass, there was an initial rush to judgment, and we discussed removing it surgically. Many people would have agreed to surgery right away, thinking, "Just get it out of me, so I don't have to deal with it anymore."

However, during an ultrasound, something about that solution didn't sit right with me. I felt a kind of trembling uncertainty in my spirit, so I decided I needed to be patient and ask more questions. Thankfully, the ultrasound tech was great—she walked me through the whole process, showing me the screen and explaining everything as she went along. Finally, I asked, "Is this mass a collection of fluid?"

The radiologist considered my question and finally answered, "Yes, indeed, it could be the residual of a hematoma." With a little patience and a few more thoughtful questions, we were able to identify the best solution. Invasive surgery, it turned out, was not the way to go. Now, I'm headed to the orthopedic surgeon, a sports medicine specialist, who will drain the fluid under imaging and break down the adhesions inside. Then a drain will be inserted to ensure everything clears out before closing it up.

While I'm sure this will be a bit uncomfortable, it's necessary to address the problem at its root. And more importantly, it's a lot less severe than if the surgeon had cut me open and carved out the mass.

This is a perfect example of a much bigger issue. When we approach challenges or people or situations in a hurry, trying to make the "problem" go away as fast as possible, we often end up in the wrong place, doing the wrong thing, and creating more problems down the road. Just like in medicine, we can't adopt a "pop a pill and fix it" approach to life. If we want to embrace life fully, we must embrace its challenges, and that means covering all the important aspects of body, mind, and spirit before taking action. In my case, I believe my spirit was trying to warn my mind that invasive surgery was not the way to go.

Awaken to the Interplay between Body, Mind, and Spirit

My experience with trying to find the best way to address my hematoma is a perfect demonstration of how the body, mind, and spirit are intertwined in everything. Yes, spirit is often the best doorway into any issue, but body and mind are no less important or relevant. A physical issue often has mental and spiritual components, just as a mental challenge shows up in the body and affects the spirit. The real trick is learning to see this connection and awake to the interplay between body, mind, and spirit.

When you're able to embrace all three—body, mind, and spirit—you will find far more satisfaction, meaning, and power in life's challenges. This is why the first step is to give up the problem-solving mentality that tries to rush toward a solution. Sure, you can keep going down the path of trying to fix problems fast, but there's nothing waiting for you at the end of that road.

What does this have to do with compassion? Well, compassion is about giving up the hasty judgments and resentments we carry—like thinking, "Why doesn't so-and-so hurry up and fix that problem everyone can see?" Compassion allows us to see the bigger picture and to understand that real solutions take time and a deeper level of care.

By embracing compassion and letting go of the quick-fix mentality, we open ourselves to the fullness of life. It's not just about solving problems—it's about embracing the journey of body, mind, and spirit, and accepting all the challenges and growth that come with it.

Compassion Takes Time

Compassion takes time—it's a quality that develops gradually and deepens as we face life's challenges. However, compassion, in many ways, is also what helps carry us through suffering and allows us to resolve what we're going through.

It requires patience and, as we will discuss later, it also requires intentionality. You have to recognize when your automatic mind is kicking in, running the same loop of negative assessments and judgments over and over again. When your mind does this, you have to *intentionally* turn your attention toward compassion.

In my well-being sessions, I like to take people through an exercise to help them see how they've been treating various aspects of their lives as problems. We explore how they can approach these things from a place of compassion instead. I invite them to recognize that the issue involves not just the mind, but the body and spirit too. Once they do, it's easier for them to recognize that the solution is to reframe how we view the "problems" in our lives and approach them with compassion as part of a larger whole.

When we try to reduce an issue to its smallest part, we're playing a con game with ourselves. We think, "If I can just fix this one thing, I'll be fine," or, "If I take this pill or solve this problem, everything will be okay." But life doesn't work that way. There's no simple fix because we aren't just dealing with one part of ourselves. Whether the problem seems physical, mental, or spiritual, they're all interconnected.

A personal example comes to mind. At one point in my life, I was incredibly stressed about my spending. My knee-jerk approach of trying to control expenses was actually me approaching the situation as a problem to solve as quickly as possible. However, it wasn't long before I realized I wasn't showing myself any compassion in the process. I was caught in the endless loop of thinking, "Damn, I'm doing it again. Spending too much money. I never learn."

But that's exactly the kind of mindset that keeps us stuck in a cycle of judgment and frustration. Once I recognized what I was doing, I slowed down. I did the "Eye of the Hurricane" breathing exercise. I moved my body a bit. And, I repeated some mantras about staying compassionate toward myself. In other words, *I took intentional action in body, mind, and spirit to shift my state*—and as a result, I was able to show myself compassion, tap back into the joy that's always available to us, and make better spending decisions at the same time.

I can't emphasize this enough: When we face any challenge, it's important to recognize that the body, mind, and spirit are all involved. If you're struggling with a body issue, bring the mind and spirit into the conversation. If you're dealing with a spiritual issue, the body and mind need to be included as well, since they are all connected. Acknowledging that connection is key to moving forward with compassion.

There's a quote attributed to Albert Einstein that perfectly captures this idea:

A human being is part of the whole, called by us "Universe," a part limited in time and space. He [or she] experiences themselves, their thoughts, and feelings as something separate from the rest—a kind of optical delusion of their consciousness. This delusion is a kind of prison, restricting us to affection for only a few persons nearest to us. Our task must be to free ourselves from this prison by widening our circle of compassion to embrace all living creatures and the whole of nature in its beauty.

Einstein's perspective on expanding our circle of compassion echoes much of what we've been discussing. It's about freeing ourselves from the illusion of separateness and broadening our capacity for empathy, not just for those closest to us, but for all living beings—including ourselves.

This aligns beautifully with the teachings of Pema Chödrön, who often speaks of compassion as a practice of continually widening our hearts. As she says, "Compassion becomes real when we recognize our shared humanity."[14] Despite the fact that Einstein embraces Western science and Pema aligns with Eastern philosophy, you could say they are like brother and sister in their approach—both urging us to stretch beyond our comfort zones and to see the world with wider eyes and a more open heart.

That's the task before us, and it's the task I'm inviting you to undertake in your own life: to move beyond the narrow confines of problem-solving and embrace the fullness of compassion. Not just for yourself or those you know, but for all of life in its complexity and beauty. It's not an easy endeavor, but it's one certainly worth pursuing.

Show Yourself Compassion

When it comes to personal challenges like managing expenses (a big one for me, as you now know), one of the

---

14 Pema Chödrön, *The Places That Scare You: A Guide to Fearlessness in Difficult Times* (Boston: Shambhala Publications, 2001).

most common traps we fall into is the automatic mental loop of self-criticism. "Well, you did it again, you loser. What's wrong with you? Why do you never get it right?" And so on. We get stuck in a cycle of judgment, beating ourselves up for not having solved the problem already. But this is exactly where compassion can break the pattern.

Again, by using a simple tool like breathwork, you can interrupt the automatic mind and shift your focus to compassion. When you pause, breathe, and let go of the constant self-criticism, you open up space for something more meaningful. This is when the spirit steps in. You begin to trust that things will work out, and you bring your whole self—body, mind, and spirit—to the table. It's about gaining that 30,000-foot view of the situation and asking, "How can I approach this with compassion, not just for the problem, but for myself as well?"

We often forget to show ourselves compassion in these moments. However, that's exactly the time that we need to pause and remind ourselves, "There I go again, being hard on myself. But I'm not a bad person for facing this challenge." You've known yourself for a long time, and you've faced similar hurdles before. It's important to acknowledge that you've always been doing your best, and there's something lovable about that persistence.

By releasing the frustration and shifting into a more compassionate mindset, your whole perspective changes. Even though the challenge still needs to be addressed, you're no longer coming from a place of self-judgment. Instead, you're approaching it with joy and acceptance: "Okay, good. Now we're going to tackle this one, and we'll do it in a way that doesn't make me wrong or foolish." That's the beauty of it—you can still address what needs to be done, but with a lighter, more joyful heart.

Whatever your problem is, take a moment to pause. Ask yourself a couple of questions:

- How can I involve my mind, body, and spirit in dealing with this?
- How can I approach this with compassion for myself and others?

These are the kinds of questions that open up new perspectives and allow you to move forward without feeling weighed down by judgment (especially self-judgment).

Remember, compassion is at the heart of what it means to be human—it's what separates us from other species. To be compassionate means to suffer with one another (or even with yourself), and to generously put yourself in their shoes.

Compassion is deeply intertwined with the Golden Rule: "*Do unto others as you would have them do unto you.*" But as you begin to practice that, remember what I mentioned at the beginning of the chapter: Compassion is not about feeling sorry for someone. That's pity, and as you know, we're not aiming for pity. Compassion is about understanding that life is full of challenges, both big and small, and we need to meet those challenges with kindness rather than judgment.

Recognize that our culture is constantly telling us that life shouldn't be difficult and that problems should be fixed as quickly as possible, but don't buy into that view. Understand that we've been conditioned to treat all challenges like problems to solve, but remember that life is not something to be broken down and solved like a puzzle. Instead, learn to see it as something to be experienced, enjoyed, and accepted.

With all that in mind, here's what it takes to fully embrace life's challenges:

1. **Give up the problem-solving mentality.** Not everything can be fixed like a mechanical issue. Life is more complex than that.

2. **Bring loads of compassion to every situation.**
   Compassion allows you to see the bigger picture
   and helps you move through a challenge with
   grace. It helps you acknowledge the real issues at
   play without judgment, and it opens the door for
   joy, healing, and peace.

When you approach challenges with compassion, you
give up the constant assessments and judgments of yourself and others. Instead, you become intentional about
how you want things to turn out. Real challenges take time
to work through—there aren't quick fixes. Compassion is
what helps you endure that time and gives you the patience
and understanding to navigate life's ups and downs.

That's the message I want to share with you: Compassion
isn't just something nice to have—it's essential for living a
life full of purpose, joy, and true well-being.

Practices for Developing Compassion

Start to develop compassion toward yourself and others—
even people you find difficult. Practicing a "Loving-Kindness
Meditation" a few times per week can help you do this.

Make a daily list of things you're grateful for, no
matter how small. You might start with two or
three things a day. Over time, lengthen the list.

When you fall into the automatic cycle of self-criticism,
use breathwork to break the pattern. Then, direct
your thoughts toward compassion, and try to adopt
a more joyful approach to solving the problem.

When dealing with any challenge in life, ask yourself
these questions: How can I involve my mind, body,
and spirit in dealing with this? How can I approach
this with compassion for myself and others?

Be willing to give up the problem-solving mentality. Not
everything in life can be fixed like a mechanical issue.

EIGHT

Acting with Intentionality

Intentionality fuels the master's journey. Every master is a master of vision.

—GEORGE LEONARD

O VER THE COURSE OF THIS BOOK, WE'VE COVERED many concepts that will help you achieve true well-being of body, mind, and spirit. Ultimately, though, our goal is to move beyond merely *understanding* the concepts of the interconnectedness of mind, body, and spirit and to intentionally start *living* them—training the mind, body, and spirit as one. If that sounds daunting, don't worry: I know from experience that practice makes perfect. While the things we've talked about may not come naturally to you at first, the more you engage with them, the more they'll become part of who you are.

As I've gotten older, I've come to appreciate how important it is to trust the process and to keep doing the work even when the results aren't immediately visible. After all, as my dad always said, "You never know how much good you're doing," both for yourself and for others. Sometimes, just keeping that truth in mind is more than enough to keep going.

So what, then, is the best way to start living these concepts? How do we intentionally align our body, mind, and spirit in everyday situations? Let's start to explore these questions by looking at a relatively simple example. Suppose you visit the doctor. Most of the time, when we go to an appointment, we simply accept the doctor's recommended treatment at face value and assume that is the whole story. If the doctor says, "This pill will fix you," or "We need to cut that out of you," we comply without question—and without considering the mind and spirit. But in our pursuit of interconnectedness, maybe there's a deeper conversation to be had. Maybe, for example, in addition to medical treatment, you could also explore what's going on with you mentally and spiritually.

Start treating your whole person (body, mind, and spirit), not just pieces of yourself. To do that, you might start a conversation with your doctor by saying something like, "I want to explore all elements of this. Yes, I want to talk about what's happening physically, but I also want to explore with you what might be happening emotionally or spiritually." And don't stop there, either. Talk to your doctor about what outcome you want from whatever treatment you mutually decide is the right course of action for you. This approach invites a more comprehensive, meaningful discussion—one that looks at you as a complete person.

I understand that this is probably a major shift in how you perceive your role as a patient. You're no longer merely a passive participant in your health care. You're now an active part of the process—and not only that, your *whole being* is part of the process. That's as it should be, because your goals, concerns, feelings, and perspective matter. And when you ask for space to explore what's happening with each part of yourself and share what you want from the treatment (beyond just a quick fix), you create space for lasting, meaningful healing that touches all areas of your life.

This is a perfect place to start your journey toward interconnectedness. Go beyond pills and surgery. They have their place, but start seeking true, wholistic well-being. Engage more fully in your own well-being journey, and give yourself the chance to heal completely in body, mind, and spirit.

Encouraging Doctors to Go Deeper

I know what you're probably thinking after reading that last section. "Getting a doctor to consider the mental and spiritual aspects of my treatment is easier said than done!" And in many cases, that's absolutely true. The question, then, is this: When working with a doctor who may be more conventionally-minded and focused on quick fixes like pills or surgery, what's the best way to invite them into a deeper conversation—one that considers the whole person, not just the immediate problem?

LIVING A WHOLE LIFE

The key to making these conversations work, especially with a conventionally-minded doctor, is to approach the situation from a place of curiosity rather than confrontation. By framing your responses as questions, you invite a richer, more thoughtful discussion. Instead of dismissing their expertise, you're asking for more insight, signaling that you're open to alternative approaches.

I recently had an experience that really drove this home for me. I took our new puppy to the vet because he was feeling unwell—lethargic, diarrhea, and a little blood in his stool. Naturally, I was worried. When we got to the vet, she didn't run any tests, didn't take a stool sample or do blood work. She just ran her hands over his head and back a couple of times and then said, "Let's start with an antibiotic, just in case."

Now, I am a fierce advocate of using antibiotics responsibly (in fact, my first book, *Becoming Good Stewards of Antibiotics: Changing the Way We Look at Things* is about that very topic). And the responsible use of antibiotics means not overusing them or turning to them as a quick fix. So I responded to the vet by saying, "Actually, if we're not testing anything, I'd rather not jump to antibiotics. I'm trying to avoid the overuse of antibiotics. Is there another route we could explore?"

Her reply was a pleasant surprise: "Oh—nobody ever asks that! Sure, we can do fluids, probiotics, and a few other things. If those don't have any effect, we can always run some tests and start him on antibiotics then if it's appropriate."

Nodding, I said, "Yep, I like those options. Let's do it." Thirty minutes later, they had given him fluids, and we were on our way home with probiotics in hand. Within a day, the puppy perked up, and not long after that he was back to his normal, happy-go-lucky self.

Notice that when the vet recommended antibiotics for my pet, I didn't confront her about inappropriate antibiotic use or accuse her of being irresponsible. In a gentle way, I requested other options and sought a more *wholistic* approach. I believe that is why the veterinarian was receptive to suggesting alternatives for me—and in fact, seemed happy to do so.

This experience was a powerful reminder of the ripple effect of asking questions and seeking understanding. If we had gone straight to antibiotics and the dog had gotten better, people would've said, "See? We nipped it in the bud. Problem solved!" But by taking the approach I did, we avoided unnecessary medication, and it drove home how important and, frankly, *easy* it is to disrupt automatic responses, whether with medical treatments or in life.

In today's medical environment, doctors have become more receptive to the patient's perspective, feelings, and concerns—at least in most cases. Back when I was an intern, things were quite different. I recall one orthopedic surgeon whom I respected a lot. He was a skilled surgeon, but if a patient ever questioned his approach, he would shut them down by responding, "I'm the doctor, not you." And that was that. Patients were expected to do what they were told, no questions asked. In those days, doctors were seen as the sole authority on health, and their word was final.

But those days are—thankfully—mostly behind us. Now, medicine is far more collaborative, and physicians are encouraged to listen to the patient's goals and concerns. You have a legitimate role in shaping your health care, and it's important to use that voice. Ask questions! Be intentional! Open up the conversation! When the doctor jumps to pills or surgery, ask something like, "What are all of my options?" or "How will this impact my mental well-being?" Invite a *wholistic* view of your care rather than just focusing on quick fixes.

Of course, taking a *wholistic* approach to well-being is about more than just changing how you interact with your health care provider. In fact, I believe the time to start is *before* you end up in your doctor's office. Take a look at your life. Do you move your body regularly? Do you stretch? Exercise your muscles? What about how you eat? Are you making choices and following patterns that will nourish your body and support your physical well-being?

The same goes for your mental health. Do you take regular pauses throughout the day to give yourself time to breathe? Is your mind a servant or taskmaster? How much of its constant dialogue do you get hooked into?

And what about your spiritual well-being? Do you choose joy, even when life throws challenges at you? Do you practice compassion and embrace gratitude?

If any of these parts seem out of balance, think about how you can bolster them. You don't have to do it all at once, of course, but taking stock of what might need more attention and then incorporating practices to give that part a more connected role in your life will work wonders for your *wholistic* well-being, now and in the future.

Fully Embracing Life's Challenges

Remember as you reflect on each aspect of your well-being that truly embracing life means embracing its challenges as well. Don't try to compartmentalize problems into smaller parts and ignore the larger context. As you now know, a physical issue often has a mental and spiritual component, just as a spiritual struggle will manifest in the body. Embracing life means you cover all of the meaningful aspects—body, mind, and spirit.

As we close out our journey, I want to bring everything together and take you through the powerful connection between intentionality, joy, compassion, and gratitude—a sequence that has become foundational in my own life and work. These four things aren't just abstract concepts; they are practices that, when woven together, create a more fulfilling and meaningful existence. Over the years, I've found that this approach offers a refreshing alternative to the traditional, symptom-based methods many physicians, including myself, were trained to utilize.

We've talked about joy, compassion, and gratitude already. So now, let me share how they relate to intentionality, which is the conscious choice to live with purpose and awareness, to guide your actions rather than just react to what life throws at you. I believe intentionality lays the groundwork for everything else. When we embrace it, joy naturally follows—not the kind of fleeting happiness we often chase, but that deeper, more sustained sense of well-being. And from that joy, compassion and gratitude naturally emerge.

Remember, intentionality, joy, compassion, and gratitude are more than practices we need to cultivate; they also become lived experiences that transform how we relate to others and to ourselves. In the world of medicine, particularly psychiatry, the focus is usually on identifying a problem and prescribing a solution—often a pill. This is a very reactive model. But I've seen time and again that while medication can stabilize symptoms, it doesn't necessarily lead to true healing. True healing happens when we focus on the bigger picture—when we introduce concepts like intentionality and compassion into the mix.

Sometimes, when I bring this up, patients and colleagues are surprised. It's a revelation to them: "Wait, Doc, you're saying there's more to healing than just medication?"

I remember a patient who said, "Oh, so you actually want to talk through things, not just hand me a prescription?" My response: Yes! I believe that healing comes from connection. Without it, we're left with only the surface-level solutions, and while those have their place, they just aren't enough to make a lasting and meaningful difference.

Just like with the other practices I've talked about, what you're really doing when you focus on intentionality is disrupting those automatic, habitual patterns of thought. It's a way to redirect your focus away from the steady stream of judgments, assumptions, and worries, some of which you're not even aware of. But once you bring those thoughts into awareness—once you say, "Hold on, why am I reacting this way?"—you start to interrupt those patterns. It's like setting off an internal alarm that wakes you up to what's going on in your own head. And once you're aware, you can begin to shift your focus.

So many of us go through life reacting without thinking, assuming the worst about people and ourselves, disconnected from what's actually happening around us. But when we start living intentionally, we slow down and engage with the world, with ourselves, and with others. And, at least in my experience, that's when real joy and compassion start to flow.

People often ask me how they can apply this to their own lives. They want to know how to break free from those automatic thought patterns, and how to bring more awareness into their day-to-day experiences. And what I've found is that most people are ready for this shift. It's almost as if they're just waiting for someone to say, "There's another way to live, and it starts with intentionality."

The beauty of this work is in realizing that we don't have to be stuck in our habitual patterns. We can choose a different way forward—one that's full of joy, compassion, and gratitude. And it all starts with that first step of living intentionally. When you embrace that mindset, everything changes. You open yourself up to deeper connections, true healing, and a life that feels richer in every sense.

Practices for Being Intentional

When it comes to your health care, don't be a passive participant. Become an active part of the process by opening up the discussion and inviting a more wholistic view of your treatment, but do so without accusations.

Start being intentional about joy, compassion, and gratitude. Slow down and engage with the world, with yourself, and with others!

Call to Action

Live Your Life—
Wholly, Purposefully, and Joyfully

Living a wholly purposeful and joyful life is something we can all do. It doesn't matter how old you are, what your circumstances are, or how much money you have. In fact, the only factor that really matters is that you understand *wholistic* well-being of body, mind, and spirit, and you know how to achieve it.

So, consider this your call to action—your invitation to start developing this interconnected well-being. Start with your body. Check in with yourself: Should you move more?

Remember, the body will rust out with disuse, *so use it*. Any exercise is helpful, so find something you enjoy and start to incorporate it into your daily routine. Maybe you like to walk. Great! Challenge yourself to walk as far as you can in six minutes. If you have more than six minutes, by all means, keep walking, but at least for those six minutes, really hustle. If you love the water, find a gym or a place with a pool and start swimming or doing water aerobics. Take a few days per week to do strength training, preferably under the guidance of a personal trainer (at least until you learn the exercises and understand proper form). And remember to stretch! Staying limber is a key part of physical well-being.

Pay attention to what and how you eat too. Yes, you can eat whatever you'd like, but practice moderation. Making an effort to give your body food that will nourish it will help too—think fruits and vegetables, protein, and complex carbohydrates. Consider talking to a nutritionist or dietician or visiting MyPlate.gov for more tips on diet. And if you're a fast eater like me, slow down! Eating isn't a race, and by taking your time, you can enjoy your food more and recognize when your body is getting full. Plus, you will find that your meals become more meditative, which is helpful for your mental well-being too.

Speaking of mental well-being, start to pay attention to how often and how deeply you get hooked into the constant, inane chatter of your mind. If you've never practiced breathing exercises, try one. "The Eye of the Hurricane" or "Box Breathing" are both good places to start. It may take some time to get comfortable with these exercises, especially since the mind is likely to struggle to stay focused at first, but that's fine. With practice, you'll be able to detach from the automatic thoughts, which in turn will allow you to break the cycle of negative thinking and develop more compassion toward yourself (and, by extension, others).

As you begin to support your physical and mental well-being, remember to focus on your spiritual well-being too. Repeat a mantra or two daily, or whenever things get challenging. Recognize that joy is a state that's always available to each and every one of us, if we choose it. Be easy on yourself when you're going through hard times, though, and aim for equanimity if joy feels out of reach. Bolster the compassion you develop through breathing exercises with a "Loving-Kindness Meditation." Act with intentionality too: Remember that joy and compassion are conscious choices, and develop practices that will help you achieve and maintain them.

Finally, remember that all of these practices and goals should never be done in isolation. They are all connected, because each aspect of ourselves is connected. You've probably noticed that when something is wrong in one area, you struggle in other areas too. When your body isn't well, your mind may be uneasy. When your spirit isn't calm and joyful, you probably don't feel well physically, and so on. It's all connected, which is why developing the ability to tune into every aspect of your well-being is foundational to living a whole life.

Reflect on Interconnectedness

When I talk about the idea of body, mind, and spirit interconnectedness, people generally grasp the concept on a superficial level fairly quickly. However, to deepen their understanding, I usually need to give them specific examples or pose some questions they can reflect on. That's why I always try to leave people with something they can carry with them. It's not enough to just hear these ideas once. The real change happens when you begin asking yourself questions and applying the concepts to your everyday life.

Start with the questions I've asked throughout this book: *Am I nourishing my body and moving it regularly? Am I hooking into negative thoughts? Do I consciously and intentionally choose joy and compassion instead of negativity and blame?* As you ask yourself these questions, others will occur to you. Your ability to reflect on your own *wholistic* well-being will deepen, and as it does, you'll instinctively know what you need to do next to support that well-being.

Ultimately, the concepts we've explored here—including but by no means limited to intentionality, compassion, joy, and gratitude—are not just abstract concepts. They're tools you can use to transform your life. And like any tool, they need to be used regularly. The more you engage with them, the deeper your understanding will grow; the more you will connect body, mind, and spirit; and the more equipped you'll be to face life's challenges with grace and compassion.

Never Stop Learning

You can always expand your understanding, just as you can always broaden your compassion. Sometimes, asking questions and seeking to know more can interrupt the automatic processes that keep us from growing and getting better.

We're so conditioned to follow the same paths over and over, often without asking if there's another way. But being a lifelong learner means you constantly question, seek alternatives, and grow in your understanding. That's the beauty of learning. We don't arrive at a point where we've learned it all or have fully cultivated compassion, joy, and gratitude. We don't arrive at a point where we can sit back and assume our minds will remain servants rather than taskmasters. We don't even arrive at a point where we can stop attending to our physical well-being! No, these are all daily practices to engage in so we can keep expanding.

This is true for people at all stages of life. Learning isn't just for the young. Aging well means continuing to grow, expanding your view of the world, and deepening your understanding of yourself and others. Whether you're 25 or 85, learning and growth—not to mention enjoying greater well-being in every aspect of yourself—are always possible. Keep asking questions, living intentionally, and cultivating joy, compassion, and gratitude. If you do, I think you'll find that you can achieve that ultimate goal: living a wholly well, joyful, and purposeful life.

Exercises for the Whole Self

1, Get your body moving. Take a six-minute
walk and check in with yourself.

2. Slow down and eat with
intentionality and mindfulness.

3. The next time your mind is racing, recognize
that the mental chatter is not who you are.
Separate yourself from the mental noise.

4. Connect with your spirit in a way that resonates
deeply with you, whether through meditation,
nature, service to others, or something else.

5. Practice breathing exercises like "The Eye
of the Hurricane" or "Box Breathing" to direct
your mind and quiet the mind's clamor.

6. When life gets challenging, choose joy. Even though transitions and change can be difficult, finding a way to shift from fear or anger to joy will help you maintain your well-being of spirit.

7. Develop compassion and gratitude by writing a list of the things you're grateful for. Start by trying to list two or three things, but let your list grow over time. This can become a nightly practice. Before you go to bed, reflect on the things you're grateful for that day.

8. Engage in a "Loving-Kindness Meditation" a few times per week. Over time, see if you can reach a place where you can even send love and kindness to people you find difficult.

9. Open up medical conversations by asking questions and bringing mind and spirit into the equation. Invite a wholistic view of your care. Don't chase quick fixes!

10. Remember that wholistic well-being doesn't have an endpoint. It's a lifelong practice. To achieve it, stay open to learning, growing, and reflecting.

Appendix

Exercises for an Interconnected Life

Throughout the book, I've offered a series of exercises to help you get in touch with your mind, body, and spirit and bring them all into a state of interconnectedness. While these exercises certainly aren't prescriptive, I've gathered them all into this appendix for convenient reference. You can do all of them on a regular basis, or pick the ones that appeal to you most on a given day and focus on those. It's up to you.

Enjoy!

Exercises for the Mind

Pause and Reflect

Are you moving in the right direction? Is there anything you need to change to live a more joyful, intentional, and purposeful life? The following exercise will help you answer those questions and others like them. All you need is time and space to journal on the following questions. You can do this exercise anytime, but it's particularly powerful at the end of the year.

- How was [*current year*]?
  - What improved from the prior year (or over the course of the current year)?
  - What became more apparent as an issue that needs to be addressed?
  - What thrilled you about [*current year*]?
  - What disappointed you about [*current year*]?

- What is your intention or hope for [*upcoming year*]?
  - What do you want to improve?
  - What issue(s) do you want to address?
  - What goals and intentions do you have?

- Energy imbalances in life show up as confusion, recurring issues, settling for going along with something, mental clamor, and/or fear and hesitation. What do you think may be out of balance? In what way?

- What else is on your mind as the current year ends and the new year approaches?

Asking yourself these questions will help you create the new year with intention by focusing on meaningful goals and themes that resonate beyond superficial resolutions.

The Eye of the Hurricane

To break free of old patterns and habits and interrupt the mind's constant dialogue, use "The Eye of the Hurricane." Find a quiet place where you won't be disturbed, either indoors or outdoors, depending on your preference. Sit comfortably (but keep your spine straight), and rest your hands on your knees or in your lap. Begin taking deep, intentional breaths. Inhale deeply through the nose, hold it for a moment, then exhale slowly through your mouth.

Visualize yourself in the eye of a hurricane, the calm center amidst life's chaos, surrounded by wind and rain. Become the stillness, even as the storm swirls around you. As negative thoughts and feelings arise, acknowledge them without judgment, but gently bring your focus back to your breathing. Each time you notice your attention has wandered away from your breathing, bring your attention back to the breath, envisioning yourself at the center of the storm all the while. Over time, you'll catch moments of inattention more quickly. Eventually, your thoughts will drift in and out without distracting you.

Start with a five-minute session once or twice per day. Over time, you can gradually increase how long you spend in each session. However, remember that even short sessions are powerful ways to cultivate peace and presence, especially in turbulent times.

Box Breathing

Like "The Eye of the Hurricane," "Box Breathing" is a powerful way to redirect the mind. Start by breathing in slowly, deeply, and calmly for a count of four (or three, or five—whatever is comfortable for you). Hold your breath for the same amount of time you breathed in. Then, breathe out (again, for the same length of time). Finally, hold your breath for the same count before taking another inhalation. Repeat this pattern ten times, once or twice per day.

Exercises for the Body

Six-Minute Walks

One of the best things you can do for your body (and your heart) is to go on regular six-minute walks. This length of time is the gold standard to determine aerobic capacity and endurance. Plus, even though it might not sound like it, six minutes is a long time to walk, especially if you're moving as quickly as possible. It gets your heart rate up, your blood pumping, and your circulation moving (all of which are good for whole-body health).

Doing this exercise is easy: Get a timer, set it for six minutes, then start walking. If you need to slow down or even stop completely to rest, feel free to do so. Incorporate these walks a couple of times per week, and over time, see if you can increase the distance you're able to go.

The Psoas Hold

Our hips revolve around the iliopsoas muscle, which connects the upper and lower body. Our kidneys and adrenals are also located in the psoas. All of this means that when that muscle gets tight, it causes pain, affects our sympathetic nervous system, and interferes with our posture. All of this can lead to headaches, fatigue, stress, and even depression.

To alleviate some of these issues, it's helpful both to stretch and strengthen your psoas. The **"Psoas Hold"** is a good exercise for this. While standing, bend your right knee and lift your upper leg. Stay balanced on your left foot (you can hold on to a chair or use a wall for support if needed) while keeping your right knee and thigh at hip level, or as high as you can comfortably lift your leg, even if it's just a few inches off the ground to start. Hold this pose for about 30 seconds, then slowly lower your right leg. Next, repeat with your left leg. As you do this exercise, focus on maintaining proper form. If your head bobs forward or you notice that your back is rounding, don't lift your leg up as high.

Seated Butterfly Pose

The "Seated Butterfly" pose is a good way to release tightness in your psoas. To do this stretch, sit on the ground with a straight spine and relaxed shoulders. Bring the soles of your feet as close together as possible, and let gravity gently pull your knees down. If you need to, support your knees with blocks, pillows, or blankets. Don't force anything, and only go as far into the stretch as is comfortable. You shouldn't feel any pain when you do this! At first, only hold the pose for twenty seconds or so; you can gradually build up to longer periods as you get looser.

Exercises for the Spirit

Forest Bathing

There are so many things that can fuel your spirit. Being of service to others, meditating, and spending time in nature are all great ways to feed your spiritual well-being. If taking in the natural world appeals to you, forest bathing might be something to try.

It's simple to do. Get outside into nature (ideally, a forest) and notice how the light plays through the leaves of the trees. Listen to the sounds around you. Breathe in the scents wafting all around you. As you do, you may find that you are able to drop into mindfulness and support your body, mind, and spirit in achieving *wholistic* well-being.

If you don't have a forest near you, going for a walk in the park offers some of the same benefits you would experience if you were forest bathing in the traditional sense. If walking in a park isn't possible, bring the outside in. If you

can, open the windows in your house or room, place some
potted plants (and maybe some rocks, pinecones, and/or
shells) around, and listen to recordings of forest sounds
while you do a breathing exercise.

Loving-Kindness Meditation

Part of fostering well-being of spirit is developing compassion, even for people you find difficult. One way to do that
is by regularly practicing a "Loving-Kindness Meditation."
Sit or lie down in a place where you won't be disturbed.
Close your eyes, and take a couple of deep breaths. Next,
imagine that you are experiencing total well-being of body,
mind, and spirit. Imagine feeling unconditional love for
yourself, exactly as you are. As you focus on this feeling, say
(either out loud or in your head; it really doesn't matter):

> *"May I be happy."*
> *"May I be safe."*
> *"May I be healthy, peaceful, and strong."*
> *"May I give and receive gratitude and compassion today."*

Take a few moments to bask in the feelings of loving-kindness these phrases bring up. Then, shift your
focus to someone in your life you're very close to. It could

be your child, your spouse, your parent, your best friend... even your pet. As you think of that being, let your gratitude and love for them wash over you while you repeat the same four phrases you said earlier. Next, think about an acquaintance you know—someone you're more neutral about. Extend the same feelings of loving-kindness to them, while repeating the phrases you used before. Finally, repeat the process with someone you find difficult. Switch the people you think of for each category each time you do the meditation to give yourself more practice.

Do this meditation a few times per week, and over time, you will find it easier to bring up loving-kindness and compassion toward everyone, including the people you struggle with.

Gratitude Journal

You can also access compassion through gratitude. A simple exercise to bolster your gratitude for life is to make a daily list of things you're grateful for, no matter how small. You might start with two or three things a day, but with practice, you'll notice the list growing. That's because you're training yourself to see the good in even the most challenging situations. As you do this, you will develop greater compassion and access joy more frequently.

Bringing It All Together

Ask Yourself Questions

When I talk about the idea of body, mind, and spirit interconnectedness, people generally grasp the concept on a superficial level fairly quickly. However, the real change happens when you start asking yourself questions and applying the concepts to your everyday life.

Start with the questions I've asked throughout this book: *Am I nourishing my body and moving it regularly? Am I hooking into negative thoughts? Do I consciously and intentionally choose joy and compassion instead of negativity and blame?* As you ask yourself these questions, others will occur to you. Your ability to reflect on your own wholistic well-being will deepen, and as it does, you'll instinctively know what you need to do next to support that well-being.

Address Challenges Wholistically

Finally, whenever you're facing a challenge, ask yourself two questions:

- How can I involve my mind, body, and spirit in dealing with this?

- How can I approach this with compassion for myself and others?

These are the kinds of questions that open up new perspectives and allow you to move forward without feeling weighed down by judgment (especially self-judgment).

Acknowledgments

This book would not exist without the help and inspiration of many extraordinary individuals, each of whom left an indelible mark on its pages. To everyone who supported, encouraged, and inspired me along the way, please know that I am deeply grateful for each of you.

A heartfelt thank you to Reverend Doctor Gail Cantor, whose wisdom and spirit have encouraged me to reach beyond the ordinary and embrace a larger, more interconnected life. And to Steve Heller, your visionary work with ZoeLife continues to be a guiding light for me and so many others. Thank you for your unwavering commitment and inspiration.

About the Author

Dr. Peter Patterson, a.k.a. "Dr. Pete," is a #1 bestselling author and a third-generation physician who has been in practice for nearly 50 years. He began his career at Mile 49 of the Alaska Highway in 1969. After general practice, he trained in pathology and laboratory medicine, spending much of his career as a hospital pathologist, working behind the microscope and directing clinical laboratories. He began working in post-acute facilities in 2012 as lab director of a mobile diagnostics company, serving nursing homes and long-term care facilities.

Dr. Pete received his MD from the University of Alberta. In the past, he worked for a Fortune 500 health care manufacturing company, where he was trained in the principles and methods of Lean continuous quality improvement. He brings the perspective of a practicing physician-manager to his current work as an author and as a consultant to long-term care facilities and networks.

Over the years, Dr. Pete has acquired an extensive background in medical quality improvement, clinical microbiology, infection prevention and antibiotic stewardship, and awakening spirituality.

He is a regular speaker at conferences and continuing education meetings. His on-the-ground experience and creative insights facilitate the transition in the world toward awareness of *wholistic* well-being.

In 2024, Dr. Pete released his first book, *Becoming Good Stewards of Antibiotics: Changing the Way We Look at Things*.

Dr. Pete currently lives in Phoenix, Arizona, with his wife, Margaret. You can find him at *www.drpetepatterson.com*.